ACTION RESEARCH IN EDUCATION

ACTION RESEARCH
IN EDUCATION

A PRACTICAL GUIDE

Sara Efrat Efron
Ruth Ravid

THE GUILFORD PRESS
New York   London

© 2013 The Guilford Press
A Division of Guilford Publications, Inc.
370 Seventh Avenue, Suite 1200, New York, NY 10001
www.guilford.com

Printed in the United States of America

This book is printed on acid-free paper.

Last digit is print number: 9   8   7   6   5   4   3

Library of Congress Cataloging-in-Publication Data
Efron, Sara Efrat.
   Action research in education : a practical guide / by Sara Efrat Efron and Ruth Ravid.
      pages cm
   Includes bibliographical references and index.
   ISBN 978-1-4625-0961-4 (pbk. : alk. paper)—ISBN 978-1-4625-0971-3 (cloth :
alk. paper)
   1. Action research in education.   I. Title.
   LB1028.24.E34 2013
   370.72—dc23
                                                        2012050760

Preface

This book was written for practicing and prospective educators. Our main goal in writing this book was to provide practical guidelines for school practitioners who would like to carry out action research in their current or future educational settings. Action research has been embraced by a growing number of teachers, administrators, counselors, specialists, school aides, and other school personnel as a viable component of their professional practice. They believe that action research can enhance their ability to grow professionally, to tackle classroom and school challenges, to make autonomous research-based decisions, and to assume responsibility for their own practice. As school practitioners who conduct and evaluate their school-based studies, they strive to question taken-for-granted assumptions, to explore new ideas to improve their work, and to understand the choices available to them and the meanings and implications of their choices. Thus, action research is a powerful strategy for enhancing educators' professionalism and improving the quality of their students' learning, thereby empowering educators to become active partners in leading school change and powerful agents of educational renewal.

This book can be used as a primary text in preservice and inservice research courses that prepare novice school-based researchers to conduct action research in their educational settings. The book is also useful for practicing classroom teachers in PreK–12 in all areas of education, as well as for other school practitioners who are interested in conducting action research for the first time, as part of their professional development. Additionally, the book can be used as a self-study text by educators who are interested in conducting action research projects in conjunction with their everyday instructional practices and activities in schools and classrooms.

As the title implies, we took a very practical approach in writing the book, which stems from our focus on meeting the needs of beginning researchers and introducing them to the knowledge, understandings, and skills necessary for conducting classroom and school investigations. The practical orientation has also emerged from our long and extensive experience with teaching and conducting action research and our close collaboration with teacher researchers. Teachers and other educators may find two distinct aspects of the book particularly beneficial for incorporating action research into their practice: an evenhanded account of qualitative, quantitative, and mixed-methods approaches and a chapter devoted to assessment. While qualitative research methods (e.g., observations, interviews, and rich narratives) enhance the sensitivity of action researchers to the nuanced world of the school, the classroom, and the students, numerical data (e.g., test scores and attendance records) provide an effective tool to assess, describe, and analyze other aspects of school life. The decision about which approach to use—qualitative, quantitative, or mixed—should be made by action researchers according to the nature of their research questions, the focus of their studies, the particular settings in which the research occurs, and their interests and dispositions. Therefore, in this book, qualitative and quantitative approaches are balanced and given equal weight. Each step of the action research process is described from the perspective of qualitative, quantitative, and mixed-methods approaches, and we explain how they differ in viewing school reality, and how the different methods and strategies are typically used in each approach.

The same practical approach and emphasis on the needs of educational practitioners led us to also include a chapter devoted to assessment, even though it is not usually included in books on action research, because we believe that assessment has an essential role in the process of action research. Assessment information can be a valuable data source as educators assess the effectiveness of their practice, examine their teaching strategies, explore a new curriculum unit, or appraise a schoolwide program. In the book we describe how to design and evaluate multiple assessment tools and the role assessment plays in educators' quest to improve their practice through action research. We discuss the contributions of each method for understanding students' achievement in order to gain a richer and more holistic insight into each student's learning and growth.

THE BOOK'S ORGANIZATION

The book's organization has grown out of the actual cycle of action research. The discussion of each step presents three perspectives: it starts with the qualitative method, continues with the quantitative method, and ends with mixed methods. While in reality action research investigation is a dynamic and fluid process, the sequential order of the chapters helps to clarify the research procedures and enable beginning researchers to undertake an action research project. However, at times, action researchers or students and their instructors may feel that their research projects require them to skip around a chapter and go back and forth between different steps of the action research process. They are invited to do that. Following is a brief overview of the content of each chapter:

▶ **Chapter 1: Introduction to Action Research.** This chapter presents an overview of educational research, explaining the differences between traditional research and action research and highlighting the role of educational practitioners as researchers in their own settings. The chapter also explores the theoretical roots of action research and its historical background.

▶ **Chapter 2: Choosing and Learning about Your Research Topic.** We start this chapter by looking at the process of identifying a topic to be explored and reviewing the literature on the topic. Suggestions for sharpening the purpose of the research and for articulating the specific questions, objectives, or hypotheses that the study aims to explore are also presented.

▶ **Chapter 3: Approaches to Action Research.** In this chapter we examine the differences between action research and traditional research. We also explore the philosophical assumptions that form the foundations for the three research paradigms: qualitative methods, quantitative methods, and mixed methods.

▶ **Chapter 4: Developing a Plan of Action.** This chapter highlights the key decisions needed for designing qualitative, quantitative, and mixed-methods practitioner research studies. We provide a guide for developing the various parts of a research plan. Issues related to the ethical considerations involved in conducting practitioner research are also discussed.

▶ **Chapter 5: Data Collection Tools.** This chapter describes the most common types of data collection strategies, both qualitative and quantitative.

Practical guidelines and examples are provided for constructing myriad data collection tools.

▶ **Chapter 6: Using Assessment Data in Action Research.** This chapter discusses the most common classroom assessment tools used in action research. Traditional and nontraditional assessment strategies are described and compared.

▶ **Chapter 7: Data Analysis and Interpretation.** This chapter provides a step-by-step description of the process and techniques for qualitative, quantitative, and mixed-methods data analysis and interpretation. We describe the most common and practical approaches for organizing, analyzing, interpreting, and drawing conclusions for different types of data.

▶ **Chapter 8: Writing, Sharing, and Implementing the Research Findings.** This chapter discusses various ways of reporting the research study. We highlight ways that the knowledge and insight gained from school practitioners' inquiry can be used to improve their practice and be shared with other educators.

In writing this book, we had in mind the educational practitioners we have had the privilege of teaching over the years. We avoided using academic and technical language and instead used language that is approachable and engaging. We also included examples and vignettes drawn from our students' experiences to demonstrate the full cycle of action research. These examples were taken from a variety of educational teaching and learning situations, school subjects, instructional topics, and age groups to authentically illustrate and bring to life the experience of action researchers. Pedagogical features that enhance the usefulness of each chapter's material include:

▶ Sample templates for assisting the development of research instruments at each of the steps involved in the research process.

▶ Checklists of suggestions and guidelines that enable researchers to assess the progress and quality of their own studies.

▶ Summary tables that highlight the particular aspects of different research strategies.

▶ Example boxes that illustrate the different sections of practitioners' action research studies.

▶ Chapter summaries that review and highlight the main points discussed in each chapter.

▶ Exercises and activities that invite students to review, explore further, or apply the methods discussed in the chapter. These activities can be done during or following the class, individually or in groups.

▶ Additional readings that direct the students to sources beyond the many references cited throughout the text.

ACKNOWLEDGMENTS

We would like to thank our editor at The Guilford Press, C. Deborah Laughton, who provided us with support, guidance, and helpful advice. Her quick responses to our inquiries, her trust in us, her professionalism, and her expertise ensured the success of this book. We would also like to thank Editorial Assistant Mary Beth Anderson for her timely and useful responses and for guiding us through the process of the book's production. Additionally, we want to express our appreciation to Louise Farkas, Senior Production Editor, and the production staff for the meticulous and helpful editing of the book. We also offer our gratitude to graphic designer Amy Charlson for her professional work and for her ability to understand our intentions even before we expressed them and then translate our simple designs into a work of art. Special thanks are due to Donna Rafanello, who read each draft of the manuscript and offered excellent editorial comments and suggestions for revisions. We also want to express our appreciation to the book reviewers, Lauren B. Birney, Assistant Professor in the School of Edcuation at Pace University, and Cheryl A. Kreutter, Assistant Professor in the Ella Cline Shear School of Education at SUNY Geneseo, who devoted time and effort to a thorough reading of the manuscript. Their feedback and suggestions were very helpful as we worked on the final draft of the book. We want to recognize with gratitude and express our appreciation to the many wonderful students we have had over the years. We are forever indebted to each and every one of you. You have enriched us with your experience, knowledge, sensitivities, and insight.

Finally, we would like to acknowledge our families. Sara Efrat would like to thank her husband, David, for his understanding, love, and support throughout the writing process and would like to dedicate the book to her children, Noa, Jesse, and Jonathan, who bring so much meaning to her life. Ruth would like to thank Cory, Ossie, Jackie, Lindsey, Ashley, and Audrey, for bringing love and joy into her life each and every day.

Brief Contents

Extended Contents

Introduction to Action Research

Ann, a third-grade teacher, is frustrated. Several of her students fail to do their homework assignments on a regular basis and seem to view homework as an option, rather than a requirement. Being aware of the important contributions of homework to students' achievements, Ann experiments with different kinds of homework, but to no avail. She seeks the help of the district curriculum coordinator who directs her to a well-known research article about how to help students develop positive attitudes toward homework. Ann is impressed by the article but realizes that the recommendations offered are not relevant to her particular setting. The situation in her class is more complex and the article does not address the challenges presented by her students. She understands that before implementing any new strategy in her classroom, she needs to gain a better understanding of the underlying causes for the homework problems in her class. Ann also concludes that she needs to educate herself by reading more about different approaches to homework.

Armed with the new information she has gathered, she can now design and implement appropriate strategies to improve her students' attitudes toward homework and increase their homework completion rate. She also decides to systematically analyze the results of her new teaching strategies and determine the effectiveness of her new approach. Based on the outcomes of her assessment, Ann will decide whether to continue, modify, or change the new strategies she has been using.

Ann's story illustrates a situation in which teachers face challenging pedagogical issues. Rather than trying to solve the problem haphazardly or blindly following strategies proposed by outside experts, Ann conceptualized a different approach tailored to her unique situation and the needs of her students. She decided that to improve her students' performance, a systematic approach was needed. Ann designed a new approach to homework assignments and improved her students' learning by following several steps: (1) gaining a better understanding of the causes for her students' reluctance to complete the homework assignments, (2) increasing her knowledge of the topic of homework, (3) implementing new instructional strategies, (4) collecting and interpreting data, and (5) assessing the effectiveness of her research-based actions. In fact, Ann was engaged in an action research study.

Action research is usually defined as an inquiry conducted by educators in their own settings in order to advance their practice and improve their students' learning (e.g., D. M. Burton & Bartlett, 2005; Fox, Martin, & Green, 2007; Herr & Nihlen, 2007; Jarvis, 1999; Menter, Eliot, Hulme, & Lewin, 2011). In education, the terms *action research* and *practitioner research* are often used interchangeably because both types of research emphasize the role of practitioners in conducting investigations in their classrooms and schools. You probably have come across several other labels that describe this type of study, among them *teacher research*, *classroom research*, and *teacher as researcher*. In this book, when we describe action research done by practitioners, we do not refer to teachers only; rather, we include other school members, such as administrators, specialists, counselors, tutors, aides, and others who are involved in education. A growing number of these practitioners have embraced action research and view it as a viable model for modifying, changing, and improving the teaching–learning process. They feel that action research enhances their ability to grow professionally, become self-evaluative, and take responsibility for their own practice. Thus, action research provides educators with a powerful strategy for being active partners in leading school improvement (Cochran-Smith & Lytle, 2009; Hopkins, 2008).

We start the chapter with a discussion of educational research and compare traditional and action research, highlighting the important role of educational practitioners as researchers in their own settings. Next, a brief historical perspective of action research is presented, followed by an explanation of the unique characteristics of action research. We end the chapter with our goals in writing the book and present an overview of the book's chapters.

WHAT IS EDUCATIONAL RESEARCH?

Before we explore action research, let's examine what we mean by research and specifically educational research. Research is an intentional, systematic, and purposeful inquiry. Using an organized process of collecting and analyzing information, the researcher seeks to answer a question, solve a problem, or understand a phenomenon (Gall, Gall, & Borg, 2006; McMillan & Schumacher, 2010).

Educational research is usually focused on studying the process of teaching and learning. Traditional educational research is often conducted by university-based researchers who carry out an investigation of others at the school setting. The ultimate goal of this type of educational research is to develop universal theories and discover generalized principles and best strategies that ultimately improve the quality of education.

To ensure that the results of traditional educational research extend beyond the local population and are applicable in a wide variety of settings, investigations are typically conducted on a carefully selected sample that represents a population of interest. The researcher is usually an outsider, external to the particular context being studied, and puts an emphasis on being uninvolved, objective, and unbiased (Mertler & Charles, 2011).

From this perspective, educational changes are mostly planned top-down in a hierarchical process. The teachers and other school practitioners are seen as recipients and consumers of knowledge produced by outside experts; their role is to effectively implement the research findings in their schools and classrooms. Thus, according to traditional educational research, there is a separation between theory and action and between research and practice (Mertler, 2012).

PRACTITIONERS AS RESEARCHERS

For many years, school practitioners have recognized the value of traditional educational research and the contributions that it has made to the field of education. Much of our understanding of the process of teaching and learning draws on studies done by researchers in the field of education, psychology, and other sciences. As practitioners, we long for scientifically proven solutions when we encounter problems that school life presents. When we confront an unruly group of students or are frustrated by countless efforts to motivate an individual student, we wish that we had a foolproof method that would allow us to solve our problems. As practitioners we also realize the limitations of implementing generalized principles and the shortcomings of applying universal theories to our practice. We recognize that for strategies to be uniformly applicable, all students must be viewed as essentially similar. However, the uniqueness of each student and the particular historical, social, economic, and cultural context of each setting belie this viewpoint. As educators we know from our experience in the complex dynamics of classrooms, with their unpredictable interactions, that there is no single solution that will produce consistently successful results. What is effective in one situation may not be productive in a different situation, and what works with one student may fail with another (Elliott & Norris, 2012).

Practitioners have grown to recognize the distinctiveness and validity of their knowledge and have realized that there is no substitute for their familiarity with the particular setting. Understanding of students' social and historical circumstances and knowing their past and present successes and failures, fears, and dreams enable the practitioners to gain insight into their students' worlds. This subjective insight provides practitioners with opportunities to explore systematically, and with care, multiple options for action, with sensitivity to the "here and now." Thus, action research offers a new relationship among the areas of practice, theory, and research that blurs the boundaries between each of them.

In action research, teachers and other school personnel take on the role of researchers and study their own practice within their classrooms and schools. The research questions arise from events, problems, or professional interests that the educators deem important. The practitioners carry out their investigations systematically, reflectively, and critically using strategies that are appropriate for their practice. Being insiders who are intimately involved and familiar with the context, practitioners are inherently subjective and directly engaged. They are not concerned whether the knowledge gained through their studies is applicable and replicable in other settings. Their goal is to improve *their* practice and foster *their* professional growth by understanding *their* students, solving problems, or developing new skills. They put their newly emerging theories into practice and carefully examine the resulting changes. From this perspective, changes in education occur in a bottom-up, democratic process, led by practitioners who are self-directed, knowledge-generating professionals (McNiff & Whitehead, 2011). Table 1.1 presents a comparison of traditional research and action research.

HISTORICAL PERSPECTIVES

The idea of action research in education is not new. The theoretical roots can be traced to progressive educational leaders from the early parts of the 20th century who lauded the role of practitioners as intellectual leaders, and encouraged them to conduct research in their own settings (Noffke, 1997). John Dewey (1929/1984) recognized the central position of teachers in reforming education. He was critical

TABLE 1.1. Comparison of Traditional and Action Research	
Traditional research	**Action research**
The purpose of research is to develop theories and discover generalized principles.	The purpose of research is to improve practice.
Research is conducted by outside experts.	Research is conducted by insiders who are involved in the context.
Researchers are objective, detached, removed, and unbiased.	Researchers are subjective, involved, and engaged.
Educational researchers conduct research *on* others.	Action researchers study themselves and their practices.
The research questions are predetermined and reflect outsiders' research interests.	Research questions arise from local events, problems, and needs.
Research participants are carefully selected to represent a population of interest.	Participants are a natural part of the inquiry setting.
Generalized rules and practices are applicable in other educational settings.	Every child is unique and every setting is particular.
The researchers' findings are implemented by practitioners.	The action researchers' findings are directly applied to their practice.
Educational changes occur top-down in a hierarchical process.	Educational changes occur bottom-up in a democratic process.
There is a separation between theory and action, and between research and practice.	Boundaries among theory, research, and practice are blurred.

of the separation between knowledge and action and argued that educators need to test their ideas and put their emerging theories into action. He encouraged teachers to become reflective practitioners and make autonomous pedagogical judgments based on interrogating and examining their practice.

John Collier coined the term *action research* (Holly, Arhar, & Kasten, 2009). Collier, a commissioner of the Bureau of Indian Affairs from 1933 to 1945, initiated community education projects on Indian reservations in the United States (Noffke, 1997). Criticizing government policies that assumed that Native American tribes all have the same needs, he described a form of research that emphasized the specific local needs of each community (Hinchey, 2008). Kurt Lewin, a social psychologist, however, is most often credited as the founder of action research. An immigrant who fled from Nazi Germany, Lewin developed the methodology of action research in the 1930s and 1940s as a means for democratic social change (Herr & Nihlen, 2007; Somekh & Zeichner, 2009). He argued that action research should be conducted with the participation of the members of the social group who are part of the situation to be changed. The action research model he developed was based on a cyclical process of fact finding, planning, action, and evaluation of the results of the action (Lewin, 1946).

Stephen Corey introduced action research to the field of education in the 1950s. He was a dean and professor of education at Teachers College and worked with schools on studies that involved teachers, parents, and students. In his seminal book *Action Research to Improve School Practice* (1953), Corey contended that educational change will not take place unless practitioners are involved in developing curriculum and instructional practices, drawing on the experiential knowledge they gain through inquiry. However, in the decade that followed, when the emphasis was placed on top-down education, action research was pushed into the background and teachers were again seen as merely conduits of curriculum designed by outside experts (Hinchey, 2008; Noffke, 1997).

In the 1970s Lawrence Stenhouse, a professor of education in the United Kingdom, coined the phrase "practitioner researcher" to describe teachers who were engaged in action research to improve their practice. Stenhouse (1975) rejected the way in which curriculum materials were typically created by experts and handed down to teachers who were then blamed for the failure of these curricula. He claimed that practitioners should be involved in examining the suitability of the new innovations to their specific students and in modifying materials as necessary. Stenhouse initiated the Humanities Curriculum Project, which encouraged teachers to be researchers who would be engaged in a systematic self-analysis of their school settings, their classrooms, and their teaching (Altrichter, Feldman, Posch, & Somekh, 2008; Eliot, 1991/2002).

Stenhouse's work inspired action research networks, and action research has been growing in popularity since the 1980s in the United States, Australia, New Zealand, and Canada (Cochran-Smith & Lytle, 1999; Hendricks, 2012). In the United States, the movement has been aligned with the teacher-empowerment movement, and action researchers facilitated the redefinition of teachers as professionals. Practitioners challenged the underlying hierarchical assumptions attached to traditional educational research and insisted that inquiry validates their knowledge and empowers them to become leaders who are involved in the process of making decisions about their classrooms and schools (Cochran-Smith & Lytle, 1999, 2009).

THE UNIQUE CHARACTERISTICS OF ACTION RESEARCH

Action research is a distinct kind of research that is different from other traditional educational research. It is *constructivist, situational, practical, systematic,* and *cyclical.*

▶ **Constructivist.** Action researchers are perceived as generators of knowledge rather than receivers and enactors of knowledge produced by outside experts. From this perspective, practitioners are professionals who are capable of making informed decisions based on their own inquiries and able to assume responsibility for their own research-based actions (Atweh, Kemmis, & Weeks, 1998; Cochran-Smith & Lytle, 1993, 2009; Hendricks, 2012; Jarvis, 1999; Pine, 2008).

▶ **Situational.** Action researchers aim to understand the unique context of their studies and the participants involved. The conclusions of these inquiries should be understood within the complexities, ambiguities, and nuances of the particular settings in which their studies were conducted (Baumfield, Hall, & Wall, 2008; Herr & Nihlen, 2007; Holly et al., 2009; Mertler, 2012).

▶ **Practical.** Action researchers choose the questions that they plan to investigate based on their own concerns and professional areas of interests. The results of their studies are immediately relevant to the improvement of their practice (Altrichter et al., 2008; Bauer & Brazer, 2012; Dana & Yendol-Hoppey, 2009; Marzano, 2003).

▶ **Systematic.** Action research is intentional, thoughtfully planned, systematic, and methodical. The research process has to be systematic in order to produce trustworthy and meaningful results (Burns, 2007; Burton, Brundelt, & Jones, 2008; McNiff & Whitehead, 2010; Stringer, 2007).

▶ **Cyclical.** Action research starts with a research question and ends with the application of the knowledge gained that leads to new questions and a new cycle of research (Johnson, 2011; Mertler, 2012; Mills, 2011; Sagor, 2011; Stringer, 2008). Following is a description of the six steps involved in carrying out a full cycle of action research and an illustration of the cyclical steps (Figure 1.1).

▶ Step 1: Identifying an issue or problem the practitioner wants to explore

▶ Step 2: Gathering background information through a review of appropriate literature and existing research on the topic

▶ Step 3: Designing the study and planning the methods of collecting data

▶ Step 4: Collecting data

▶ Step 5: Analyzing and interpreting data

▶ Step 6: Writing, sharing, and implementing the findings

In reality, action research is much more dynamic, fluid, and—at times—messier than is implied by the linear description of the process presented in Figure 1.1. Nevertheless, to clarify the research procedures and enable you to undertake

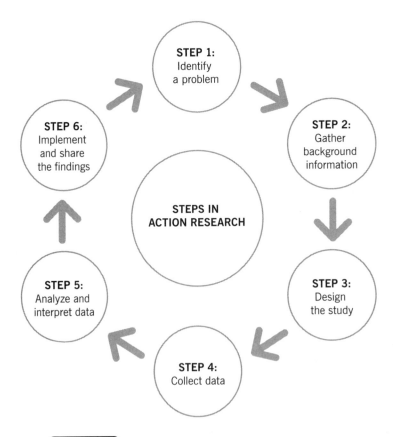

FIGURE 1.1. The six cyclical steps of action research.

an action research project, we divided this book into distinct and sequential steps. Additionally, the research-cycle process often does not end with the implementation of findings. When the study's results are put into action, you may need to assess the outcomes and determine whether the desired changes have occurred or other strategies are required. Thus, the cyclical process continues from one study to the next as your practice improves incrementally.

The field of action research grew out of various educational traditions and is marked by a heated debate about the nature of educational knowledge and the meaning of research in the context of education. Generally, the diverse approaches to action research tend to be classified under two competing perspectives: the *qualitative* and *quantitative* approaches. However, this book de-emphasizes these traditional dichotomies and moves beyond the theoretical "either/or" choices. Instead, we chose to focus on the practical ways that inquiry can be used to address the complexities of the issues educators face in their practice day in and day out.

The practical orientation of the book also led us to the decision not to align ourselves with qualitative research only, as is often done by many action researchers. Although we recognize that practitioners can never be objective observers, neutral data collectors, or detached interpreters of school reality, we also recognize the invaluable contributions of quantitative approaches to action research. While qualitative research methods, such as observations, interviews, and rich narratives, enhance the sensitivity of action researchers to the nuanced world of students and others in the school setting, numerical data provide an effective tool to assess, describe, and analyze other aspects of school life. The decision about which methods to use—qualitative, quantitative, or mixed—should be made by practitioners based on the nature of their research questions, the focus of their studies, the particular settings in which the research occurs, and their interests and dispositions. Therefore, in this book, qualitative and quantitative approaches are balanced and are given equal weight.

CHAPTER SUMMARY

1. *Action research* is usually defined as an inquiry conducted by practitioners in their own educational settings in order to advance their practice and improve their students' learning.

2. In education, the terms *action research* and *practitioner research* are often used interchangeably because both types of research emphasize the role of practitioners in conducting investigations in their classrooms and schools.

3. Action research provides educators with a powerful strategy for being active partners in leading school improvement.

4. Research is an intentional, systematic, and purposeful inquiry. Using an organized process of collecting and analyzing information, the researcher seeks to answer a question, solve a problem, or understand a phenomenon.

5. Traditional educational research is often conducted by university-based researchers who carry out an investigation *on* others at the school setting. The ultimate goal of this type of educational research is to develop universal theories and discover generalized principles and best strategies that ultimately improve the quality of education.

6. According to traditional educational research, changes are mostly planned top-down in a hierarchical process and there is a separation between theory and action, and between research and practice.

7. In action research, teachers and other school practitioners take on the role of researchers and study their own practice; their research questions arise from events, problems, or professional interests that the educators deem important.

8. The practitioners carry out their investigations systematically, reflectively, and critically, using strategies that are appropriate for their practice.

9. The goal of action researchers is to engage in a study to find out how to improve *their* practice and foster *their* professional growth by understanding their own students, solving problems, or developing new skills.

10. The idea of action research in education is not new. From the early parts of the 20th century, educational leaders lauded the role of practitioners as intellectual leaders and encouraged them to conduct research in their own settings.

11. Since the 1980s, action research has been growing in popularity in the United States. Aligned with the teacher-empowerment movement, action researchers facilitated the redefinition of teachers as professionals.

12. Action research is a distinct kind of research that is different from other traditional educational research; it is *constructivist, situational, practical, systematic*, and *cyclical*.

13. There are six steps involved in carrying out a full cycle of action research: (a) identifying an issue or a problem the practitioner wants to explore, (b) gathering background information through a review of appropriate literature and existing research on the topic, (c) designing the study and planning the methods of collecting data, (d) collecting data, (e) analyzing and interpreting; and (f) writing, sharing, and implementing the findings.

14. Although the diverse approaches to action research are often classified under two competing perspectives—qualitative and quantitative—this book focuses on the practical

ways that inquiry can be used to address the complexities of the issues educators face in their practice day in and day out.

15. While the qualitative research enhances practitioners' sensitivity to the nuanced world of school and classroom life, quantitative research offers an effective tool to assess, describe, and analyze other aspects of school life. Educators can benefit from the contributions of each.

16. The decision about which methods to use—qualitative, quantitative, or mixed—should be made by practitioners based on the nature of their research questions, the focus of their studies, their particular settings, and their interests and dispositions.

CHAPTER EXERCISES AND ACTIVITIES

1. What are some of the advantages and disadvantages of traditional educational research for teachers' daily practice?

   a. List one or two examples in which traditional research can contribute to your practice or to your students' learning.

   b. List one or two examples in which traditional research on an issue, although important to you, may have no immediate relevancy for your practice.

2. In your opinion, what are some advantages of conducting action research by school practitioners and what are some of the barriers they may face?

   a. List one or two examples of action research conducted in a classroom, school, or other educational setting.

   b. List one or two examples in which a practitioner may encounter barriers to conducting action research in his or her own practice.

3. What are some of the ideas and themes that have underscored the history of action research from the early parts of the 20th century? Do you see some of these themes still evident today?

4. This chapter highlights some of the distinct characteristics of action research. Consider these characteristics from the perspectives of a practitioner, an administrator, a parent, and a student.

5. Review the six steps involved in carrying out a full cycle of action research (Figure 1.1). Reflect on the issues and concerns that may arise with the implementation of each of these steps.

ADDITIONAL READINGS

Adelman, C. (1993). Kurt Lewin and the origin of action research. *Educational Action, Research 1*(1), 7–24.

Lankshear, C., & Knobel, M. (2004). *A handbook for teacher research.* New York: Open University Press.

Reason, P., & Bradbury, H. (2008). *The Sage handbook of action research: Participative inquiry and practice* (2nd ed.). London: Sage.

Rudduck, J., & Hopkins, D. (1985). *Research as a basis of teaching: Readings from the work of Lawrence Stenhouse.* Oxford, UK: Heinemann Educational Books.

Whitehead, J., & McNiff, J. (2006). *Action research living theory.* London: Sage.

Winter, R. (1987). *Action research and the nature of social inquiry: Professional innovation and educational work.* Averbury, UK: Aldershot.

CHAPTER 2

Choosing and Learning about Your Research Topic

A research process starts by identifying the topic of your choice and becoming knowledgeable about it. This chapter helps you select an area of interest and articulate a problem statement that will guide your research by providing a clear purpose for your investigation. We present the process of locating and organizing literature related to your research around themes, followed by suggestions on how to write the literature review. With the knowledge gained through developing the literature review, you will be able to formulate a specific research question that will guide your study.

CHOOSING YOUR RESEARCH TOPIC

The first step in the teacher research process is to identify a meaningful area of interest. Your classroom and school are the best sources for your questions, puzzles, and problems. Reflect on your daily practice: Is there anything you want to change, improve, or validate? For example, are you considering changing the way you assess students' knowledge? Do you want to better understand the problematic behavior of a particular student? Are you wondering how a specific educational policy will affect your own educational setting?

Be sure to select a topic that is significant for your work. Action research is time consuming and you need to feel that your time is well spent on something that is worthwhile, that is personally meaningful and contributes to your personal and professional growth. At the same time, be realistic. Choose a topic that you can complete within your time constraints and available resources. Some examples of research problems include:

1. What are the advantages and disadvantages of year-round schooling?
2. How do my second-grade students deal with social conflict?
3. What is the impact of inclusion on my ELL (English language learner) students?
4. How can I successfully integrate differentiated instruction into my language arts classroom?

Brainstorming with a partner or in a small group will help you choose a meaningful topic for your study and clarify its focus. Group members/partners should ask questions and help each other refine and sharpen the research focus. You may want to follow these steps prior to meeting with your group or research partner:

1. Jot down a list of issues that interest you.
2. Review the list and prioritize the items.
3. Choose the issue that you are most passionate about.
4. Share your issues with your group and explain your choice, noting the following:
    a. Why is this topic significant for you personally or professionally?
    b. How would exploring this issue be helpful to your students?
    c. How will the investigation be helpful to others (e.g., peers, parents, and the education field in general)?
    d. What are some of the obstacles that may stand in your way (e.g., time, resources, and access)?

Before you launch your investigation you may want to look for general information on the topic you are considering. This will help you to make an informed choice about the focus of your study.

FRAMING THE RESEARCH PROBLEM STATEMENT

The next step is to articulate, in writing, your research problem. The problem statement (often referred to as "the general statement of the problem") serves as an introduction to the research and will guide the direction of your study. Your problem statement presents a clear purpose for your study. For example:

1. **The study is designed** to explore the effects of problem-solving mathematics curriculum on second-grade students' motivation and success in mastering basic math functions.

2. **The purpose of the study is to investigate** how a democratic classroom influences students' behavior in class.

The purpose of your study may consist of several research questions. These questions can be further divided into several subquestions (see Figure 2.1). To make your study manageable we suggest that you limit yourself to no more than three to five subquestions. In addition, the problem statement usually includes the following:

1. Definitions of the central concepts and terms that may not be familiar to the reader. For example, define the terms *problem-solving curriculum* or *democratic classroom*.

2. A description of the personal and professional context for the study. You may describe a situation or concern that motivated you to choose the topic.

3. An explanation of your role in the study. For example, clarify if you are the teacher in the classroom where you will conduct the study.

4. An examination of who, besides yourself, might be interested in the study and who will benefit from the knowledge gained. For example, peers, colleagues, parents, and policymakers.

Purpose					
Research Question 1			Research Question 2		
Subquestion 1	Subquestion 2	Subquestion 3	Subquestion 1	Subquestion 2	Subquestion 3

FIGURE 2.1. A schematic representation of purpose, research questions, and subquestions.

For example, Polly, a middle school language arts teacher, is interested in examining how to best implement differentiated instruction in her own classroom. Box 2.1 presents Polly's research problem statement.

Here are some practical suggestions that you may consider as you write your study's problem statement:

1. Have a clear rationale for conducting your study.

2. Narrow your broad topic of interest to a more refined focus. For example, "How successful is inclusion in my class?" may be changed to "How do

---

BOX 2.1. Research Problem Statement of a Sixth-Grade Teacher Conducting Research to Determine the Success of Applying Differentiated Instruction in Her Classroom

INTEGRATING DIFFERENTIATED INSTRUCTION INTO THE CLASSROOM

The range of abilities within today's classrooms has grown significantly. Teachers have to be responsive to learners with diverse academic, social, and emotional needs (Tomlinson, 2001; Tomlinson & McTighe, 2006). As a sixth-grade teacher of language arts in an inclusive classroom, I work with students who have varying skill levels. My students' reading abilities range from the 10th to the 90th percentile of sixth-grade students nationwide based on the Measures of Academic Progress (MAP) tests administered annually to students in my district. The most challenging aspect of my work is to develop a responsive curriculum and educational environment that effectively reaches each student in my classroom.

Within the context of this study, *differentiated instruction* is defined as "a systematic approach to planning curriculum and instruction for academically diverse learners" (Tomlinson & Eidson, 2003, p. 3). This educational approach offers opportunities for each class member to be engaged by providing "different avenues to acquiring content, to processing or making sense of ideas, and to developing products so that each student can effectively learn" (Tomlinson, 2001, p. 1). I have found differentiating instruction to be an effective way to meet the needs of the diverse learners in my class, keep them engaged, and enable them to perform better on assessments. Additionally, my school district has, in recent years, stressed the importance of differentiation and has made this approach a high priority for all of its teachers. However, many of the teachers still struggle with finding the best ways to differentiate instruction, considering the limited resources and the extra time that is required for doing this on a regular basis. This study will provide us with research-based knowledge that is drawn from our local setting and is applicable to our practicing teachers.

regular education students relate to students with special needs in my class-room?"

3. Choose an issue that you are able to explore within the limited time and resources that you have.

4. Choose a topic that is not too obscure or new to enable you to locate a sufficient number of research articles on your topic.

5. Choose a research question that does not call for simple yes or no answers.

You may find that collaborating with others or with a partner will help you refine and improve each other's problem statements. Figure 2.2 provides a quick checklist for you and your research partners to evaluate the research problem statement.

DEVELOPING THE LITERATURE REVIEW

Action researchers aim to link theory to practice and connect what happens in their educational settings with the broader knowledge about teaching and learning. After stating the research problem, the next step is to familiarize yourself with what has been written about your topic and arrange this information into a coherent essay called the *literature review*. A literature review is a summary and synthesis of research put forward by others that is pertinent to your own inquiry. In your synthesis you combine the relevant ideas and research reported in the

✓	Evaluation Criteria
	Is the problem clearly stated? Is it concise?
	Is the problem researchable?
	Is the significance of the problem discussed?
	Are all the major terms defined and explained?
	Is it clear who will benefit from the study besides yourself?
	Is the proposed research feasible and doable within the constraints of your time, access, and resources?

FIGURE 2.2. A checklist to guide the self-evaluation of the research problem statement.

different readings into a meaningful and coherent whole. The synthesis allows you to gain a better understanding of the background and context of the study you are about to undertake. In addition, the literature review can establish the rationale for your study by highlighting the importance of your own research question. Often, as a result of reviewing the literature, the purpose of your study may become more focused or even shift.

Sources for the literature review include peer-reviewed journal articles, professional books, conference papers, institutional publications, media reports, and documents located on websites. We suggest that you consult your instructor for specific guidelines as to what types of sources are acceptable for your literature review.

Some qualitative action researchers question whether reviewing the literature prior to the data collection process may lead to bias and preconceived notions about the investigated topic (Glaser, 1992). However, more and more qualitative researchers see the value of conducting a literature review before starting the data collection. These researchers claim that being informed about current research, theoretical positions, and potential methods of data collection helps action researchers clarify and refine their own studies (Corbin & Strauss, 2007). Therefore, take time to immerse yourself in reading and summarizing what others have written on your topic. Doing so will allow you to:

- ▶ Place your research project within an existing knowledge base.
- ▶ Trace the conceptual threads, themes, debates, and questions related to your topic.
- ▶ Situate the study within a historical context or theoretical perspective.
- ▶ Identify the need for your research.
- ▶ Choose possible procedures and methods to use in your study.
- ▶ Narrow and further refine your research question.

Additionally, as you complete your study, you may want to return to the literature and compare and contrast the findings from your study with what you learned from past research. Keep in mind that the literature review process is not complete until you finish your study, as new research is constantly added and disseminated.

The process of preparing to write the literature review usually follows several sequential steps: locating sources for the literature review, reading literature to identify themes, and constructing a literature review outline.

Step 1: Locating Sources for the Literature Review

The process of writing the literature review begins with locating sources that allow you to gather background information about your topic. This can be done by using an Internet search engine to identify information related to your topic quickly and easily. However, although there is much excellent material online, there is also a lot of questionable, unsupported information and you must examine the credibility of your sources. By comparison, academic journal articles, professional books, and conference presentations are reviewed by peers before being published. It is important that you use references that have been subjected to this review process.

When possible, use *primary sources* rather than *secondary sources*. Primary sources are descriptions of the original research reported by the researchers who conducted the study. Secondary sources are publications in which authors describe ideas, works, and studies done by others. An example of a primary source is a study conducted by Gort (2006) on bilingual students who received instruction in both their dominant language and second language. Brisk (2011), in her article that was published in the *Handbook of Research in Second Language Teaching and Learning*, incorporated Gort's study as she provided an overview of current knowledge and research on the development of writing of elementary-age bilingual learners in their second language. Thus, Brisk's article is a secondary source.

The greatest disadvantage in using secondary sources is that you have to rely on text citations and summaries of reports done by others without being able to check the original or primary source. Nevertheless, when your research time or access to published research is limited, you may find that using some secondary sources is convenient and helpful.

Increasingly, educational electronic databases, such as ERIC, EBSCO Host, Pro Quest, and JSTOR offer the full text of journal articles that can be easily downloaded. If an article you are looking for is not accessible online, it can still be obtained from a university library or through an interlibrary loan system. You may ask the university librarian to help you locate and access the sources needed for your literature review. While most online databases are not free, accessing them through the university or a public library will yield a great number of free full-text articles. We recommend that for the most part you use articles that were published within the last 10 years. Nevertheless, make sure that you do not overlook seminal works or major authors that have influenced and shaped the subject of your study or can offer a historical perspective.

Before beginning your library search, transform the problem statement into library search terms by defining your research focus and deciding on the specific issues to be included. The database search is conducted by using keywords or descriptors. (Keywords and descriptors refer to the main words and terms that describe your topic.) To increase the likelihood of accessing desired sources, it is helpful to ensure that the terms you use are identical to the keywords used in the educational databases. You may want to use the ERIC thesaurus to identify the general descriptors or keywords used.

Following are suggested steps for your online search:

1. *Identify the central terms and concepts in your topic.* Write a list of keywords based on these terms and concepts.

2. *Develop a list of synonyms for your keywords.* Most databases have a thesaurus that you can use to find synonyms.

3. *Create a list of keywords in order of importance to your research.*

4. *Conduct a database search by starting with the most important keyword.* If there are too many results, add a second or third term to narrow your results.

5. *Narrow or broaden the search as needed.* Almost all databases use basic Boolean commands to narrow or broaden searches. The command "and" between two search keywords narrows the search and the command "or" broadens the search by allowing synonyms.

Repeat the process if there are too many or not enough suggested articles and books. You can narrow the search by omitting the least important keyword, or broaden the search by adding different keyword descriptors or synonyms.

Another suggestion for locating additional resources on your topic is to examine the references cited by the articles that you did obtain, especially if these articles are recent. As you identify and locate reference sources, first read the abstracts or skim through the articles to determine whether they are relevant or useful for your study. The articles you are looking for should:

▶ Be related to your topic of interest.

▶ Be published in a "peer-reviewed" research journal.

▶ Be published within the last 10 years. However, you may choose to include older references that are highly relevant to your study, have greatly impacted the field, can provide a historical perspective, or are landmark studies.

▶ Include articles that discuss the theoretical framework, as well as articles that describe research studies on your topic.

▶ Present different positions or viewpoints when the issue you study is controversial.

The review should be comprehensive but not overwhelming. Usually, time constraints limit the number of articles that can be reviewed. The number of sources reviewed may depend on the expectations outlined in your research project guidelines or the course syllabus. It is a good idea to collect more articles than are required so that you can choose the sources that have the greatest relevance to your research topic.

At times, the articles you find do not exactly address your particular research focus. For example, the article may not discuss children of the same ages, research strategies, or methods you are planning to investigate. Don't despair; in these situations, you can use those articles that are most related to your topic. For example, Leslie, a student teacher, wants to explore the benefits of teaching a foreign language in the primary grades; however, she could only locate articles that describe research conducted with middle school students. Her solution is to review the articles that she found for the literature review, and in her own study, she plans to explore which findings from the middle school studies also apply to younger students.

Step 2: Reading Literature to Identify Themes

Conducting a literature review requires you to read a bit differently than usual. The purpose in reading research articles, books, or reports is to focus specifically on information that directly relates to your own investigation. This information is organized around themes that are pertinent to your study. The themes are usually made up of perspectives, approaches, ideas, or results from relevant existing studies. As you review the literature relevant to your investigation, you identify the themes that drive your narrative. The references that you cite support your themes and serve as evidence for the arguments and assertions that you have made. Thus, the literature review is a topical essay consisting of analysis and synthesis of your readings around themes, rather than an annotated bibliography (Machi & McEvoy, 2009).

To develop the literature review, start by discovering the relevant themes in each study that you read. As you develop each theme, cite information from your sources that serves as evidence material. Finally, present the themes in a logical order according to the relationship among them and their importance to your own investigation. Using headings to identify your themes makes the structure of the literature review clearer for you and the reader.

You may find it helpful to create a map or a matrix to keep track of your sources and link them by using software packages such as Endnote®. The following are steps that we've found useful for identifying themes to be discussed in the literature review:

1. Begin by skimming quickly through each article (or other documents) to get a general idea of its content. Identify and mark the paragraphs or sections that are specifically meaningful for your research.

2. Read the marked sections again, this time slowly and in depth, paying attention to the themes that emerge. In the margin, write down these themes.

3. Take notes on each article as soon as you finish reading it and write a narrative summary of each relevant theme. We suggest that for each reference you use an electronic "index card" (article thematic review template).

4. Include the complete citation on the "index card." If you obtained the source via the Internet, note when the record was retrieved and the web address.

5. Summarize each theme on the card. The length and details of the description depend on the importance of the information for your study; the more relevant the content is to your topic, the more detailed the summary should be. You may make notes about the different ways a theme is perceived by different authors. For example, note agreement, disagreement, and contrasting or complementary findings.

6. Note whether the theme was already discussed by another author. Feel free to add any other information that you find useful.

7. Read each article critically and record your response, agreement, or criticism of each source. Consider the following issues: How was the research paradigm identified? Were terms adequately defined? Was there sufficient information about the research setting, participants, data collection procedures, and findings?

8. Be meticulous! If you identify a very strong or unique statement that you want to quote, quote it precisely and don't forget to include the page number(s) and other publication information.

Title of article (follow APA style): _____

Author(s): _____

Journal: _____

Year of publication: _____ Volume: _____ Issue: _____ Pages: _____

For electronic sources: Relevant issues/themes: Web address: _____

Digital object identifier: _____

Summary of Theme I: _____

Summary of Theme II: _____

Summary of Theme III: _____

Quotes (including page numbers): _____

_____

FIGURE 2.3. Article thematic review template.

Figure 2.3 shows a template for an article thematic review.

Step 3: Constructing a Literature Review Outline

After you've read and recorded all of your assembled articles, you may still be uncertain about how to organize the various issues into a theme-based, coherent, and well-integrated narrative. You may find the following method helpful in constructing a thematic outline (Mills, 2011). Transfer from the article thematic review (Figure 2.3) those themes that emerged from each article into a literature review theme organizer (see Figure 2.4). Similar themes can often be found in more than one article and some articles may discuss several themes. Figure 2.4 may help you choose which themes are most pertinent to your research and which are superfluous and can be eliminated.

Now you are ready to create an outline for the literature review. It can be written in a narrative style or as a series of bullets. Analyze the similarities and differences between the themes and subthemes and turn them into topics and subtopics. Make sure you record the name(s) of the author(s) next to each theme.

Also, consider multiple perspectives and approaches presented by different authors on the same topic or subtopic, recognize points of agreement and disagreement, and compare and contrast research findings and conclusions. Add the author(s) you will use for each of the subtopics and the year(s) of publication.

Author(s)	Date of Publication	Themes Discussed in the Article					

FIGURE 2.4. Literature review theme organizer.

Decide on the logical order of your themes and subthemes. The rule of thumb in constructing the literature review outline is that issues least related to your own research focus are discussed first and the most related are discussed last. Additionally, it makes sense to organize items from the general to the specific, from historical to contemporary, from theory to practice, and from definitions to examples. Suppose, for example, that you want to examine the role of homework in middle school. You may start by providing a historical perspective on the role of homework. Next, describe contemporary debates surrounding the issue, presenting the arguments proposed by those who support and those who object to assigning homework. Finally, explore homework from the point of view of teachers, students, and parents, concluding by pointing out the limited research on students' perceptions of homework. Figure 2.5 illustrates an example of a linear outline of a literature review on the topic of classroom as a democratic community.

Some action researchers discover that visual mapping is an effective means of organizing graphically the topics and subtopics of their literature review. In a literature topic map they display the central topic and subtopics as they relate to each other and to the issue under investigation. Sources are linked to each theme and subtheme (Creswell, 2011; Hendricks, 2012). For example, Chris, a preservice

---

Classroom as a Democratic Community

1. History of Democratic Education from the Turn of the 20th Century to the Present (Spring, 2010; Tozer, Senese, & Violas, 2009; Tyack, 1974)

2. Different Visions of Democratic Education (Parker, 2003)
   a. Dewey's Vision of the Democratic Classroom (Dewey, 1916)
   b. Diverse Contemporary Perspectives of Democratic Education (Banks et al., 2005; Kahne & Westheimer, 2003; Mikel, 2011; Parker, 2003)

3. Democracy in Practice
   a. Learners and Teacher: Dialogical Relationships (Apple & Beane, 2007; S. Frank & Huddleston, 2009; Freire, 1970)
   b. Classroom as a Just Community (Apple & Beane, 2007; Banks et al., 2005; Edelstein, 2011; Goodlad, Soder, & McDaniel, 2008).
   c. Planning and Evaluation (Apple & Beane, 2007; Goodlad et al., 2008; Parker, 2003)

4. Problems and Critique (McQuillan, 2005; Schutz, 2008)

5. Examples of Implementations of Democratic Education in the Classroom (Goodlad et al., 2008; Michelli & Keiser, 2005).

FIGURE 2.5. Example of literature review.

student, who serves as a long-term substitute teacher in a self-contained special education class, explores the topic of cooperative learning (CL) within the special education classroom. As he reviews the literature he creates a topic map that illustrates the way he plans to structure the information he obtained from his readings. Figure 2.6 shows an excerpt from Chris's literature topic map that focuses on the benefits of CL for students with special needs in the general classroom.

Once your literature review outline or topic map is completed, you are ready to write the literature review. Follow the outline to construct the literature review as a topical essay. (Your outline's topics and subtopics may become the formal subheadings of your essay.)

Step 4: Writing the Literature Review

There is no single format for writing a literature review, and the structure generally emerges from the nature of the particular literature that is reviewed. However, there are usually three main sections: (1) an introduction, (2) the main section of the review, and (3) a summary and concluding remarks that end with the specific research question(s). Remember, the arguments you make in the literature review

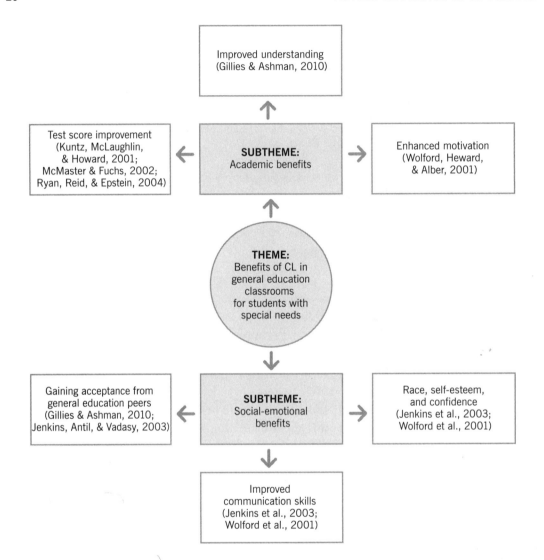

FIGURE 2.6. Excerpts from a literature map: The benefits of collaborative learning for special education students.

section of your research report cannot be based on your personal opinion and beliefs. Every idea, proposition, or assertion needs to be supported by "evidence," such as a citation from a credible article. On the other hand, do not accept studies' findings blindly. Read critically to ensure that your arguments are supported by trustworthy theory and data. Where possible, assess the studies that you review noting their strengths and weaknesses (Booth, Colomb, & Williams, 2008; Machi & McEvoy, 2009).

Introduction

In the introduction to the literature review you may use an advanced organizer to lay out the topics to be discussed. Terms are explained and defined, unless these terms were introduced and clarified in the problem statement section.

Main Section of the Review

The main section of the review follows the outline structure and is organized thematically. Under each subtopic discuss the appropriate theories or studies. Depending upon the significance of the source to your own study, the discussion can be brief or lengthy. In the beginning of the main section of your review, you may briefly state a theme or propose an argument, and then cite references that support your assertion. For example, a group of teacher researchers who study ethics and moral education in the classroom begins the main section of their literature review by briefly stating the essential role of moral education in the classroom and the importance of teachers' values in their teaching. Relevant references are used to establish these claims. Box 2.2 is an example of the opening paragraph of the main section of the literature review.

On the other hand, as your discussion of the literature becomes more relevant to your own research focus, you may want to elaborate and describe, at length, a particular study, an idea, or a source that pertains to one of your themes. For example, the teacher researchers discussed above review different approaches to moral education and include a detailed description of care ethics, which is one of these approaches. They analyze the work of Nel Noddings (1992, 2002, 2003), one of the central proponents of this approach. Box 2.3 is an example of one of the paragraphs from their literature review.

Transitional sentences or phrases should be used between ideas, sections, and paragraphs to facilitate the organization of the literature review. Terms like *in*

BOX 2.2. An Opening Paragraph from the Main Section of the Literature Review

Many educators and researchers agree that moral meanings pervade all aspects of the teacher's work (e.g., Campbell, 2003, 2008; Hansen, 2001; Richardson & Fenstermacher, 2001). It is also agreed that teachers' practice emerges from their values (Ayers, 2004; Brown, 2004; Efron & Joseph, 2001; Greene, 1978, 1995; Hansen, 2001; Palmer, 2007; Van Manen, 1994). Even when teachers submit to the expectation that they'll leave their personal self at the classroom door, their moral identities are unintentionally revealed through their words and actions (Alsup, 2006; Brookfield, 2005; Osterman & Kottkamp, 2004).

---

addition, contrary to, other studies, and *similarly* signal the logical flow of ideas in your review and the relationships among studies, theories, and ideas. Additionally, it is your responsibility to point out to the reader where there are agreements, inconsistencies, or gaps in the literature. You may want to use terms such as *however, by comparison, contrary to findings reported by* X, or *similar findings were reported in a study by* X.

You should communicate to the reader how the studies fit together. Point out controversies, agreements, and disagreements among researchers in the field. When different authors are in agreement, do not restate the point but present it once and reference all the authors. If one of the authors expands on the issue and provides

---

BOX 2.3. A Paragraph from the Literature Review

Nel Noddings (1992, 2002, 2003) viewed classroom relations and trust as the foundations of ethics education. Her approach, named "care ethics," proposed that the caring and trust relationships between the teacher (the "caregiver") and the students (the "cared for") are at the heart of moral education. In her book *The Challenge to Care in Schools* (1992) Noddings suggested that the caring relationship is expressed in the attention ("engrossment") given by the teacher to the feelings, desires, and concerns of the students. The caring teacher responds to the students' own perceptions of their needs and wants, and acts upon them while at the same time leading the students toward a better set of values. Noddings proposed that caring relationships between teachers and students and among the students are developed through demonstration of genuine concern for students and informal interactions with them, as well as planned classroom activities.

additional information, start with what is common to all the authors before adding the new information. For example, a paragraph in a literature review may start with a sentence that offers general information, followed by specific information reported by one of the sources cited in the first sentence (see Box 2.4).

Sources must be referenced in a scholarly format throughout the review. In educational studies, the *Publication Manual of the American Psychological Association, Sixth Edition* (APA, 2010), is often used. Make sure that your review does not end up as a series of quotations from sources. As a rule, quotations should be used sparingly and only when they highlight essential points or are particularly well phrased. Don't forget to reference each quotation, and, when available, include the page number. Similarly, also report the page number when referring to a specific table, figure, or equation in the text that you are reviewing. On the other hand, when you paraphrase or summarize ideas presented by the author(s) of the articles you review, you need to reference the source but you are not required to include the page number.

Summary and Concluding Remarks

Provide closure for the review by writing a short summary. In the summary, the major themes across *all* studies reviewed and their implications need to be highlighted. You may include a critique of the studies you reported or point out practices that have emerged that may contribute to your own research. You can also point out the limitations of the current knowledge and recognize unresolved issues or remaining questions. An existing gap in knowledge and practice would make

---

BOX 2.4. An Opening Paragraph from the Literature Review:
Moving from the General to the More Specific

Scientific experiments are an essential part of science education. The use of multimedia in science education has greatly enhanced and simplified students' access to a variety of experiments (Killdeer, 2004; Lows & Davies, 2012; O'Connor, 2011). According to Lows and Davies, electronic websites allow students to participate in experiments that are too expensive, too complex, or too dangerous to carry out in a school science laboratory.

Note. The sources for the literature review described in this example are fictitious references.

the case for the need for your own particular research. Your concluding remarks provide the rationale for formulating your study's specific questions by identifying the need for your study. A concluding sentence might be "Although prior research provides an in-depth look at the use of problem-solving skills, not enough is known about the ways high school students incorporate those skills into the study of history. Therefore, this study will explore the following questions. . . . " Another example might be "Although a great deal of research has been conducted on school recess in grades 3–5, very little research has explored this issue from the children's point of view. For that reason, my research question is. . . . "

Here are a few other suggestions for writing the literature review:

1. The literature review is devoted to a review of published studies conducted by others. You may express your opinion and criticize studies; however, the literature review is not an editorial or opinion page.

2. Every idea presented in the review must be attributed to someone, using a citation that indicates the author's last name and the publication date.

3. To avoid plagiarism, be sure to cite the sources for your ideas and arguments rather than present them as your own.

4. Every citation you make in the text of your review must appear in full in the reference list at the end of the paper. Similarly, no references may appear in the list if they are not cited in the paper.

5. Follow a standard citation format, such as APA style. The reference section at most public libraries will own a copy of the APA *Publication Manual* (2010). You may also access the APA website at *www.apastyle.org*.

6. Abbreviations should be explained and defined when they are first introduced. Write out the full term first and enclose the abbreviations in parentheses; from there on, an abbreviation may be used. For example, the first time you use the term *NCLB*, write it as follows: "No Child Left Behind (NCLB)." Subsequently, you can use the abbreviation NCLB alone.

It is a good idea to have another "set of eyes" read the first draft of your literature review. Someone unfamiliar with your topic will be able to point out grammatical errors, confusing statements, missing but necessary explanations, and any weakness in the organization of your paper. Figure 2.7 is a checklist of questions that you can use for a critical reading of the literature review.

✓	Assessment
	Is there an introduction to the review that indicates how the literature review is organized?
	Is the organization of the literature review clear?
	Is the literature review organized around themes?
	Do the ideas flow logically and smoothly from one paragraph to the next?
	Are there transitions between topics and from topics to subtopics?
	Are the ideas presented in the context of relevant research and theory?
	Are different or contrasting positions on the topic reported?
	Are the ideas and arguments supported and properly referenced?
	Does the literature review adhere to APA writing standards?
	Are the quotations properly used and the page numbers of quotations indicated?
	Does the review end with a meaningful summary of the main ideas discussed?

FIGURE 2.7. A checklist of questions for assessing the literature review.

FORMULATING SPECIFIC RESEARCH QUESTION(S)

You have already formulated a broad focus in the general problem statement that identified the overall purpose of your study. Now that you have become more knowledgeable about your topic, it is time to refine the questions that will guide your inquiry.

To articulate the specific research question(s) begin by describing precisely what you want to investigate. This usually means translating the general problem statement into more specific and focused questions. A good question should be clearly stated and formulated in researchable terms. The way the specific research questions are constructed indicates the methods you are going to use in your study. Are these methods going to be qualitative, quantitative, or mixed?

Questions in Qualitative Action Research

Questions in qualitative research are usually open-ended. The most common way to state research questions is by using the words *how* and *what*, rather than to articulate questions that lead to yes or no answers.

The question should identify who or what you are going to investigate in the study. For example, you may choose to focus your research on (1) individuals or groups (e.g., students, teachers, or administrators); (2) actions, interactions, behaviors, attitudes, and feelings; (3) curricula, programs, and teaching strategies; or (4) your own values, beliefs, and educational philosophy, and their impact on practice. Following are two examples of questions in qualitative action research:

1. How do my preschool students resolve problems on the playground during recess time?

2. What are the social and emotional impacts of standardized testing on the students in my school?

Qualitative research by its nature is evolving; therefore, it is acceptable to change or refine the focus of the specific research questions as your study proceeds, if you find it necessary to do so.

Questions in Quantitative Action Research

Research questions that are concerned with measuring variables that can be quantified are usually specific and involve assessing "how much" or "how many." These research questions are often followed by *hypotheses*, especially in experimental studies. Hypotheses are educated guesses, or predictions, about the outcomes of the study.

You should state your hypothesis in such a way as to be *observable* and *testable*. For example, do not state that a new teaching method is "good" or that positive attitudes toward inclusion are "important," because terms such as *good* or *important* are too vague and open to many interpretations, and cannot be quantified, observed, or measured. Your hypothesis should guide the design of the study whose results will allow you to conclude whether the hypothesis was confirmed. (Note: In research, we do not say that we "prove" the hypothesis. Instead, we use the term *confirm* because there is always a margin of error involved in any decision about the hypothesis.)

In the context of quantitative research, there are generally a limited number of variables that are being tested. For example, a hypothesis may predict that there will be a positive correlation between students' math and science scores or that there will be no difference in the attitudes of boys and girls toward their school. Following are two examples of questions in quantitative action research:

1. Is there a correlation between middle school students' scores on math and science tests?

2. What is the impact of integrating technology into the classroom on students' achievement test performance?

Questions in Mixed-Methods Action Research

In a mixed-methods research study you may want to pose several specific research questions, each calling for a different form of data collection. Some questions may lead to qualitative data and others to quantitative data. For example, in a study about year-round schools, one question may call for numerical data, such as students' test scores or attendance. Another question may call for qualitative data, such as in-depth interviews to explore students' motivation or parents' attitudes. Following are two examples of questions in mixed-methods research:

1. What is the effectiveness of differentiated instruction on my fourth-grade math students' learning? How do they perceive the value of this approach (qualitative interviews)? Is there an improvement in their end-of-unit test scores (quantitative data)?

2. How does a peer-mentoring program at the high school level help motivate at-risk students? Do the at-risk students feel more motivated to complete their homework and participate in class activities (qualitative data based on observations and interviews)? Is there an increase in attendance for the at-risk students and a decrease in their behavior problems and referrals (quantitative data of attendance and referrals)?

Examples of Research Problems: From the General to the Specific

In writing the research questions, start with the general research topic that is of interest to you. For example, you may wish to study the topic of bullying in elementary school. Next, narrow your focus as you articulate your problem statement. For example, you can focus on different types of bullying with an emphasis on cyberbullying. After conducting the literature review, narrow your statement to a specific question. For example, how does the use of a role-playing method impact the incidence of bullying within a fifth-grade classroom? If you plan to conduct a quantitative study, you may add a hypothesis, such as "The number of cyberbullying incidents reported will be significantly lower after the role-playing intervention, compared with their incidence prior to the intervention." Figure 2.8 provides a diagram of this process.

Note that although qualitative, quantitative, and mixed-methods researchers may start with the same general research topic and problem statement, their research questions and approaches are different and reflect their chosen paradigm. The following example illustrates how a general problem statement can lead to three different types of research questions. Each of these questions suggests the type of procedures that will be used to collect the data needed to answer the research question. Are the methods going to be qualitative, quantitative, or mixed? Figure 2.9 summarizes the process of starting with a general research topic, followed by a general problem statement, which then leads to specific qualitative, quantitative, and mixed-methods questions.

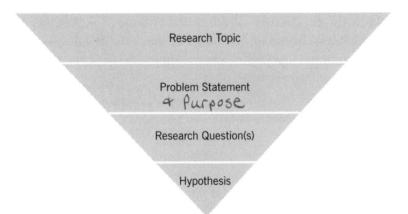

FIGURE 2.8. The process of moving from a general topic to the specific research question and hypothesis.

```
┌─────────────────────────────┐
│      RESEARCH FOCUS:        │
│       Parents reading       │
│      to their children      │
└─────────────────────────────┘
                │
┌─────────────────────────────┐
│     GENERAL PROBLEM         │
│        STATEMENT:           │
│   What impact does parents' │
│   reading to their preschool│
│  children have on the       │
│  children's reading         │
│  development?               │
└─────────────────────────────┘
```

1. QUALITATIVE RESEARCH QUESTION:	1. QUANTITATIVE RESEARCH QUESTION:	1. MIXED-METHODS RESEARCH QUESTION:
How does parents' reading to their preschool children influence (a) the children's attitudes toward reading and (b) the children's motivation to read on their own?	QUESTION: Is there a relationship between the amount of time parents read to their children (measured as minutes per day) and these children's attitudes toward reading (measured on a survey of attitudes)? HYPOTHESIS: There will be a positive correlation between the amount of time that parents read to their children and the children's attitudes toward reading.	How does parents' reading to their preschool children influence the children's motivation to read? Is there a relationship between the amount of time parents read to their preschool children and these children's reading readiness?

FIGURE 2.9. General research topic, problem statement, qualitative research question, quantitative research question and hypothesis, and mixed-methods research question.

CHAPTER SUMMARY

1. The first step in the teacher research process is to identify a meaningful area of interest that is significant for the action researcher work; classroom and school are the best sources for research questions, puzzles, and problems.

2. Brainstorming with a partner or in a small group often helps action researchers choose a meaningful topic for their study and clarify its focus.

3. The research problem statement (often referred to as "the general statement of the problem") presents a clear purpose for the study, serves as an introduction to the research, and guides the direction of the study.

4. The problem statement often includes definitions of the central concepts and terms, a description of the personal and professional context for the study, an explanation of the researcher's role in the study, an examination of who, besides the researcher, might be interested in the study, and a description of who will benefit from the knowledge gained.

5. Although qualitative, quantitative, and mixed-methods researchers may start with the same general research topic and problem statement, their research questions and approaches are different and reflect their chosen paradigm.

6. The purpose for the study may consist of several research questions; these questions can be further divided into several subquestions.

7. A *literature review* is a summary and synthesis of research put forward by others that is pertinent to the researcher's own inquiry; it establishes the rationale for the study by highlighting the importance of the research question.

8. Sources for the literature review include peer-reviewed journal articles, professional books, conference papers, institutional publications, media reports, and documents located on websites.

9. The process of preparing to write the literature review usually follows several sequential steps: locating sources for the literature review, reading literature to identify themes, and constructing a literature review outline.

10. When possible, use primary sources (descriptions of the original research reported by the researchers who conducted the study) rather than secondary sources (publications in which authors describe ideas, works, and studies done by others).

11. Before beginning your library search, transform the problem statement into library search terms (called descriptors) by defining your research focus and deciding on the specific issues to be included.

12. The literature review is organized around themes that are pertinent to your investigation. The themes are usually made up of perspectives, approaches, ideas, or results from relevant existing studies.

13. The outline for the literature review can be written in a narrative style or as a series of bullets.

14. The review should be organized logically around themes and subthemes going from issues that are least related to the study to the most related, from the general to the specific, from historical to contemporary, from theory to practice, and from definitions to examples.

15. Visual mapping is an effective means of graphically organizing and displaying the topics and subtopics of the literature review.

16. While there is no single format for writing a literature review, there are usually three main sections: (a) an introduction, (b) the main section of the report, and (c) a summary and concluding remarks that end with the specific research question(s).

17. The introduction to the literature review may include an advanced organizer to lay out the topics that are going to be discussed.

18. The main section of the review follows the outline structure and is organized thematically; the length of the discussion of each source depends on its significance to your study.

19. You should communicate to the reader how the studies fit together, pointing out controversies, agreements, and disagreements among researchers in the field.

20. Provide closure for the review by writing a short summary in which the major themes across *all* studies are reviewed and their implications are highlighted.

21. A specific research question begins with a precise description of the goals of the investigation by translating the general problem statement into more specific and focused questions.

22. Questions in qualitative research are usually open-ended, using words such as *how* and *what*, rather than questions that lead to yes or no answers.

23. Research questions that are concerned with measuring variables that can be quantified are usually specific and involve assessing "how much" or "how many"; these research questions are often followed by hypotheses, especially in experimental studies.

24. In a mixed-methods research study there are usually several specific research questions; each may be calling for a different form of data (qualitative or quantitative).

CHAPTER EXERCISES AND ACTIVITIES

1. Write two or three possible topics for your investigation and explain briefly why they are of interest to you. Follow the steps outlined at the beginning of the chapter to make a final choice of topic for your study.

2. Using the checklist in Figure 2.2, assess your problem statement. If working with a group, evaluate each other's statement.

3. Develop an outline of your literature review using the format in Figure 2.5, or create a visual topic map (see example in Figure 2.6).

4. Using the checklist in Figure 2.7 read critically a draft of your literature review. If working with a group, read the literature review written by a peer and respond thoughtfully to his or her writing. Point out what is done well but also highlight what needs to be revised, added, edited, or changed to refine the writing.

5. Choose a topic of interest for a study and develop three research questions for exploring the topic: one research question to be based on the *qualitative* approach, another on *quantitative* approach, and the third on the *mixed-methods* approach. Compare and contrast the three questions you have written and suggest how each one will guide your choice of data collection tools. If working with a group or a peer, choose a topic of mutual interest. (You may find the example in Figure 2.9 helpful in completing this task.)

ADDITIONAL READINGS

Berry, R. (2004). *The research project: How to write it* (5th ed.). New York: Routledge.

Blaxter, L., Hughes, C., & Tight, M. (1996). *How to research*. Berkshire, UK: Open University Press.

Boote, D. N., & Beile, P. (2005). Scholars before researchers: On the centrality of the dissertation literature review in research preparation. *Educational Researcher, 34*(6), 3–15.

Fink, A. (2009). *Conducting research literature reviews: From the Internet to paper* (3rd ed.). Thousand Oaks, CA: Sage.

Hart, C. (2003). *Doing the literature search: Releasing the social science research imagination*. London: Sage.

Rumsey, S. (2008). *How to find information: A guide for researchers* (2nd ed.). Berkshire, UK: Open University Press.

Trimmer, J. F. (2004). *The new writing with a purpose* (14th ed.). Boston: Houghton Mifflin.

Zerubavel, E. (1999). *The clockwork muse: A practical guide to writing theses, dissertations, and books*. Cambridge, MA: Harvard University Press.

CHAPTER 3

Approaches to Action Research

As educators, teachers, administrators, and school support personnel, we all want to improve how we work with our students and advance the way education is practiced in our classrooms and schools. Research and data-driven decisions are often offered as the way to achieve these goals. However, in the middle of the demanding, ever-changing, and, at times, chaotic environments of schools, we are required to make constant and important decisions, and sometimes research is far removed from our thinking. If you consider the word *research*, you realize that it means searching again and again to answer our questions or to find solutions to our problems.

In this chapter we highlight three research perspectives—qualitative, quantitative, and mixed—and provide a brief overview of the elements that distinguish each approach: (1) assumptions about school reality, (2) research purpose, (3) the researcher role, (4) research process, and (5) common research methods. We end the chapter with helpful suggestions for how to choose your own research approach.

EDUCATIONAL RESEARCH APPROACHES

Action research draws from a wide range of educational research approaches and is implemented in a variety of forms. Underlying the different approaches are alternative assumptions and sets of beliefs about knowledge, school reality, and the purpose of the research. In turn, these assumptions shape the choices that are made by practitioners about the questions that they pose, the way they collect and analyze their data, and the type of conclusions derived from the data. Kuhn (1970) defined these alternative sets of assumptions and perspectives, or worldviews as "paradigms."

Since you, as an action researcher, are becoming a generator of knowledge, it is important that you understand the differences between three paradigms that have informed and helped shape contemporary action research. Clarifying the different assumptions that underlie each perspective and the practical implications associated with each one will assist you in developing your own inquiry. Based on this understanding, you will be able to make your own choices about the types of questions you want to ask and about the strategies and techniques for collecting and analyzing the data to answer your questions.

QUALITATIVE EDUCATIONAL RESEARCH

Qualitative research is designed to study school situations and events as they unfold naturally. The focus of the investigation is on the meanings of these experiences for the individuals and groups in these settings. (Examples of books on qualitative research include Bogdan & Biklen, 2006; Glesne, 2010; Marshall & Rossman, 2011; and Merriam, 2009.)

Assumptions about School Reality

Schools are complex, socially constructed institutions that comprise multiple realities. The meaning assigned to school experience is varied, shaped by individuals' subjective interpretations, and influenced by their personal, cultural, and historical background. Actions, behaviors, expectations, norms, and beliefs are strongly influenced by the uniqueness of each context and perceived differently by each individual. Thus, qualitative research results cannot be generalized across time and locations.

Research Purpose

Meaningful school change and the improvement of school experiences for students should emerge from the perspective of those who are involved in each setting. Therefore, the purpose of qualitative research is to gain insight into and understanding of how students, teachers, parents, and administrators make sense of their educational experience. The knowledge and insight serve as a base for bringing about needed change.

Researcher Role

Researchers often become immersed in the educational site where their studies take place. Interactions with those under study enable researchers to acquire familiarity with the situation and gain the trust of participants. Researchers must acknowledge their own personal values and how these values shape their perceptions and interpretations.

Research Process

The study emerges from broad open-ended questions. Researchers spend extended time at the educational settings, observing and interviewing people through the daily school routine. Researchers describe through rich narrative and visual media, such as pictures and videos, the subjective meanings that individuals in the schools ascribe to their actions and experiences. The focus is on a holistic understanding of the complex interdependencies that distinguish the educational, social, and cultural environments that are being examined. The data collected are analyzed and organized into categories, trends, and patterns.

Common Qualitative Methods

Case Study

Case study research aims to understand a particular phenomenon (such as a program, process, event, organization, or concept) by selecting a particular example of that phenomenon as the focus of the study. To shed light on the larger phenomenon, the researcher explores in depth the selected entity, actions, and the reasons for these actions. Although case study research usually focuses on a single entity (e.g., an individual, a class, or a program), at times, two or more cases are selected for comparison purposes. For example, in order to understand the realities of including high-functioning autistic children in mainstream classrooms, the researcher describes the social, emotional, and learning experiences of one high-functioning autistic middle school student and tries to provide explanations for the student's actions and interactions with peers and teachers. In a *multiple case study*, the researcher replicates the same study with different high-functioning autistic middle school students so he or she can compare and contrast the findings. (Examples of books on case study research include George & Bennett, 2004; Hancock, 2011; Merriam, 1998; Stake, 1995; and Yin, 2009.)

Ethnographic Research

Ethnographic research is focused on the cultural and social life of schools, classrooms, and communities. The researcher immerses him- or herself in the group that is the subject of the study, exploring their lived experiences and identifying their shared values and beliefs. For example, through many interactions and discussions with high school dropouts, their families, and their peers, the researcher tries to understand how students who dropped out view education and its role in shaping their economic future. (Examples of books on ethnographic research include Denzin, 1997; Eisenhart, 2001; Firmin & Brewer; 2006; and Madison, 2011.)

Narrative Research

Narrative research presents stories of life experiences told by individuals in their own words, accompanied by reflections on the meaning of these stories within a broader educational context. The use of narrative complements the desire to recapture past experiences and to describe the teacher's professional and personal self within the context of his or her practice. As an example, a researcher may ask teachers to use storytelling narratives to share their experiences or memories. The teachers then analyze how these past experiences have contributed to informing their moral world, values, and beliefs. (Examples of narrative research books include Andrew, Squire, & Tamboukou, 2008; Clandinin, 2006; Clandinin & Connelly, 2000; Holley & Colyar, 2009; and Webster & Mertova, 2007.)

Critical Research

Critical research centers on a social justice agenda. The purpose of the study is to expose repression, domination, and inequities and bring about social change. To raise the consciousness of those who are marginalized in society and seek a change in these inequities, researchers often invite them to be involved in the inquiry. For example, the researcher invites new immigrant parents to participate in a discussion of school district testing policy to find out if this policy puts students with limited English knowledge at a disadvantage. (Examples of books on critical research include Anyon et al., 2009; Carr & Kemmis, 2009; Denzin, Lincoln, & Smith, 2008; Steinberg & Cannella, 2012.)

QUANTITATIVE EDUCATIONAL RESEARCH

Quantitative research is designed to gather numerical data from individuals or groups using statistical tests to analyze the data collected (Slavin, 2007). Cause-and-effect relationships can be studied best in experimental studies (Mertler & Charles, 2011). In nonexperimental quantitative studies, researchers study relationships between variables as they exist, without any attempt to change them (Slavin, 2007). Statistical data can also be used in nonexperimental studies to describe information related to occurrences of phenomena and to measure the degree of association between phenomena. (Examples of books on quantitative research include Gall et al., 2006; and Gay, Mills, & Airasian, 2011.)

Assumptions about School Reality

The social reality of school operates according to stable, fixed, and verifiable rules and laws that are relatively constant across time and settings. This reality is objective and is separated from and independent of school participants' feelings, perceptions, and beliefs. Objective researchers can, through scientific methods, discover and measure these universal rules. This information then can be applied to describe, explain, and predict behavior with a calculated degree of certainty.

Research Purpose

The goal of quantitative educational research is to produce an effective and efficient educational system designed to improve the academic achievements of all students. This goal can be achieved by discovering universal, scientifically based rules or methods that are proven to enhance the quality of the teaching and learning process.

Researcher Role

Educational researchers take a neutral, objective, and dispassionate position, trying to minimize their engagement with the study's participants. Appropriate procedures are employed to prevent researchers' personal biases from influencing or affecting the investigation process in order to ensure scientifically accurate findings.

Research Process

The process usually starts with research questions about a limited number of clearly defined variables. In *experimental* research, researchers focus on answering questions related to cause-and-effect relationships. The questions are followed by hypotheses that make a prediction about the outcomes of the study. A research study is then designed to test hypotheses by controlling the impact of all variables: those being studied as well as outside variables that might influence the study's outcomes. In *nonexperimental* (sometimes called *descriptive*) research, the purpose is to measure or numerically describe existing groups, settings, or phenomena, compare two or more groups, or describe statistically the strength of the association between two or more variables. In both types of quantitative studies, researchers systematically choose the research participants and develop a set of procedures and strategies for gathering, analyzing, and interpreting numerical data.

Common Quantitative Methods

Experimental Research

Experimental research is designed to measure cause-and-effect relationships (Fraenkel, Wallen, & Hyun, 2011). It is conducted to test the effect of planned interventions, called the *independent variables*, on groups or individuals. The effect of the independent variable is assessed by gathering data on the outcome measure, called the *dependent variable*. For example, you may want to test the efficacy of cooperative learning group work (the independent variable) on the reading scores (the outcome, or dependent variable) of your students who have learning challenges.

Causal–Comparative (Ex Post Facto) *Research*

Causal–comparative *(ex post facto)* research is also used to investigate causal relationships between something that happened in the past and subsequent responses (McMillan, 2011). There is no planned intervention because the independent variables have either occurred prior to the start of the study or are variables that cannot be manipulated. For example, a researcher may want to compare the social skills (outcome variable) of college freshmen who were home-schooled with those of similar students who attended public or private high schools. The independent variable in this study, type of schooling, has already occurred by the time the study is conducted.

Correlational Research

Correlational research investigates the degree of relationship between two or more variables in a given situation. The relationship can be quantified and its direction (positive or negative) and strength (high, moderate, or low) can be assessed. For example, a study may be carried out to measure the relationship between students' performance on state- and district-administered math tests. Keep in mind, though, that even when we find a correlation between variables, this does not show that one variable caused the other (Mertler & Charles, 2011).

Descriptive Research

Descriptive research represents the current conditions of the topic under investigation without trying to change or manipulate them. These studies summarize existing phenomena by using numbers to describe groups or individuals (McMillan & Schumacher, 2010). The most well-known large-scale descriptive study conducted in the United States is the one conducted by the U.S. Bureau of the Census (Dane, 2011). An example in education and public policy may be a study that is done in a large metropolitan area to document the number of students who drop out of high school before graduating.

MIXED-METHODS RESEARCH

For years, a schism between qualitative and quantitative approaches dominated the field of educational research. The debate emphasized the differences between the two worldviews or paradigms. In the last few decades, mixed-methods research has been gaining influence as a third, alternative approach. The mixed-methods approach proposes to cross boundaries between worldviews and blend (or combine) qualitative and quantitative research methods and techniques into a single study. (Examples of books on mixed-methods research include Creswell & Plano Clark, 2011; Hesse-Biber, 2010; Tashakkori & Teddlie, 2010; and Teddlie & Tashakkori, 2009.)

Assumptions about School Reality

Solutions to the problems that school presents are at the center of this pragmatic mixed-methods approach, rather than philosophical discussions about school reality. All approaches that contribute to understanding and solving school problems are embraced and their value is judged by the consequences. The emphasis is on finding out "what works" and acting upon it. From this perspective, the research problem rather than philosophical and ideological assumptions, should always guide the study.

Research Purpose

The goal of mixed-methods research is to draw on the strength of both quantitative and qualitative research to enhance school improvement. Combining both techniques in a single study enables the researcher to use multiple methods to explore different aspects of the same question.

Researcher Role

The two paradigms, quantitative and qualitative, can live peacefully together in one study. The researcher can assume an objective or subjective stance, or attitude, depending on the question under investigation.

Research Process

The researcher employs both quantitative and qualitative data collection strategies, methods, and analyses, either simultaneously or sequentially. Thus, the different data tools that are used complement each other by highlighting different aspects of the same question. The workability of the methods and the usefulness of the results are the most important factor in planning the study.

Common Mixed Methods

Embedded-Design Research

Embedded-design research is used in studies in which both methods of data collection, quantitative and qualitative, are included, but one paradigm dominates the study. One approach is nested within the larger method of data collection. Either the nested or the dominating approach may be qualitative or quantitative. For example, in an experimental districtwide study designed to assess the effects of an innovative reading circle on students' reading-understanding skills, a qualitative interview with gifted students is embedded within the larger pretest–posttest experimental study.

Two-Phase Research

Two-phase research addresses different questions within the research problem in a two-phase study. The qualitative and quantitative methods are employed separately, simultaneously, or sequentially, without much mixing, to investigate each of these questions. An example might be the impact of early diagnosis and treatment on the development of children with attention-deficit/hyperactivity disorder (ADHD). The researcher assesses the social skills of these students through qualitative observations, and uses quantitative procedures to evaluate the students' school performance using standardized assessment tools.

Integrated Research

Integrated research combines quantitative and qualitative methods throughout the research process to answer the same question. The methods are employed concurrently with equal weight. For example, in a study to assess the impact of inclusion on relationships among students, two data collections tools are used, each yielding numerical and narrative data: (1) a survey that contains numerical and open-ended questions and (2) and an observation protocol that includes unstructured observations and a checklist.

A summary of the characteristics that distinguish among qualitative, quantitative, and mixed-methods approaches is presented in Table 3.1.

CHOOSING AN APPROACH FOR YOUR RESEARCH PROJECT

The three paradigms—quantitative, qualitative, and mixed methods—present strikingly different ways of viewing school reality and, consequently, different methods and strategies for inquiry. Action research draws upon each of these educational research paradigms. No approach is right or wrong, none is considered

TABLE 3.1. Characteristics of Qualitative, Quantitative, and Mixed-Methods Approaches

	Qualitative	Quantitative	Mixed methods
Assumptions about school reality	There are multiple school realities and their meanings are shaped by individuals' historical and cultural backgrounds.	School reality operates according to stable, fixed rules relatively constant across settings that can be objectively discovered.	Solutions to problems that school presents are at the center rather than philosophical discussions about school reality.
Research purpose	Understand school experience from the perspective of those involved to improve schools.	Discover universal rules and methods to improve education and the quality of teaching and learning.	Draw on the strength of both quantitative and qualitative approaches to enhance school improvement.
Researcher role	The researcher interacts extensively with individuals at the study's setting. The researcher acknowledges his or her own subjectivity and biases.	The researcher maintains a neutral and objective stance to ensure scientifically accurate findings.	The researcher assumes both objective and subjective stances, depending on the question under investigation.
Research process	The researcher is immersed in the setting and describes the subjective meanings that individuals place upon their actions and experiences.	The researcher investigates relationships among a limited number of variables that are measured, quantified, and generalized.	The researcher employs both quantitative and qualitative data collection methods and analysis, either simultaneously or sequentially.
Common methods	Case study research Ethnographic research Narrative research Critical research	Experimental research Correlational research Descriptive research	Embedded research Two-phase research Integrated research

"the best," and each has contributed to practitioner knowledge and understanding. However, these approaches differ in several ways. Each perspective (1) offers different kinds of questions or problems, (2) seeks different types of findings, (3) calls for different strategies, and (4) is assessed by different criteria.

Prior to launching your own project you should decide which of the three approaches will best serve as a model for your study. As you ponder your choices, we suggest considering the following: action research framework, your personal worldview, and your research question(s).

Action Research Framework

The inherent nature of action research affects the methods you choose for your investigation. As mentioned before, action researchers study their work, and the study's findings contribute directly and immediately to their practices. Thus, the purposes of the study they undertake, as well as the methods they choose for their investigations, are influenced by the possibilities and limitations of conducting research in their own classrooms and schools. For example, conducting experimental research is possible and at times desirable. However, generalization of the findings to other settings cannot be done with a high degree of confidence, because of the small size of most action research projects, the limitations in selecting a representative sample of participants, and the tenuous control practitioners have over the variables in the study. Still, for action researchers, the focus is most likely not on whether the inquiry's findings can be generalized to other settings but rather on whether the findings can be useful for improving their own practice. Similarly, action researchers may choose to conduct critical research because of their desire to be advocates for marginalized students in society at large and to bring about social justice and equity. In reality, though, the likelihood of change is greater when the focus is on the local community. Action researchers are therefore advised to conduct studies to explore and seek change within their local settings, classrooms, schools, and communities.

Personal Worldview

We all bring distinct assumptions about school reality and the impact of research on our practices that ultimately influence how we design and conduct our studies. Our views are mostly unconscious and unarticulated. As an autonomous practitioner you want to become aware of the tacit assumptions that undergird your perspectives on school reality and implicitly shape your decisions throughout the research process. Self-awareness is key to purposeful inquiry, in which the choices you make regarding the questions, methods, and strategies best reflect your values and professional needs.

Research Question

The final factor to consider in choosing the approach for your study is the research question you want to answer or problem that you want to solve. Certain questions call for particular types of methodology; the research approach should match the question you ask as the problem drives the choice of methods. For example, if you want to evaluate the gains in students' learning as a result of a new strategy you have adopted, numerical test scores might be a good source of data. On the other hand, if your question focuses on understanding the attitudes and feelings of students toward this strategy and how it impacts their motivation, a qualitative, in-depth interview might be your best approach. If your research focuses on understanding students' perceptions of the new teaching strategy *and* how it impacts their academic achievement, a mixed-methods approach might be the way to go.

As you choose your research approach, it is a good idea to brainstorm with a partner or in a small group. Reflect on the three considerations highlighted above (action research framework, personal worldview, and research question) and contemplate how they inform your choice of research method. The checklist of questions in Figure 3.1 may help guide your decision making.

✓	Questions
	1. What are my assumptions about the nature of school reality?
	2. What are, from my perspective, the purposes for conducting action research?
	3. How do I see my role as a researcher?
	4. How will the action research framework affect my choice of a method?
	5. How might my research question impact my choice of method for my study?
	6. What research method is practical and doable within my situation?

FIGURE 3.1. A checklist of questions to guide the choice of a research approach

CHAPTER SUMMARY

1. Action research draws from a wide range of educational research approaches and is implemented in a variety of forms.

2. Alternative assumptions and sets of beliefs about knowledge, school reality, and the purpose of the research underlie the different approaches to educational research.

3. Clarifying the different assumptions that underlie each perspective and the practical implications associated with each will assist you in developing your own inquiry and choosing the types of questions you want to ask and the strategies and techniques for collecting and analyzing the data to answer your questions.

4. There are three common worldviews (i.e., paradigms) that traditionally have shaped educational research. The three research paradigms are *quantitative, qualitative*, and *mixed methods*.

5. Each research paradigm is discussed in this chapter in terms of (a) assumptions about school reality, (b) research purpose, (c) the researcher role, (d) research processes, and (e) common research methods.

6. Common methods that are used in qualitative research are *case study, ethnographic, narrative*, and *critical* research.

7. Common methods that are used in quantitative research are *experimental, casual–comparative (ex post facto), correlational*, and *descriptive* research.

8. Common methods that are used in mixed-methods research are *embedded design, two-phase*, and *integrated* research.

9. Qualitative, quantitative, and mixed-methods approaches differ in several ways. Each perspective (a) offers different kinds of questions or problems, (b) seeks different types of findings, (c) calls for different strategies, and (d) is assessed by different criteria.

10. In choosing the method for their research project, action researchers may want to consider their action research *framework, personal worldview*, and *research question(s)*.

11. For action researchers, the focus is most likely not on the ability to generalize the inquiry's findings to other settings but rather on the usefulness of the findings for improving their own practice.

12. As autonomous practitioners, action researchers need to be aware of the tacit assumptions that undergird their perspectives on school reality and implicitly shape their decisions throughout the research process.

13. The purposes and methods of action research study are influenced by the possibilities and limitations of conducting research in the practitioners' own classrooms and schools.

14. The research approach should match the questions being asked as the research questions drive the choice of particular research approach and the type of methodology.

CHAPTER EXERCISES AND ACTIVITIES

1. Clarify your own assumptions or deliberate with peers or colleagues the following points.

   a. The nature of school reality

   b. The purpose of conducting research

   c. The researcher role

   d. The research processes

   If working with a group, you may want to compare and contrast your different perspectives.

2. Reflect on the *qualitative, quantitative*, and *mixed-methods* research approaches discussed in the chapter.

   a. Deliberate on the strengths and weaknesses of each of these approaches.

   b. Consider the relations that these perspectives have to your personal experience as a teacher (or as a learner).

   c. What research approach seems to be most feasible in your current or future educational settings and why?

3. As discussed in the chapter, each research approach—*qualitative, quantitative*, and *mixed methods*—offers several research methods (e.g., case study, experimental research, and integrated research). Depending on your choice of research approach, which method would be most appropriate for exploring your study's question(s)? Explain your choice.

4. Look for one or more published studies that discuss a topic relevant to your research project, and answer the following:

   a. Identify which research approach was used in the study—*qualitative, quantitative,* or *mixed method?*

   b. Which of the common research method(s) within the *qualitative, quantitative,* and *mixed-methods* approaches does each of the studies reflect?

   c. How does the study question reflect the approach chosen by the writer(s) of each of the chosen studies?

5. Revisit the research question(s) you have developed for your study. Consider whether the research approach matches your questions.

ADDITIONAL READINGS

Anfara, V. A., & Mertz, N. T. (Eds.). (2006). *Theoretical frameworks in qualitative research*, Thousand Oaks, CA: Sage.

Ary, D., Jacobs, L. C., Sorensen, C. K., & Walker, D. (2013). *Introduction to research in education* (9th ed.). Independence, KY: Wadsworth.

Creswell, J. W. (2012). *Qualitative inquiry and research design: Choosing among five approaches.* Thousand Oaks, CA: Sage.

Denzin, N. K., & Lincoln. Y. S. (2011). *The SAGE handbook of qualitative research.* Thousand Oaks, CA: Sage.

Guba, E. G. (1990). *The paradigm dialogue.* Newbury Park, CA: Sage.

Hoy, W. K. (2009). *Quantitative research: A primer.* Thousand Oaks, CA: Sage.

Johnson, R. B., & Christensen, L. B. (2010). *Educational research: Quantitative, qualtitative and mixed.* Thousand Oaks, CA: Sage.

Krauss, S. T. (2005). Research paradigms as meaning taking: A primer. *The Qualitative Report, 10*(4), 758–770.

Morris, T. (2006). *Social work research methods.* Thousand Oaks, CA: Sage.

CHAPTER 4

Developing a Plan of Action

Action research is a process of self-reflection in which you have the central role during all the phases of your action research project. This chapter focuses on the development of a plan of action for your inquiry. By now, you have selected the approach (qualitative, quantitative, or mixed method) that will guide your study based on your understanding of the major paradigms that underlie action research and the methods that each perspective entails. You have also expanded your knowledge of the topic you have chosen to investigate and have formulated your research question(s). It's time now for the next step of your action research project: developing the research plan with a focus on the data collection procedure.

The research plan serves as a guide for the inquiry process. It invites you to step back before you launch your investigation and to carefully consider the essential issues involved. Consider questions that will guide the procedures involved in implementing your study. For example: How will you collect the data? How will you choose the participants for your study? What will be the scope of the study and how long will it last? What will be your role as an action researcher throughout the investigation? How will you ensure soundness of the data you plan to collect?

When you implement your plan, you may need to revise, adapt, and modify it to respond to and accommodate unexpected school circumstances. For example, you may have to schedule an interview with a colleague but the colleague's plans have changed, and he or she is no longer available or interested in participating in your study. You now need to find another interviewee or modify your data collection plans. In another example, you may decide to survey another group of students because of a low response rate from your first attempt to collect survey data. However, thinking ahead and identifying the steps involved in putting together a practical, logical, and purposeful plan will prevent aimless and haphazard inquiry. Carefully planning the study's procedures in advance is especially helpful for a novice action researcher.

The starting point and the key for developing your research plan is your research question. The question is a trigger for planning the process that will enable you to find meaningful answers. The question guides your decisions regarding the scope of the inquiry, the participants you choose, and the data collection and analysis techniques you select. You should also pay attention to the practical implications of conducting your inquiry within the context of your day-to-day work and its effect on your practice. Consider issues such as What is your role in the research setting? Are you a teacher, a specialist, or an administrator? Are you a student teacher, parent, tutor, or a visitor? Additionally, be cognizant of the amount of time you may be able to dedicate to the project and whether this study is compatible with your other professional obligations and responsibilities. Also be sure to get the proper permission to conduct the study from all involved.

The research plan should be described in sufficient detail to provide you with a clear blueprint to guide your investigation. A meaningful and efficient research plan usually necessitates reflecting on the following elements:

1. Considering your role as a researcher
2. Establishing the research scope
3. Identifying the research site and participants
4. Choosing data collection procedures
5. Ensuring the study's validity and trustworthiness
6. Developing ethical guidelines
7. Creating a "to-do" list

CONSIDERING YOUR ROLE AS A RESEARCHER

At the center of the discussion about the researcher role is the question about the subjective or objective stance you are assuming during the collection, analysis, and interpretation of the data. There is a long debate between qualitative and quantitative researchers about how subjectivity should be addressed in educational research. Qualitative researchers perceive subjectivity as an integral part of the research process. They often reinforce the personal dimension of the study by disclosing past and present involvement with the topic, as well as their personal experiences during the research process. On the other hand, quantitative researchers view objectivity as essential for conducting educational research. They detach themselves from the study participants to avoid influencing the research process and compromising the credibility of the findings.

However, the role of educational practitioners who investigate their own practice is much more complex. Realistically, objectivity cannot be achieved as the practitioners are intimately involved and building relationships with their students, colleagues, administrators, and parents. By the same token, these ongoing relationships may limit the practitioner's ability to be open to new and different perceptions, viewpoints, and understandings.

In short, in action research there needs to be a balance between objectivity and subjectivity. As a researcher, you should strive for a *disciplined* subjectivity, acknowledging explicitly the following connections: (1) your own values, beliefs, and commitments that are related to the study; (2) your past involvement and experience with the topic; and (3) your relationship with the participants. Recognizing these connections personally and publicly will mitigate your subjectivity and prevent bias from creeping in and influencing the study. Understanding your role as a researcher will also facilitate the process of understanding your findings.

Qualitative research emphasizes the concept of reflexivity as it relates to acknowledging how the researchers' perspectives and positions shape the research. *Reflexivity* means self-awareness and taking into account the potential impact of one's values, worldview, and life experience and their influence on the decisions made and actions taken during the research process. Reflexivity suggests that the action researchers acknowledge and disclose their subjectivity and monitor its potential effect on their data collection and data interpretation (Guillemin & Gillam, 2004; Rallis & Rossman, 2012; Rossman & Rallis, 2010).

The researcher role statement in Box 4.1 was written by Mindy, a sixth-grade teacher, who investigated the topic of differentiation. Mindy's statement reveals reflexivity as she reflects on her role, subjectivity, and bias and their impact on her investigation. She deliberates on ways that will ensure her ability to contemplate truthfully the perceptions and meaning her participants make of their experience with differentiation.

subjectivity

BOX 4.1. A Researcher Role Statement

The topic of differentiation has been a part of my professional teaching career since before I even set foot in a classroom. I was introduced to the topic in one of the first courses I took for teacher certification that focused on the issues pertaining to the education of children with disabilities. It was here that I began to understand the challenges of teaching the different types of learners who make up today's inclusive classroom. The concept of adapting the practice to the different needs of individual students has resonated deeply with me as it complements my perception of teaching and learning and my belief in constructivist, democratic, and student-centered education. I also know that, as a student, I flourished and thrived when I was taught by caring teachers who took the time to see me as I am and tried to encourage me to shine, in spite of my shyness. I wanted to provide such an experience to my own future students. As I continued my graduate studies, and even more so during my substitute teaching and student teaching, the varied levels of learners in any classroom became obvious to me as well as the complexities that are involved in teaching curriculum that can be understood by all. Confronting such a reality led me to find ways to reach each student in my classroom and to search for strategies for adapting my instruction to his or her needs, strengths, and challenges.

Now, as a sixth-grade general education teacher of reading, language arts, and social studies, I am challenged by this aspiration each day and continually find myself searching for new ways to meet students at their own varied level of learning. In any particular period during the day, I can have a classroom of 25 students that will include special education students with individualized education plans (IEPs), and students for whom English is a second language, students who have been identified as gifted, as well as various levels of learners in between. More than ever, I am convinced that in a diversified classroom of learners, a teacher cannot simply teach the curriculum the same way to each student; different modalities of instruction can reach more students. However, I have never explored systematically students' and parents' perspectives on differentiation and whether they feel it affects the learning experience in the classroom. In this research my focus is on them.

I know that my personal convictions and passionate feelings toward this topic, as well as my presence in the setting, may impact my research. I acknowledge my biases and am aware that my preconceptions may enter into the data collection, analysis, and interpretation process and that I need to take measures to monitor my bias and subjectivity. My goal is to hear and understand students and parents and learn from them and from the way they make meaning of our class reality and how they experience it. This requires me to listen carefully and with sensitivity to their voices. Aware of the possibility of bias I will constantly and honestly reflect on how my subjectivity shapes what data I collect, analyze, and interpret.

- your values
- your background
- who you're working with
- who your participants are and why you chose them
- teaching experience

ESTABLISHING THE RESEARCH SCOPE

The scope of your study is determined by your research question and the purpose of your study. The scope affects decisions such as the length of time you will dedicate to conducting the investigation, the number and nature of the data collection tools you will utilize, and the participants who will be involved. For example, how many interviews will you conduct? How many observations will you be able to carry out? How many surveys will you administer and to whom?

In a qualitative inquiry, the study is an evolving process and the action researcher is usually expected to carry out the study for a prolonged period of time using a variety of data collection techniques. Optimally, the research project continues until the practitioners feel they have obtained all the information needed for answering the research question and sense that the continuation of the inquiry will not yield any additional insight. By comparison, in quantitative action research, the scope of the study is more defined and predetermined, and the research is planned ahead of time in greater detail. The investigation ends when the data are collected and analyzed.

As you plan the scope of your study, consider its purpose by reflecting on points such as Are you engaged in your research project to inform your practice or enhance your professional growth and skills? Are you motivated to undertake the study to solve a particular problem you encounter in your work? Are you required to conduct the study as part of formal coursework? Are you contemplating presenting your findings within your district or at a state or national conference? Is your intention to publish your findings or post them online? The answers to these questions will influence the scope of your study.

Another consideration that impacts the extent of your inquiry is the external conditions that are not within your control. These include issues such as the school calendar, the length of the curriculum unit or program that you plan to investigate, standardized testing dates, or the due date of an assignment you are completing for a course. Other external concerns may be your ability to access information within your school (e.g., test scores and attendance records) and the district or school policy pertaining to research conducted within the school. If, on the other hand, the research project is part of your coursework, educational degree program, or student-teaching requirements, the course syllabus may dictate the parameters of your research project. Consult with your advisor, mentor, or class instructor as to the extent of data collection required, time frames, and scope of the project.

The research project should always be manageable and doable. Remember that your first obligation is to your students, colleagues, parents, and administrators.

While your aim should be for an in-depth inquiry, be realistic as you plan and implement the study within the framework of your practice. Identify the boundaries and constraints of your proposed study and consider how they may affect your ability to investigate effectively. Moreover, be sure that the process of conducting your research does not negatively impact the quality of your practice.

Having a manageable project is especially true if this is the first time you are conducting action research and are unfamiliar with the process. We suggest viewing this project as the first step in a career-long professional development process as an action researcher. Use the experience of this study to become comfortable with the process of being a researcher, to acquire the skills needed for conducting school research, and to learn to appreciate its potential for your professional growth. The main focus is on the experience of being a researcher, rather than on the specific results of the study.

• Think about the journey & the process!!

IDENTIFYING THE RESEARCH SITE AND PARTICIPANTS

Since action research is embedded within the classroom and school setting and the results of the inquiry have immediate local application, knowledge of the participants and the contextual factors is of particular importance.

Research Site

Details about the overall school community offer a fuller description of the study within its particular context. These details will include information about the students, parents, staff and faculty, and the neighborhood where the school is located. Depending on the specific focus of the study, additional information may be required. For example, if your research focuses on gifted education, it will be helpful if you also indicate the special programs and services available to gifted students. Most of the school and district demographic information is easy to obtain and is available on state-mandated websites. Additional details may be obtained from the school's administration office, as well as from publications such as school newsletters and brochures.

Box 4.2 presents an excerpt from a research site section as written by Orin, a student teacher in a middle school who is doing an action research project for the research class he is taking. The study is focused on students' and teachers' perspectives with regard to the use of a portfolios assessment system in science class.

Goes in methods section

- demographics
- Title 1?
- population
- be detailed

EXAMPLE

BOX 4.2. An Excerpt from a Research Site Section

The middle school in which my study is conducted is one of six middle schools in a public school district in a big metropolitan city in the Midwest. It is a lower- to middle-class socioeconomic community with a diverse population. There are approximately 670 seventh- and eighth-grade students consisting of 48.2% African Americans, 3.5% Asian Americans, 23.9% Caucasians, 23.2% Latinos, and 1.2% Native Americans. About 32.8% of the students receive a free or reduced-price lunch.

---

* Never assume the reader knows anything!!

Research Participants

The identification of who and how many participants will be asked to take part in your study depends on two factors: (1) determining who will be able to provide valuable information for your study, and (2) criteria for participant sample selection. As is the case with all action research, practical considerations of what is doable within your time constraints is a factor in your decision.

. demographics of specific class!

The participants of the research study are the people who affect or are affected by the issue under investigation. Their actions, behaviors, or perceptions should contribute valuable information that will enable you to answer your research question. For example, in an action research study that assesses the impact of a new fourth-grade language arts textbook on students' motivation, the fourth-grade students will be the primary group participants for the study. At other times the researcher may want to add complementary groups of participants to obtain additional perspectives. For example, in this study of fourth graders' motivation, the researcher may add teachers and parents as participants to obtain a fuller picture. Teachers' perspectives may provide information about the students' participation in class discussions, while parents may share students' informal views and their willingness to do their homework.

Although all of the participants within the group that is the focus of your investigation may be eligible to be included in the study, you will probably need to select a smaller sample for practical considerations. A set of criteria may guide your choice of a suitable sample.

The process of sample selection differs between qualitative and quantitative action research. Both are small-scale studies that involve a relatively limited number of participants and are focused on local settings. However, there are distinct

Define the terms!
- social-emotional learning
- positive reinforcement
- At-risk students

differences between the two approaches in terms of the number and identification of the participant sample.

Qualitative action research does not have a formulated set of rules about the size of the sample or how it is selected. It is not uncommon to have a sample size of one to four individuals who have experience and in-depth knowledge about the topic being investigated. If, on the other hand, your inquiry is focused on an event, a program, a new approach, an organization, or a setting, you may prefer a broader spectrum and select more participants to ensure that diverse perspectives are represented. Sample selection is based on the relevancy of the participants' experiences regarding the topic of the study and their ability to enable you to obtain rich data and valuable information that will contribute to the understanding of the issue under investigation (Onwuegbuzie & Leech, 2007). Additional considerations may include their willingness to participate, their knowledge of the issue, their ability to articulate their opinions, and their ability to contribute to your understanding of the topic. Some qualitative researchers assert that because participants in qualitative research are not expected to represent anyone but themselves, it is more appropriate to talk about specific individuals or a group rather than about a "sample." However, others emphasize the specific purpose for choosing the participants for the study (Cohen, Manion, & Morrison, 2011).

There are several options available for selecting the sample for your study:

1. Selecting a *purposive* sample: The participants are chosen deliberately according to a predetermined purpose (Maxwell, 2013). Some of the common samples in this category are:

    a. *Typical case* sampling: Participants selected are judged to be typical of the group under study.

    b. *Extreme case* sampling: Particular individuals are judged to be the most outstanding examples of a characteristic or behavior (at either end of the continuum) are studied.

    c. *Representative* sampling: The participants are selected for possessing or exhibiting the range of characteristics or behaviors in connection to the issue under investigation.

2. Selecting a *volunteer* sample: When access to participants is difficult, the researcher selects the participants from among volunteers, such as friends or participants who are motivated enough to be part of the study.

3. Selecting a *convenience* sample: Participants are chosen from among the nearest and most accessible individuals.

Action Research Can be written in first person!! make it personal

For example, Jesse, a sixth-grade student teacher, may be experimenting with a new, more democratic classroom management style and wants to find out how it is perceived by his students. Jesse may choose students who represent the *typical* behavior of the majority of the students in the class. On the other hand, he may decide that it would be more beneficial to choose students who exhibit *extreme* classroom behaviors, such as very disruptive and very quiet pupils. Yet another option is to choose those that *represent* a range of student behaviors in the classroom. At times, though, limiting circumstances may preclude the use of preconceived selection criteria. For example, Jesse may not have a choice and will have to study only students who volunteer to participate in the study. Moreover, time and other constraints may lead him to choose a *convenience* sample, such as selecting students because they are easily accessible during his free time.

Whatever sampling strategy you choose to use for your study, be sure to clearly explain the basis for your selection process. If you need to change your sample selection during the course of the study, which can happen in evolving qualitative research, be sure to explicitly present the reasons for the change in the final report (Peshkin, 2001).

For an example of a research participants section we turn again to Orin, the student teacher who investigated teachers' and students' perspectives on the use of portfolio assessment in the science class. Box 4.3 presents an excerpt from his description of his study participants

EXAMPLE FOR PARTICIPANTS

BOX 4.3. A Description of Research Participants

The participants in my study included two female science teachers and 14 seventh- and eighth-grade students. One of the teachers is in her thirties and has been teaching in the school for 2 years. The second teacher is in her forties and has 8 years' teaching experience, 4 of them in the current school. I chose these two teachers for my inquiry because I work with them as a student teacher; they are a convenience sample. *because you already work w/ them · includes students*

The 14 seventh- and eighth-grade students (6 males and 8 females), were chosen from the two teachers' science classrooms. The teachers who participated in the study assisted in the process of selecting a representative sample as we worked together choosing students that the three of us felt best represented the diverse range of achievements in science, motivation and attitude toward the subject, and behavior in class. Two of the students were at the top of the class, four were average, and three needed extra help. We were also cognizant of including one student for whom English is a second language, two students with learning challenges, and two students with behavior problems.

· can put into a table as well

Quantitative action research relies on numerical data gathered in the study. Although such research may aim at studying a large group of people, such as all parents in a district, it is often difficult and impractical to study these large groups, called *populations*. Instead, a *sample* is selected from the population of interest, and information gathered about this sample is generalized back to the population. That is, we make inferences about the population characteristics that are of interest to us based on the data obtained using the sample (Myers, Well, & Lorch, 2010). In quantitative studies, the sample *size* is also an important consideration. In most traditional educational research studies, a sample size of at least 30—and ideally more—is required in order to use more robust statistical tests and to make valid inferences (Mertler & Charles, 2011). Single-case experimental investigations may also be conducted to explore cause-and-effect relationships by studying one individual or a small group.

There are several common ways that are used to select a sample for quantitative studies:

1. Selecting a *random* sample. Every individual in the total population (e.g., teachers, students, or parents) has an equal chance of being selected. The final sample is most likely to represent the population from which it was selected.

2. Selecting a *systematic* sample. The sample is selected in a systematic way from the population. For example, every fifth or tenth person is selected.

3. Selecting a *stratified* sample. The population is first divided into subgroups based on certain demographic characteristics, such as grade level or gender. Next, using random selection, a sample is selected from these subgroups. The final sample represents, proportionally, the demographic subgroups in the population.

4. Selecting a *convenience* sample. This is the most common way to select a sample for researchers, who study those who are most easily available and accessible.

In action research, most samples are chosen from a population that is of interest to the researcher. For example, Valerie, a high school athletics director, is interested in assessing athletes' attitudes toward school. She constructs a 10-item survey asking students for their gender, grade level, and the sport(s) they play. Because of school policies, she cannot ask the athletes to write their names on the surveys. Out of the list of 200 athletes in the school, Valerie gives the survey to a *random* sample of 40 to 50 athletes. Valerie may also decide to give the survey to every third or fourth student in her list of athletes; this would be an example of a *systematic* sample. It is also possible that Valerie will have to use data from a *convenience* sample, where she asks some of the athletes to complete the survey and uses the results from their surveys. In all cases, because not all athletes were included in the study, Valerie will have to take this into consideration as she analyzes the survey data and be cautious in extending the findings to *all* athletes at the school. She may want to look at the demographic information available (gender, grade level, and sport) to determine how well they represent the total population of athletes.

Statistical tests that are used to analyze the data are based on large sample sizes and results are usually reported in terms of probabilities ("p value") or level of statistical significance. (The concept of probability and statistical significance is discussed in Chapter 7.) In action research, unlike traditional educational research, the study focuses on participants in the researcher's own setting, and therefore their number is often limited. For example, David, a first-grade classroom teacher of 21 students, wants to examine the use of a computer software program by his students to practice letter recognition. He uses a test to assess his students' performance before and after using the program. While David realizes that he does not have a large enough class size to meet the expected minimum sample size requirements of traditional educational research, his goal is not to generalize his findings to other classrooms but rather to improve his students' reading skills.

Additionally, in traditional quantitative research, the goal of the researcher is to choose a representative sample that resembles the population within an acceptable margin of error (Dane, 2011). The concept of representation in traditional quantitative research refers to the extent to which the sample being studied is representative of the population at large. For example, let's say that a university researcher wants to test a new problem-solving strategy in math in high school. The purpose is to demonstrate the value of using the strategy in schools all across the country. The researcher selects a representative sample of high school classrooms from different areas of the country to pilot test the math problem-solving strategy. Math scores of students in classes using the new strategy are compared to scores of similar students in classrooms using the current strategy. If the scores of the students in the pilot study are significantly higher than those of the other students, there is evidence to document the effectiveness of the new strategy over current approaches, and the new strategy would be recommended for implementation in all high schools. In contrast, in action research, the goal is to study the researcher's own classroom or school rather than to generalize the results to other locations. For example, a high school math teacher who would like to test the efficacy of a new math problem-solving strategy will use it with students in his or her own classroom, regardless of whether they represent some larger population of students elsewhere.

Table 4.1 summarizes the most common approaches to sample selection that are used in qualitative and quantitative action research.

In a *mixed-methods* action research, the number and identification of participants depend on the particular research tools you plan to employ (Kemper, Stringfield, & Teddlie, 2003). For the qualitative component of your study, you may choose individuals who fit the selection criteria discussed above. For the quantitative portion of your research, try to include as many of the available and eligible participants as needed. For example, assume Suzanne, a preservice student teacher, would like to investigate how to conduct effective parent–teacher conferences in the fourth grade. She plans to collect her data using both qualitative and quantitative tools that include observation, survey, and interview. For each strategy, she selects a different number and type of participants, as appropriate. For the observations, Suzanne selects three parents who represent different levels of parental involvement. The second tool is an exit survey that Suzanne intends to give to all parents after the conferences. After receiving the survey's numerical results, she plans to conduct phone interviews with five parents to further discuss how they perceive the experience and benefits of the conferences. These parents will be selected to represent children of different levels of academic performance. Using the three data sources will provide Suzanne with a more complete perspective on ways to conduct effective parent–teacher conferences.

One of the advantages of action research is the familiarity the researcher has with people in the study setting. Your choice of participants from among students, parents, and colleagues is made on the basis of your firsthand knowledge of who among them is best suited for your study. If you are a guest in the setting, you may

TABLE 4.1. Selecting Samples in Qualitative and Quantitative Action Research	
Qualitative studies	**Quantitative studies**
• Purposive (typical cases, extreme cases, representative)	• Random
	• Systematic
• Volunteer	• Stratified
• Convenience	• Convenience

ask your mentor, advisor, or cooperating teacher to assist you in obtaining your sample.

In your research plan, describe the participants. For example, if the participants in the study are five students, indicate their age and grade level, gender, services provided by the school, or any other relevant information that is approved by the school administration to share and is not confidential. Additionally, explain why you have chosen these particular students from all eligible students in your class.

When planning the study, you may not have all the required information about the participants and the setting. In such cases, you may want to indicate what specific information you plan to gather later. As you develop the research plan, provide the details you currently have and note what additional information is still needed.

what kind of data is doable? interesting?

CHOOSING DATA COLLECTION PROCEDURES

The research question guides your choice of inquiry procedures. The process of constructing data collection tools, therefore, begins by contemplating your research question, deciding what information you need to collect in order to answer this question, and determining what kinds of strategies will be most effective in providing this information.

Be cognizant of the fact that many of the same data collection tools can be structured to be used in a variety of research studies and to yield both narrative and numerical data. For example, surveys can be constructed with open-ended questions to provide narrative data, as well as structured rating items that provide numerical data.

Each data collection strategy can be carried out in a variety of ways. You may, for example, interview individuals or groups presenting questions face-to-face, by telephone, or online. These interviews may be structured or unstructured. Each strategy provides a different type of information; therefore, in order to get a fuller picture it is suggested that you use more than one data collection tool. Using different sources will also increase your ability to compare and contrast the information you collect. Using multiple data sources is referred to as *triangulation* and is discussed in greater detail in this chapter in the section titled "Ensuring the Study's Validity and Trustworthiness." Table 4.2 focuses on the most common data collection tools and their definitions and outlines their possible usefulness as well as some of their limitations.

TABLE 4.2. Most Common Data Collection Tools: Their Definitions, Usefulness, and Limitations

Tool	Definition	Usefulness	Limitations
Interview	Purposeful conversation between two or more people in which an interchange of views about a selected topic occurs.	Presents individuals' perspectives, expressed in their own words, on the topic explored.	May be time-consuming; usually limited to a few interviewees.
Observation	Purposefully observing people, events, and interactions as they occur.	Provides an authentic view of what is taking place, mostly within a natural context.	Represents only observable behaviors and requires other tools to determine the intentions of the people being observed.
Surveys	Collecting information from a large number of people, mostly numerical; narrative data may also be gathered.	Easy to reach a large number of participants while maintaining anonymity; allows for diverse perspectives on a topic.	Self-report surveys may be sensitive to misinformation; response rate may be a problem.
Artifacts and documents	Documents and artifacts produced in the context of the class, school, or district.	Provide personal, demographic, and historical formal and informal data that are easily obtained and can be used to represent the setting, groups, and individuals.	Obtaining some documents may be difficult due to school policy and legal issues.
Assessment data	Teacher-made and standardized test scores representing students' achievement.	Allows monitoring of student progress and evaluation of the effectiveness of teaching strategies, curriculum, or programs.	Assessment tools may not accurately capture student performance, the content taught, or the effectiveness of the teaching strategy.

As you plan your study and ponder which strategy to choose, we suggest that you consider the following:

1. Which strategies will yield the information needed to gain deeper insight about the issue you are exploring?

2. Which strategies will provide you with different perspectives on your topic?

3. Which strategies are most suitable for your particular situation and are most likely to be enacted within your setting?

4. Which strategies will yield data within the boundaries of the time available to you?

For example, let's say that a school board is considering a proposal to provide more time for middle school students to prepare for state-mandated standardized achievement tests. A reduction in recess time seems to be the solution favored by the majority of the board members. Jenny, a sixth-grade social studies teacher in that school, is concerned about the effect of a shorter recess on her students. She decides to conduct a study to explore the impact of recess on her students' academic progress and classroom behavior. Jenny is considering five different strategies to answer her research question: interviews, observations, student work, a survey, and teacher-made tests. Interviews and surveys would allow her to obtain the students' perspectives on the value of recess. Observations would offer her an opportunity to systematically watch and record her students' behavior, class participation, and on-task performance. Test scores would present her with numerical objective data, and students' work samples would reflect their ability to understand the materials presented in class.

The scope of Jenny's research and time frame are limited by the fact that the next school board meeting is in 4 weeks. An additional consideration that impacts Jenny's decision is how doable and practical these research strategies are within the constraints of her teaching responsibilities. For example, will she be able to conduct observations while fulfilling her duties as a classroom teacher? Will she be able to conduct in-depth interviews of students of different ability levels and with behavior issues and transcribe them? Can a numerical survey reflect the nuances of students' feelings and thoughts? What kinds of documents will Jenny choose from among her students' work that will reflect her students' progress over time?

After deliberating the usefulness and limitations of each strategy, Jenny decides not to use interviews, since they would take too much of her limited time. Instead, she will add five open-ended questions to her survey to allow students to express their opinions in their own words. Jenny would also like to observe her students. To avoid compromising her teaching responsibilities, she asks her colleague, Marianne, to videotape the class while she is teaching. Jenny decides against including samples of students' work as part of her presentation to the school board because of the short time she was given for her presentation. Finally, knowing the inclination of the school board to trust statistical test data, Jenny chooses to use her students' test scores for her presentation.

ENSURING THE STUDY'S VALIDITY AND TRUSTWORTHINESS

You have to be confident that your research findings are valid in order for the results of the study to be useful for your practice and to enable you to shape your decisions and future actions. The term *validity* refers to the degree to which the study, the data collection tools, and the interpretation of data accurately represent the issue being investigated. Validity is valued in both qualitative and quantitative research; however, it is addressed differently by each approach. In *qualitative* studies, which are essentially subjective and focused on participants' perspectives, validity refers to the extent to which data reflect participants' views of the issue being explored. In fact, practitioners often prefer the term *trustworthiness* to describe the kind of data used in qualitative inquiry. In *quantitative* studies, validity is most often an issue that relates to the appropriateness of the tools used to collect data, the soundness of the study's design, and the extent to which findings can be generalized to other groups.

Qualitative Studies

The most common methods to enhance the trustworthiness of qualitative action research studies are triangulation, disciplined subjectivity, thick description, member checking, peer review, and data audit.

Triangulation is the practice of relying on more than one source of data by using multiple methods or obtaining varied perspectives. While the image of a triangle suggests using three sources of information, using two or more methods might be more feasible, depending on your particular research question or circumstances. For example, Julie, an assistant principal, seeks to obtain the perspectives of students, teachers, and parents on the restructuring of the student council. Obtaining data using different sources, such as interviews and surveys, would allow Julie to triangulate the information gathered and thus establish the trust-worthiness and credibility of her interpretations (Richards, 2009).

Disciplined subjectivity invites you to acknowledge your personal preconceived ideas with regard to the study and to monitor your biases. In our discussion about the researcher role in this chapter, we emphasized the value of acknowledging the researcher's own subjectivity. The trustworthiness of the study requires reflexivity, an ongoing self-reflection with regard to the setting, participants, and the topic as the researcher collects, analyzes, and interprets the data (Guillemin & Gillam, 2004).

Thick description refers to a detailed and rich account of the research context and a presentation of the participants' perspectives in their own words. This thick description allows the audience to perceive authentically the participants' views and "enter" into their world by seeing, hearing, and sensing their experiences. Since qualitative research findings emerge from the participants' perspectives, an intense and detailed narrative allows your audience to better understand your interpretation of the data, thereby enhancing the trustworthiness of the study.

Member checking allows you to ensure that you present the participants' perspectives honestly and accurately. This can be accomplished by sharing with the participants the interview and observation transcripts and discussing with them your analytical thoughts and interpretation.

Peer review provides you with an additional "set of eyes" and helps you to determine the credibility of your interpretation and the accuracy of your findings. To achieve this, you can recruit a colleague, a friend, or a collaborative research group member to review your data and interpretation and provide you with constructive feedback.

Data audit is a process that records and lists the raw data: transcribed notes from observations and interviews, original documents, photographs, and other artifacts. This information allows your audience to assess whether the interpretations, insights, and conclusions you offer reflect coherently and honestly the information gathered throughout the study.

Quantitative Studies

Traditional experimental studies in educational research are designed to test the effectiveness of an intervention (the independent variable) and the impact it has on the dependent (outcome) variable. In other words, researchers are looking for cause-and-effect relationships and articulate their predictions about these relationships by stating their hypotheses prior to the start of the study. In most cases, experimental and control groups are used and their scores on some measure are compared before and after the intervention. This is especially true with traditional large-scale studies with important consequences, such as purchasing new textbooks for the students in a district or training teachers how to use a new instructional method. Researchers have to carry out tightly controlled studies in order to document that the changes they have observed are due to the independent variable (intervention) and not other causes, called *extraneous* variables (Ravid, 2011). Those extraneous variables are unplanned and uncontrolled variables that may be related to and influence the study's outcomes. For example, the time of day that the study takes place, the quality of classroom teaching, or the type of tools that are used to assess the students—all of these can impact the outcomes and mask the true effect of the planned intervention.

When we are able to document that the changes we observe are due to the planned intervention and are not caused by other possible extraneous variables, our study is said to have high *internal validity*. There may also be threats to the study's *external validity* when the sample selected is not representative of the general population to which the results are generalized. As an example, problems may be related to the fact that the group used in the pilot study is composed of volunteers who are highly motivated and do not represent the general population. In studies conducted by educational practitioners, though, the goal is not to generalize to other populations of participants, so the problems listed above generally do not create serious issues that threaten the validity of the findings.

As an action researcher, if you want to investigate cause-and-effect relationships, you should try to control as many of the relevant variables as you can. For example, assume that Darlene, a second-grade teacher, wants to try a new method to teach vocabulary. For one month, she tests the students every Friday on the 10 vocabulary words taught that week using the current instructional method. For the next month, she uses a new teaching method and again tests the students at the end of each week. After 2 months, Darlene compares the total number of correct words achieved by each student. Ideally, the 2 months should be similar on several relevant variables, such as the number of school days, the difficulty of the words taught, and student attendance. If, for example, there is a flu epidemic in the second month of the study, Darlene's students may not do as well on their vocabulary tests because they missed too many school days and not because of the instructional method used. Because Darlene cannot control many of these variables, she should consider them when she analyzes her data.

Validity also depends on the quality and appropriateness of th
to collect data and whether they measure what they purport to be i
is true in both traditional and action research in education. For exa
comprehension test that measures students' ability to read a passaⱨ
to questions about the passage is not a valid test of reading fluenⱦ
math test that includes computation exercises is not a valid indicatⱸ
ability to solve math word problems.

In quantitative research, the issue of reliability is also important. *Reliability*
refers to the consistency of the tools used to gather data. As a researcher, ask yourself whether similar results would have been obtained if you were to repeatedly
use the same or equivalent data collection tools or procedures. In studies where
trained observers or raters participate in the data collection process, the agreement between them can serve as an index of reliability and consistency (Mertler &
Charles, 2011). In other studies, results from repeated testing using the same tool
or using equivalent forms of the same test can be compared in order to determine
the reliability of the assessment tool. In general, longer tests are likely to be more
reliable. For example, a math test with only a few questions leaves too much room
for guessing and, therefore, may not be as reliable as a longer test. If your study
includes data gathered through the use of commercially available tests (such as
standardized achievement tests), it would be a good idea to include information
about their reliability. (See Chapter 6 for further discussion of reliability.)

To illustrate the process of establishing content validity and reliability of
teacher-made tests, let's look at Travis, a middle school social studies teacher. Travis and the other social studies teachers in the district met in the summer to review
the curriculum, articulate their learning objectives, and write district assessments
to be used throughout the year. Matching the assessments to the learning objectives ensured the validity of the assessment tools. The assessments that were constructed included at least three items to measure each learning objective. This was
done to increase the tests' reliability by providing students with several opportunities to demonstrate their knowledge.

Mixed-Methods Studies

The procedures for ensuring the trustworthiness and validity of qualitative and
quantitative approaches are different; therefore, make sure to describe the strategies you will use for each. In the qualitative sections, this may include triangulation, thick description, peer review, and so on. In the quantitative methods portion

of your research, discuss the validity and reliability of the data collection tools, as well as the threats to internal validity, when appropriate (Creswell, 2009).

DEVELOPING ETHICAL GUIDELINES

Although action research is conducted by practitioners in their own practice, it is still considered research and should be monitored and conducted by following ethical guidelines. You should ensure the safety, confidentiality, and well-being of those you study or those who may be affected by your study. Ethical consideration of your students and your colleagues should be key elements of your action research study (Mertler, 2012) and you should protect the interests and well-being of all the study's participants (Stringer, 2008). As you plan your inquiry, you need to consider the following issues as they relate to your action research.

Obtaining Permission to Conduct the Study

Check with the appropriate "gatekeepers" (e.g., teachers or administrators) and obtain permission to conduct the study and collect data. Even if you carry out the inquiry in your own classroom, you may need to get the approval of your administrators (Samaras, 2011). Make sure you document the exchange of messages giving you permission for the study. In some cases, depending on the school policy and the nature of your study, you will need to obtain parents' permission as well. If the inquiry is part of your academic course requirements, your instructor will provide you with the necessary guidelines and advise you about the process. In many cases, universities, as well as school districts, have an established research review process that involves submitting a proposal to an ethics and review committee (Denzin, 2009; Pritchard, 2002).

Confidentiality of Data Collected

Whenever you collect data for your study, you need to ensure the confidentiality of your findings. Regardless of the information you collect — observations, interviews, test scores, school records, and the like—the rights of participants should be guaranteed. Avoid identifying by name or providing other identifying information about your students or other participants, such as colleagues or parents, and be sensitive to people's desire to remain anonymous. You may use pseudonyms or general descriptions such as "suburban school in a large metropolitan area." Use group data when possible to protect individuals. For example, report test scores for the class as a whole instead of scores for individual students. To protect the anonymity of the study's participants, names and other contact information need to be removed from documents used in the study such as writing samples, surveys, and tests. Additionally, with so much data currently stored in electronic formats, be sure to protect participants in case the data are compromised in any way.

Informed Consent

In many studies, participants (or their parents or legal guardians if they are minors) have to consent to participate in the study. Don't assume that you can design any study or collect any data that you want just because you are investigating in your own setting. Additionally, make sure you have the proper permission to record or videotape the participants. Unless the data you collect are part of your professional responsibilities, you have to notify the participants about your action research and provide them with an opportunity to ask questions about it. We suggest sending a letter of introduction to the participants or to their parents or guardians if they are minors. In the letter identify yourself and your role in the school, describe the purpose of your study, and outline what the research participants' involvement in the study will entail. You should also ensure the participants' confidentiality and privacy and explain that they can withdraw from the inquiry if they wish to, without any negative consequences. This information may encourage the cooperation of the participants (or their parents or guardians) and will allow them to make a thoughtful decision about whether to sign the informed consent form (Bouma & Ling, 2004; Samaras, 2011). Boxes 4.4 and 4.5 are examples of a letter of introduction and an informed consent form, respectively, that were sent by Orin, the student teacher who investigated portfolio assessment, to the parents of his students.

Respect toward the Research Site

As an action researcher, respect the needs, goals, and priorities of the school or classroom where you conduct your inquiry. The quality of your study depends, to a large extent, on participants' cooperation. Treat them with respect, share with them the purpose of the investigation, keep open communication, and invite their feedback. Acknowledge your appreciation and express your gratitude for their

BOX 4.4. Sample Letter of Introduction

Dear Parents and Guardians,

My name is Orin _____; I am a student teacher in _____ school and a student in the MAT (Master of Art of Teaching) program at the University of _____.

As part of my student-teaching practice I am working with Mrs. _____ and Mr. _____, your children's science teachers. It was my privilege and pleasure to work with your sons and daughters. As part of my graduate studies I am required to conduct a research project and chose to focus my research on the portfolio assessment system in the science class. This study is done with the permission of the school principal, and the full cooperation and support of your child's science teachers. The purpose of the study is educational and the results will contribute to the knowledge and understanding of the value of portfolios from the point of view of the students and their teachers.

The study involves (1) an observation of two sessions of science classes where portfolio assessment system is practiced, (2) reading your son/daughter's portfolio on the topic of Earth, and (3) a 30-minute interview. During the interview, your child is free not to answer any of the questions asked and you or your child may terminate the interview at any time.

I assure you that your child's privacy and anonymity will be respected and protected throughout the process and no real names or identifying information will be included in my final research report. Participation in the study is voluntary. If you are not comfortable with having your child participate in the study, you may at any time withdraw your child's participation.

I would like to formally ask for your permission to allow for your child's participation in this research project by filling out the Informed Consent Form attached. Thanks in advance for your cooperation and support.

Please feel free to contact me if you have any questions about the study or your consent.

Sincerely yours,
Orin

contributions. When you present your findings, be sure that it's done truthfully, but with sensitivity, and with the greatest care not to hurt the participants' feelings and self-image.

Safety of the Participants

Study participants should not be put in harm's way or suffer in any way in the name of research. If there is any possibility of a conflict between your research goals and your professional responsibilities as a practitioner, your first concern should be the welfare, well-being, and needs of your students, their parents, and your colleagues. Be sure to inform participants (or their legal guardians) that they can stop their participation in the study at any time.

BOX 4.5. Sample Informed Consent Form

I give my consent to have my son/daughter, _____, participate in a research project regarding the use of portfolio assessment in the science class. I understand that if I give this consent my son/daughter will be interviewed and observed during two sessions of science class, and his/her portfolio on the topic of Earth will be read by the researcher.

   I understand that participation in this study is voluntary; I can withdraw my son/daughter from the study at any time during the study without any negative consequences.

   I further understand that my child's anonymity will be protected, and the name of the school or the teachers will not be revealed when reporting the results of the study.

Please sign and return the form.

Your name (please print): _____

Your child's name: _____

Your signature: _____

Date _____

_____ I understand the information above and **AGREE** to allow my son/daughter to participate in the research project.

_____ I understand the information above and **DO NOT AGREE** to my son/daughter's participation in the research project.

Accurate Interpretation and Presentation of the Data

You should maintain the highest standards and be honest and accurate when gathering and interpreting your study's data. While it may be tempting at times, do not overextend your findings and do not report as conclusive findings that you cannot confirm with a high degree of certainty.

CREATING A "TO-DO" LIST

Creating a "to-do" list will help you to (1) carefully schedule the implementation of your data collection plan, (2) assess the time required for each activity, and (3) ensure the feasibility of completing your study within the time available. Figure 4.1 shows a section from a "to-do" list that includes an outline of the major activities of the plan, the time and location of each activity, the people involved, and the materials required for each activity.

Allow yourself some leeway to accommodate unplanned changes and unforeseen delays that often occur in executing the plan. Remember that the plan you have developed so far is focused on the data collection phase of the study. Be sure to budget additional time to analyze and interpret the data gathered in the study and to write the final report.

FINALIZING THE RESEARCH PLAN

Once you have completed writing the research plan, reread it carefully and critically, preferably with a friend, a research colleague, or your advisor/instructor. The starting point for your reading is the research question. Evaluate if all the aspects of the plan will enable you to successfully answer your research question

Date	Activity	Location	Participants	What Is Required
Monday, April 12, 10:15– 11:00	Interview	A quiet place to talk in the teachers' lounge	Mrs. Smith (a fifth-grade teacher)	Recording device, interview guide, paper, and pen

FIGURE 4.1. A section from a "to-do" list.

within your time frame and circumstances. Consider whether you have thoughtfully addressed the various elements of your research plan and made appropriate choices that will allow you to efficiently and successfully carry out your investigation.

Start by stating your research question and analyze its components. Figure 4.2 (on page 80) presents a series of questions for each of the seven elements that were addressed in this chapter. As you review your plan, self-check and respond to the questions below.

CHAPTER SUMMARY

1. The research plan serves as a guide for the inquiry process; it allows the action researcher to step back before launching the investigation, and to carefully consider the essential issues involved. This is especially helpful for a novice researcher.

2. When implementing the research plan, the researcher may need to revise, adapt, and modify it to respond to and accommodate unexpected school circumstances.

3. The research plan should be described in sufficient detail to provide the practitioner with a clear blueprint to guide the investigation.

4. The research question is the key for developing a research plan that will enable the researcher to find meaningful answers.

5. A meaningful research plan usually necessitates reflecting on the researcher's role, the scope of the study, the data collection techniques, the research participants, the study's validity and trustworthiness, and ethical guidelines.

6. Reflexivity means taking into account and openly discussing the potential impact of the practitioner's preconceptions, values, and personal and professional experiences on decisions made and actions taken during the study.

7. The scope of the study affects the length of time dedicated to conducting the investigation, the number and nature of the data collection tools utilized, and the participants who will be involved.

8. The process of constructing data collection tools begins by contemplating the research question, deciding what information should be collected in order to answer this question, and determining what kinds of strategies will be most effective in providing this information.

9. Since action research is embedded within the classroom and school setting and the results of the inquiry have immediate local application, knowledge of the participants and the contextual factors is of particular importance.

Your Research Question: _____	
Elements of Plan	**Questions and Choices to Consider**
Your role as a researcher	• What values and preconceived notions do you have that may impact your study? • What is your relationship with the participants and with the topic? • How will you address your subjectivity and biases? • How will you monitor your subjectivity throughout the study?
Scope	• What is the purpose of your study and with whom will you share it? • Is the study manageable within your daily practice? • What are the external constraints that will impact the execution of the study? • How will you address these limitations?
Research site and participants	*Site*: • What are the unique characteristics of the local setting? • How do these characteristics impact the inquiry? *Participants*: • Who and how many people will be involved in the data collection? • What criteria will you use for selecting the sample of participants and why? • Does the sampling allow you to obtain multiple perspectives on the issue being investigated? • What are the demographics of the participants?
Data collection procedures	• What and how many data collection techniques are you going to use? • What is the purpose of each strategy and how will it enable you to answer your research question? • Will you be able to triangulate the data gained through these strategies? • Are these strategies doable within your particular situation?
Validity and reliability	• What methods will you use to ensure the trustworthiness of the findings? • How will you secure triangulation or multiple sources? • How will you check the accuracy of your data? • What strategies will you use to ensure the validity and reliability of your data collection tools?
Ethical considerations	• How will you protect the confidentiality of the data collected? • What permissions and informed consents are needed and how will you obtain them? • How will you protect the rights of the participants and ensure their privacy? • How will you maintain high respect toward the site of your study?
"To-do" list	• When and where will the different activities take place? • Who will be involved in each activity? • What materials will be needed? • Is your timetable realistic, flexible, and feasible?

FIGURE 4.2. Summary of the elements of the data collection plans.

10. The identification of who and how many participants will be asked to take part in the study depends on who will be able to provide valuable information for the study and the criteria for participant sample selection.

11. Details about the overall school community offer a fuller description of the study within its particular context.

12. *Qualitative* action research does not have a formulated set of rules about the size of the sample or how it is selected. Types of samples selected include *typical extreme cases, representative, available*, and *convenience*.

13. *Quantitative* action research relies on numerical data and, therefore, sample *size* is an important consideration. Types of samples selected include *random, systematic, stratified*, and *convenience*.

14. In *mixed-methods* action research, the number and identification of the participants depend on the particular research tools the researcher plans to employ.

15. When planning the study, the researcher may not have all the required information about the participants and the setting. As the research plan is being developed, the researcher needs to include the details currently available while also noting what additional information is still needed.

16. Practitioners engaged in action research have to be confident that their findings are valid in order for the results of the study to be useful for their practice and to enable them to shape their decisions and the actions that follow.

17. The term *validity* refers to the degree to which the study, the data collection tools, and the interpretation of data accurately represent the issue being investigated. Validity is valued in both qualitative and quantitative research; however, it is addressed differently in each approach.

18. Qualitative researchers prefer the term *trustworthy* over *validity* because they assert that qualitative studies are essentially subjective, and the focus is on the researcher's ability to see and present the issue being explored through the eyes of the participants.

19. The most common methods for enhancing the trustworthiness of *qualitative* action research studies are triangulation, disciplined subjectivity, thick description, member checking, peer review, and data audit.

20. In *quantitative* studies, validity is most often an issue that relates to the appropriateness of the tools used to collect data, the soundness of the study's design, and the extent to which the findings can be generalized to other groups.

21. In *quantitative* studies, validity also depends on the quality and appropriateness of the measures used to collect data and whether they accurately measure what they purport to.

22. The procedures for ensuring the trustworthiness and validity of qualitative and quantitative approaches are different; therefore, make sure to describe the strategies you will use for each.

23. In *quantitative* research, the issue of reliability is also important. *Reliability* refers to the consistency of the tools used to gather data.

24. It is essential that action researchers follow ethical guidelines when conducting their studies; they should ensure the safety, confidentiality, and well-being of those they study or those who may be affected by their study.

25. Action researchers may find it helpful to create a "to-do" list that includes an outline of the major activities of the plan, when and where each activity will take place, the materials required for each activity, and the people involved.

CHAPTER EXERCISES AND ACTIVITIES

1. Write down your research question in a center of a page, circle it, and jot down around it ideas triggered by the question. Write down the types of information, choices, tasks, and actions you will need to take in order to answer the question. Once you complete this visual map, review it with a practical eye and consider what is doable within the context of your own professional and personal circumstances. (This brainstorm activity may be done alone, with a peer, or with your research group.)

2. Reflect on *your role as a researcher* and jot down your subjective connection to the topic of your study. Consider the influence of your subjectivity on the decisions you make and actions you take.

3. Identify the *site and the participants* for your study. Plan how to access this site and obtain permission to conduct the study. Indicate how you will select your sample, and describe who will participate in the study.

4. Explain the *types of data* that you plan to collect and how they will allow you to answer your research questions. (Table 4.2 and the questions on page 69 may assist you in choosing the most useful data collection strategy.)

5. Describe how you will ensure the *validity* and *trustworthiness* of your study. If you are conducting a quantitative research or a mixed-methods study, be sure to include an explanation of how you will ensure the reliability of the tools you will use to gather numerical data.

6. Reflect on the *ethical issues* related to your own study. Consider how to ensure the safety, confidentiality, and well-being of those involved in the study and describe the procedures you will take to protect their rights. (The examples in Boxes 4.4 and 4.5 may be helpful in case you are required to use a consent form.)

7. Using the example in Figure 4.1, create a tentative "to-do" list for your study.

8. Using Figure 4.2, review all the elements of your proposed plan. Jot down potential problems or challenges that you may encounter while implementing the research plan. (This brainstorm activity may be done alone, with a peer, or with your research group.)

ADDITIONAL READINGS

Denzin, N. K., & Giardina, M. D. (Eds.). (2008). *Qualitative inquiry and the politics of evidence.* Thousand Oaks, CA: Sage.

Hancké, B. (2010). *Intelligent research design: A guide for beginning researchers in the social sciences.* Victoria, Australia: Oxford University Press.

Israel, M., & Hay, I. (2006). *Research ethics for social scientists: Between ethical conduct and regulatory compliance.* London: Sage.

Merriam, S. B. (2009). *Qualitative research: A guide to design and implementation.* San Francisco: Jossey-Bass.

Mills, G. E. (2011). *Action research: A guide for the teacher researcher* (4th ed.). Upper Saddle River, NJ: Pearson.

Schram, T. H. (2006). *Conceptualizing and proposing qualitative research* (2nd ed.). Upper Saddle River, NJ: Pearson Education.

Teddlie, C., & Tashakkori, A. (2008). *Foundations of mixed methods research: Integrating quantitative and qualitative approaches in the social and behavioral sciences.* Thousand Oaks, CA: Sage.

Warin, J. (2011). Ethical mindfulness and reflexivity: Managing a research relationship with children and young people in a 14-year qualitative longitudinal research (QLR) study. *Qualitative Inquiry, 17*(9), 805–814.

CHAPTER 5

Data Collection Tools

Our classrooms and schools are rich with data. As educators, we are continuously bombarded with information and intuitively "collect data" every day. When we listen to our students or to their parents, when we observe how students behave on the playground, when we try a new curriculum or revise an existing practice, or when we review students' portfolios—all these activities are an integral part of our work. We do not consider them "research" because they seem to be natural elements of the educational routine. But, in reality, that is what they are. They provide us with insights into the life of our classroom and an understanding of the consequences of our actions. These same activities are used when we collect data for teacher action research. However, in teacher research, the data collection effort is purposeful, deliberate, organized, and systematic. The information we gather from our data may serve as evidence that confirms our insights and validates our intuition.

The selection of data collection tools and strategies derives from the nature of our research questions, rather than from theoretical orientations (Check & Schutt, 2011; Merriam, 2009). As you explore the many types of data collection tools detailed in this chapter, ask yourself the following questions: What do I want to know? Which data sources will best enable me to collect the information I need? and Can I obtain the information that I am looking for? Do not limit yourself to a particular theoretical orientation; rather, choose the data collection methods that will be most useful in understanding the research problem and answering the questions you raise. Therefore, ask yourself: Will qualitative data or quantitative data provide me with meaningful information? Or will a mixed-methods approach—collecting both quantitative and qualitative data—offer me a better understanding of the research problem than either approach alone?

Due to the inherent complexity of classroom life, it is hard to divide the research tools and methods into qualitative and quantitative when carrying out action research. The same tool may generate qualitative or quantitative data depending on the strategy developed. For example, an open-ended observation may lead to a subjective, holistic, "thick description," whereas closed-structure observation, based on predetermined categories, like a checklist, will result in numerical data. Similarly, artifacts may include qualitative data, such as those found in self-reflective journals, as well as quantitative information, such as attendance records. Therefore, unlike most of the chapters in the book, we did not organize this chapter around the qualitative, quantitative, and mixed-methods framework but rather structured it around the major data collection tools.

In this chapter, we discuss several common data collection tools that educators like you have found to be most useful for gathering information in investigating their practice. For each method, we provide some general guidance and practical tips that, we hope, will contribute to the effectiveness of your data collection process. We also include examples to illustrate how the methods work in educational settings.

We organized the chapter around four types of teacher research instruments most appropriate to the classroom and school world: (1) observation, (2) interview, (3) survey, and (4) artifacts and documents.

OBSERVATION

Observation refers to looking at a setting purposely. The act of observation provides a powerful insight into the authentic life of schools and classrooms. You can systematically observe the activities, people, and physical aspects of your educational setting. Observations allow you to view the school, the classroom, or specific individuals in those settings and to see things that you may unconsciously miss in the often-chaotic dynamics of teaching. In contrast with interviews, in which the participants' voices guide your understanding, observation allows you to be aware of nonverbal behaviors, gestures, and body language (Good & Brophy, 2007; Wragg, 2012).

The observation strategies available to you as a teacher researcher lie on a continuum, from qualitative to quantitative, from open-ended to closed-ended, from unstructured to structured, and from holistic to preordained.

Qualitative Observation

During qualitative observation, you should look, listen, learn, ask, ponder, and record your observations. The qualitative observation may be semistructured or unstructured. In a *semistructured* observation, you start by developing a set of issues such as students speaking out of turn and patterns of class participation. The observation is designed to generate data that illuminate these issues as they arise naturally in the classroom setting. An *unstructured* observation is usually not based on a given agenda; rather, you will look at what is taking place in the classroom setting before deciding what is significant in the situation for your investigation (DeWalt & DeWalt, 2010). In the following section, we describe the qualitative unstructured observation tools that are typically used by educators in their educational settings: the observation protocol, the behavioral log, and tools such as photographs, videotapes, and audiotapes. We based our description on our experience as educational researchers and teachers of action research, as well as on many sources that include DeWalt and DeWalt (2010), C. Frank (1999), Good and Brophy (2007), LeCompte and Schensul (2010), O'Reilly (2012), Rodriguez and Rayave (2002), and Wragg (2012).

The Process of Conducting Qualitative Observation

Overall, the focus of your observation should emerge from the research question(s), but at the same time you should be cognizant of the general context of the setting. Envision how the observation will help you in answering the research question. You also need to make a decision about where, how often, and how long the observations will be (Hopkins, 2008). Ask yourself questions such as What am I going to look for? and How will I describe the observation in words for future analysis and interpretation?

Determine what your role will be during the observation. Do you plan to conduct the observation at a distance, getting involved as little as possible with the observed setting? Are you going to be a full participant/observer, engaged in some level or another with the students or taking part in the life of the setting you observe? Or is your role going to be something in between, such as observing teacher–student interactions in another class or observing your own students during lunchtime, or another situation in which you have no teaching responsibilities? Keep in mind that even if you do not purposely intervene, your presence in the classroom can affect the behavior of the people in the setting and change it. When you observe your own class, consciously look from a perspective of an outsider. Step back from the daily routine of your work and look at the setting as if you are seeing it for the first time. Make the familiar and known new and unexpected. Be sensitive and question what is assumed and what is taken for granted (Hendricks, 2012; Hopkins, 2008; Rodriguez & Rayave, 2002).

We suggest starting with a broad sweep of the classroom to acquaint yourself with the environment and the people involved. Gradually narrow your focus and zero in on the people, behavior, and interactions that are at the center of your study and that are most relevant to your research question. Every now and then broaden your observation to see the full picture before you zoom in, once more, on the specific activities or students directly related to your investigation. This will allow you to be sensitive to the specifics without being blind to the broader picture.

Observation Protocol

The observation protocol contains field notes that are detailed descriptions of what you see, hear, and sense during the observation, and the thoughts, feelings, and understandings these observations provoked. The richer the description, the more meaningful the observation. Through thick description narrative, the setting should be "brought to life" and the reader should have the feeling of "being there." Observation protocol includes two kinds of field notes: *descriptive* and *reflective*.

Descriptive Notes

Descriptive notes aim to record what happened during the observation without inferring feelings or responses to what is happening. In the descriptive notes, describe the physical setting; provide a verbal portrait of the participants; record the acts, activities, and events that take place; and document conversations verbatim. Draw a classroom seating chart of the physical layout of the setting including desks, tables, other furniture, computers, and other teaching tools, such as a smartboard. Figure 5.1 shows an example of a classroom seating chart.

Several researchers (e.g., Angrosino, 2007; Bogdan & Biklen, 2006; DeWalt & DeWalt, 2010; Lofland, Snow, Anderson, & Lofland, 2005; H. F. Wolcott, 2005) suggest that before you start, you should concentrate on the aspects that are directly connected to your own topic. Consider the following general questions:

1. **Who** is in the setting? For example, indicate the number of people present, and their gender and age group.

2. **When** does the group meet together? For example, the time of the school day and the length of the session.

3. **Where** is the meeting taking place? For example, the physical setting, the ways the group uses the space, and the ambience of the room.

4. **What** is happening here? For example, what are the people in the setting doing or saying to one another? In what events, activities, or routines are the students engaged?

5. **How** is the situation organized? For example, what rules or norms govern the situation?

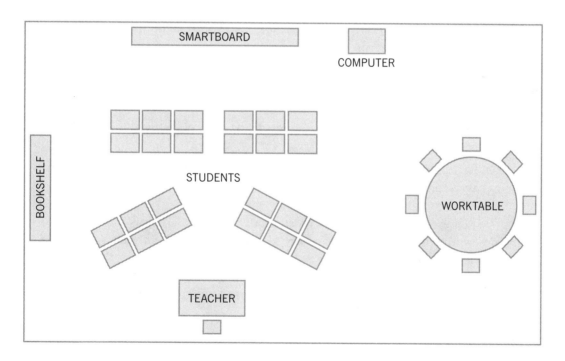

FIGURE 5.1. Classroom seating chart.

As you focus your observation on the issues directly related to your own investigation, direct your attention to the following aspects:

1. Portray the *individuals* or *groups* that you chose to follow: for example, their physical appearance, mannerisms, and gestures.

2. Describe *activities:* for example, provide a detailed depiction of activities related to the focus of your study.

3. Note particular *interactions:* for example, who was involved and what occurred?

4. Record *dialogues:* for example, direct quotes, unique phrases, and revealing statements.

Reflective Notes

Reflective notes are used to record reflections and insights about what is happening in the setting. These notes may include:

1. Reflections on the *meaning* of what is observed: for example, your insights and emerging interpretations.

2. Reflections on the observation *methods:* for example, reflect on procedures and materials used in the process, and think of some suggestions for future observations.

3. Reflections on *problems* encountered: for example, ethical dilemmas and conflicts.

4. Reflections on your own *frame of mind:* for example, attitudes, expectations, and biases.

The reflective field notes are written in a way that clearly sets them off from the descriptive notes. Some researchers use brackets or parentheses to indicate their reflective notes, whereas others draw a line down the center of the observation protocol form to divide the descriptive notes from the reflective notes. (See Figure 5.2 for a sample observation protocol form.)

Observation Steps

The following are some guidelines and suggestions to help you plan and carry out your classroom observations:

| Research question(s): _____ |
| Date of observation: _____ Time frame: _____ |
| Location of observation: _____ |
| Who are the foci of the observation? _____ |
| Activities: _____ |
| Purpose of observation (behaviors, interactions, responses): _____ |
| How does the observation reflect what I want to know? _____ |
| What is important here? _____ |
| What would I want to focus on more closely if/when I return to this setting? _____ |
| _____ |

Descriptive Field Notes	Reflective Field Notes

FIGURE 5.2. Sample observation protocol form.

1. Find a place that provides a good view of what is going on, without being conspicuous.

2. Spend some time at the beginning of the observation without taking notes and then confine your attention to the general characteristics of the setting.

3. Identify the people, activities, and interactions that will be the focus of your attention.

4. Draw a diagram of the classroom.

5. Record your descriptive and reflective field notes on the observation protocol form.

6. Start with a broad sweep and gradually narrow your focus to particular participants or interactions that are most valuable for your research.

7. Record what happens in the class. It would be helpful to note the progression of the classroom activities and topics discussed.

8. Write down behavioral descriptions in the descriptive field notes section as they occur; be sure to set them off from the reflective field notes.

9. After completing the observation, take some time to review your notes and add any descriptions and reflections you may have missed. Respond to questions such as What is important here? and What would I want to focus on more closely if I return to this class?

Behavior Log

The behavior log is a useful observational tool for a more focused observation. This type of log is a running record used to keep track of the behaviors exhibited by an individual student or a small group of students during a given situation (e.g., student group work, playground). The running record enables the teacher to identify patterns of behavior. It provides an examination of the dynamic between what preceded and followed the behaviors and allows for a comparison between an individual's conduct at different times or in different situations (Cohen et al., 2011).

In the behavior log, record the sequence of events and describe what preceded and what followed the studied behavior. You may record a student's inappropriate behavior every time it occurs (see Figure 5.3).

Another option is to keep an interval behavior log where you record what is happening at regular intervals, such as every 5 minutes (see Figure 5.4). For

Child _____ Grade _____ Date _____ Observed Setting _____			
Time	Specific Behavior	Environmental Reaction	Comments

FIGURE 5.3. Sample behavior log.

Child *Tina*		Grade *4*	Date *12/7*	Observed Setting *Math Class*

Time	Specific Behavior	Environmental Reaction	Comments
9:05	A math worksheet is on the table in front of Tina. She is fidgeting, looks around.	The students are working. Laura, who sits next to Tina, glances at her every now and then. The teacher grades papers.	Does Tina understand the assignment?
9:10	Tina grabs Laura's pencil and drops it to the floor.	Laura pulls Tina's book. The teacher looks at Tina.	Is the teacher aware of Tina's behavior? Why doesn't she get involved?
9:15	Tina bounces on the chair. Her worksheet is pushed aside.	Laura calls out: "Tina is making noises. I can't work!" The teacher gets up. Stands next to Tina. Tina points angrily at the worksheet. "It is boring," she exclaims.	It seems that the teacher recognizes that Tina needs help.

FIGURE 5.4. Sample interval behavior log.

example, let's say you observe a child, who is diagnosed as having attention deficit disorder, while he or she is working on math exercises. Every 5 minutes record his or her behavior; note also the reaction of the people in the context (e.g., peers and the teacher) to his or her actions during that time. In a separate column add interpretive comments.

Photographs, Videotapes, and Audiotapes

Observational tools like photographs, videotapes, and audiotapes can enhance your capacity to capture student behaviors, attitudes, and social interaction through images and sounds.

Photographs

Photographs provide a useful means of representing a setting and its members. They offer powerful visual images that complement the observation protocol and reinforce the verbal descriptions. For example, if you investigate students' interactions during lunch, you may take a set of photographs of the lunchroom at 5-minute intervals over a 30-minute time span for several days. Together the pictures depict patterns of seating arrangements, behaviors, and interactions in that setting on a typical day (Allen, 2012).

Videotapes and Audiotapes

Videotapes and audiotapes are useful when you want to observe your own teaching and you lack the time or the ability to take observational notes while you teach the class. The advantages of video- and audiotapes is that they provide a permanent record you can review to notice, with greater accuracy, students' behavior, attitudes, and social interactions, and other aspects of the classroom dynamics that are not easily captured or remembered (White, 2012) .

For example, Sarita is an English as a Second Language (ESL) preservice teacher enrolled in her practicum class. She is working on improving her skills in engaging students in classroom discussions. As part of her effort she collaborated with her supervisor in studying the effect of the strategies she has read about while researching this topic. During the data collection phase, Sarita videotaped herself posing thought-provoking questions while working with a small group of seventh-grade ESL students. To obtain students' responses to Sarita's questions, her student-teaching supervisor recorded students' involvement in the conversation using a *behavior log*. The combination of these two observation strategies enabled Sarita and her supervisor to examine the effect of her teaching strategies on the level and quality of students' engagement in the discussion. The following are some suggestions for conducting classroom observations:

- ▶ As with every research activity that involves participants, ask the permission of the people in the setting, and in the case of young children, their parents' permission, before you tape them. (Follow the ethical guidelines outlined in Chapter 4.)
- ▶ Test run the taping equipment to ensure that it works properly.
- ▶ Consider carefully where you are going to post the video- or audiotape recorder. Is the focus going to be on a specific student, on a particular group of students, or on you? The location of the equipment will determine what images and voices will be prioritized.

▶ Mark all tapes with dates, time, and participants' identities and other pertinent information.

▶ Record the observational notes from videotapes and transcription from audiotapes following the observation protocol process described above.

Quantitative Observation

In contrast to the open-ended qualitative observation, structured closed-ended observations (like tally sheets, checklists, and rating scales) are focused on predetermined categories. Whereas in qualitative observations the behavior is recorded as it happens, in quantitative observation a particular set of behaviors or activities is listed in advance and checks are made to record them as they occur. As a teacher observer you adopt a nonparticipant role, noting the frequency or the level of the behavior being studied. Whereas qualitative observation techniques result in subjective narrative descriptions, quantitative observation techniques require that you systematically direct your attention to specific measurable behavior that results in numerical data. Quantitative observations allow a comparison among settings, individuals, and situations, and frequencies, patterns, and trends.

Tally Sheets

A tally sheet is used to track the frequency of a target behavior or event at a specific point in time. Figure 5.5 is an example of a tally sheet showing how many times during class Johnny raises his hand and asks for help.

Behavior	Math	Reading
Johnny raises his hand to answer his teacher's questions.	⊬⊦⊦ ⊬⊦⊦ |||	⊬⊦⊦ ||

FIGURE 5.5. Tally sheet of recorded behavior.

Checklists

A checklist is made up of a predetermined list of behaviors or activities that are the focus of the observer's attention. In order to develop a useful checklist, the observed behaviors should be defined and be separated into their components (e.g., "The students concentrate on their work"; "The student sways on his chair."). Checklists allow you to track the development of behaviors over time or across settings. For example, Stephanie, a preschool teacher, may want to observe Mary, one of her students, during free-play time and record the way she interacts with her peers. Stephanie does that by placing a checkmark next to the behaviors exhibited by Mary. Mary's behaviors might include pushing, cooperating, playing with other children, or taking toys from others (see Figure 5.6 for a sample checklist).

Rating Scales

A rating scale is used to record the extent to which a specific behavior or situation exists. The response choices range on a continuum from one end of the scale to the other (e.g., strongly agree to strongly disagree). Rating scales are also called Likert scales (named after Rensis Likert, the developer of the scale) or Likert-type scales. Figure 5.7 shows a sample of a rating scale that is focused on a specific student's behavior.

Figure 5.8 presents a list of suggestions and considerations to keep in mind as you plan your qualitative or quantitative classroom observations.

Child _____ Grade _____ Date _____ Observed Setting _____	
Behavior	**Observed**
Mary is playing with other children.	✓
Mary takes a toy from another child.	
Mary is pushing another child.	✓
Mary is talking with the teacher.	

FIGURE 5.6. Sample checklist.

| Circle the appropriate response: |
| 1. The work of student (name of student) has improved throughout the semester. |

| **Strongly Agree** | **Agree** | **Undecided** | **Disagree** | **Strongly Disagree** |

FIGURE 5.7. Sample behavior rating scale.

✓	**Suggestions**
	1. Ask the permission of the people in the setting you observe.
	2. Allow the focus of the observation to emerge from the research question(s).
	3. Decide where, how often, and how long the observations will be.
	4. Determine how involved you will be in the setting during the observation.
	5. Record your descriptive and reflective field notes in the observation protocol form.
	6. Start with a broad observation and gradually narrow your focus on particular participants and interactions in the setting that are directly relevant to your question.
	7. Describe in great details the participants, interactions, and activities at the center of your study.
	8. Write the descriptive notes without evaluation or judgment while your reflections in the descriptive notes may include your insights, thoughts, and feelings about what you observe.
	9. Draw a classroom seating chart of the physical layout of the setting.
	10. Use a behavior log and interval behavior log for a more focused observation.
	11. Decide on the focus of your observation: Will it be an individual student or the whole class?
	12. Decide whether you are looking for specific behaviors or will record any behavior that you observe.
	13. Decide whether you will focus only on the teacher, on teacher–student interaction, or on student–student interaction.
	14. Capture the setting's environment by using photographs or video- or audiotapes.
	15. Mark all observation protocols, behavior logs, interval behavior logs, and tapes with dates, time, and participants' identities and other pertinent information.

FIGURE 5.8. A checklist of suggestions for planning and collecting data using classroom observation.

INTERVIEW

The interview is a major data collection strategy in teacher action research. It provides an opportunity for in-depth conversations and allows teacher researchers to ask questions of students, teachers, administrators, parents, and others connected with school. This method of inquiry provides an understanding of the participants' experiences from their own perspectives because it allows them to voice their ideas, opinions, values, and knowledge on issues related to the investigation. Interview data complement and substantiate observation data. The observation can also serve as a springboard for the interview questions. For example, through observation you can record student action and interaction during free time. Interviewing some of the same students would allow you to gain an understanding of their behavior from their own perspectives. Interview data can be collected in an unstructured, semistructured, or highly structured process.

Unstructured, Semistructured, and Structured Interviews

Unstructured Interviews

The unstructured interview is an informal, though purposeful, conversation. The questions are broad and are presented in a casual style; the interviewer lets the conversation proceed naturally on its own course. Following the conversation we suggest that a brief summary of the exchange be jotted down, and important information be highlighted. For example, Herald, a first-grade teacher, investigates the value of daily homework. As part of a natural conversation, Herald asks the parents, when they pick up their children from school, "How did your son or daughter's homework go yesterday?" He then records the parents' responses in a teacher journal.

Semistructured Interviews

The semistructured interview is based on questions that were prepared prior to the interview. These are open-ended questions. During the interviews, participants are invited to co-construct the narrative and raise and pursue issues that are related to the study but were not included when the interview questions were planned. Additionally, when more clarification is needed or unexpected information is revealed, the teacher interviewer asks follow-up questions and probes further to encourage the participant to extend and deepen his or her responses (Kvale & Brinkmann, 2009; Seidman, 2012). For example, Ashley studies the activities provided to students in the after-school program at her school. She constructs a set of questions, but as she interviews the different program instructors and tries to dig deeper into their experiences, additional questions emerge. In interviewing the dancing club facilitator, for example, she starts by asking a general question: "Tell me about the dance club you facilitate." But, through the teacher's answer, she realizes that different students wish to focus on different kinds of dance. Some want hip-hop dancing, others would like to learn mostly salsa dances. A third group would prefer to spend most of the time on classic ballroom dancing. Ashley asks several questions exploring this issue, though initially she was not aware of the fact that the instructor faced this problem and therefore did not prepare any questions related to this issue.

Structured Interviews

The structured interview is also based on prepared questions. However, unlike semistructured interviews, in the structured format the interviewers frame the questions using an exact wording, replicating the order of the questions and providing identical questions to all participants (Seidman, 2012). For example, Norm, a social studies teacher, considers purchasing a new computer software program for his classroom. He interviews teachers from several school districts who currently are using the program. He uses the same questions to elicit their opinions about the program. Using the same standardized set of questions allows Norm to gain comparable data across people and sites.

Each of the formats of interviews above has advantages and disadvantages (Opdenakker, 2006). In choosing an interview format, consider the fact that as educators studying our own settings, we are familiar, in some way or another, with the people we interview; more important, we aim to gain their trust and encourage them to open up and speak freely. Taking a formal stance by sticking to the standard prepared questions is often unfeasible. Still, preparing a set of questions that will elicit the information you need for your study is very helpful and will allow you to relax and present the questions informally. Your participants will sense your confidence, which will enhance their tendency to speak freely, and in depth, about issues related to your study.

As you plan the interview questions, be sure that some of the essential themes that you explored through other sources of data used in your study are represented. This will allow you to triangulate, compare, and contrast the data during the analysis and interpretation phases. If the interview is poorly planned, the data may be difficult to analyze.

We suggest developing an interview guide with two sections. Section I will be completed before the interview and Section II immediately after. In Section I, start with the research question and then provide concrete information about the interview and the interviewee. Then outline a set of interview questions that you want to explore. As each interview evolves, you may change the wording and order of the questions, add questions, or extend the scope of the original questions. Section I of the interview guide can also be used for note taking during the interview. Section II provides a narrative description of the person you interview: for example, his or her body language, willingness to share information, and level of comfort. (See Figure 5.9 for a sample interview guide form.) In the data-obtained section you may want to reflect on the main ideas and insights gained through the interview. Then reflect on the process: Do you want to change anything? Are there any additional questions that you want to add in the future? (C. Frank, 2011; Rubin & Rubin, 2012; Seidman, 2012).

The Interview Process

In this section we discuss how to develop and conduct a successful interview and how to facilitate an individual, a focus group, or an online interview. The suggestions for the steps used in each stage of the interview are drawn from our experience as well as from the following sources: C. Frank (2011), Gubrium and

---

Section I:

Research Question(s): _____

Date and Setting: _____

Interviewee Demographic Information: _____

Interview Questions: _____

_____

Notes: _____

_____

Section II:

Interviewee Description: _____

Data Obtained: _____

Reflections (on the Process): _____

_____

FIGURE 5.9. Sample interview guide form.

Hollstein (2002), Kvale and Brinkmann (2009), Rubin and Rubin (2012), and Seidman (2012).

We start with guidelines for developing the interview questions, followed by suggestions for the interview process, and we cover different types of interviews: individual, focus group, and online.

Developing the Interview Questions

By using interviews as an inquiry method, you are looking for the participants' perceptions, knowledge, opinions, experience, and beliefs with regard to your research topic. The challenge in constructing interview questions is to phrase the questions and order them in a way that elicits the information you need (Foddy, 1993). Remember to write the questions on the interview guide form (Figure 5.9). Keep these ideas in mind as you construct your interview questions:

1. *Brainstorm* the concepts, topics, and ideas related to the focus of your inquiry that you might want to explore.

2. *Examine* your written ideas, grouping similar topics together. These clusters of ideas are categories from which you will develop the interview questions.

3. *Select* the categories that are most meaningful to your research focus.

4. *Develop* broad, as well as more focused, open-ended questions for each selected category.

5. *Sequence* the categories; within each category sequence the questions in a logical order. (Some suggestions can be found below.)

6. *Prepare* a draft of your interview guide, Section I.

7. *Pilot test* the interview questions with several people not involved in the study.

Patton (2002) presents six types of interview questions:

1. *Background/demographic questions* elicit respondents' descriptions of themselves. For example, ask questions about their age, education, years of experience, and prior occupation.

2. *Sensory questions* elicit how the respondents perceive their environment. For example, ask, "Please describe your classroom."

3. *Knowledge questions* elicit what the respondents know about a particular topic. For example, ask, "Tell me what you know about. . . . "

4. *Experience/behavior questions* help determine what the respondents do or have done through descriptions of their experiences, actions, activities, and behaviors. For example, ask, "What experiences did you have on the field trip?"

5. *Feeling questions* are used to understand the respondents' emotions regarding an experience or a situation. For example, ask, "Do you feel anxious, worried, confident, or intimidated about . . . ?"

6. *Opinions/beliefs/values questions* elicit the respondents' beliefs, intentions, and values as related to a certain issue. For example, ask, "What do you believe should be the way to react to . . . ?"

Following are some suggestions for phrasing interview questions:

1. Develop interview questions that will provide you with the information needed to answer your research questions.

2. Group the questions by topics and sequence them in a logical order. For example, if you are asking eighth-grade students about bullying, you should group all the factual questions (when, where, how often, who is involved) in the first section, and questions about the reactions of different members of the school in the next section.

3. Start the interview with simple, uncontroversial topics before you address more complex, more challenging, and potentially more sensitive issues. A common mistake is to ask about a hot topic before promoting a level of rapport that allows respondents to be open and expansive in their answers.

4. Begin the interview with broad ("grand-tour") questions, such as "What were your first impressions about the reading program?" and follow up with probing, more specific questions to elicit detailed and elaborated answers, or to clarify responses. Broad questions are often rephrased more specifically as probes: for example, "Describe what specifically made an impression on you."

5. Phrase questions clearly and free of words, idioms, or syntax that will interfere with respondents' understanding. Questions that are too vague will fail to elicit a comprehensive response.

6. Ask open-ended questions that are not answered with a quick response such as "yes" or "no" or can be answered by choosing between fixed alternatives. For example, ask "Why have you decided to join the Karate Club?" rather than "Did your friends suggest that you join the Karate Club?" or "Did you join the club because your friends suggested it or because you like karate?"

7. Avoid asking leading questions. A leading question is one that implies the preferred response or influences the direction of the response. For example, "Don't you think that the new reading program is better than the one we used before?"

8. Choose the degree of directness you will use in asking questions when the issue is sensitive and when respondents may hesitate to share their honest opinions. For example, rather than asking "How do you feel about . . . ?" you may ask the question indirectly: "How do the teachers in your school feel about . . . ?" or "How do some teachers feel about . . . ?"

9. Ask questions about one issue at a time and do not combine two or more questions together. For example, the question "How do you feel during math and science classes?" should be replaced by two separate questions.

10. Encourage respondents to be as specific in their answers as possible. Follow up on abstract answers by probing and asking for concrete examples. For example, when you ask a teacher "What is your classroom management style?" add "Can you give me a specific example of how this style is demonstrated in your teaching?"

Conducting the Interview

Before the Interview

Before you conduct the interview, choose your interviewee carefully. This person should be knowledgeable, be verbally skilled, and be willing to be interviewed. The issue of convenience should also be considered; often, teacher researchers choose participants who are more readily available. Be sure to arrange a time and place for the interview that is convenient for both you and the interviewee. Try to find a quiet place where you are not likely to be interrupted and where you will be able to record the interview. Don't forget to bring with you a recording device (with an extra blank tape if needed), your interview guide, a note pad, and a computer or electronic tablet for jotting down ideas, impressions, and new questions that occur to you as you listen. We suggest testing your recording device before the interview.

During the Interview

Take notes during the interview, even if you use a recording device, to allow you to capture the essence of the responses, note body language and any change of tone, and jot down any ideas or follow-up questions. It is important to take time to develop rapport with your interviewee. Start the interview by introducing yourself; thank the person for agreeing to be interviewed, and be attentive to the interviewee's responses. Explain the topic of your interview and why you chose him or her as an interviewee. Guarantee confidentiality, and request permission to record the interview. (See Chapter 4 for a fuller discussion on the ethical aspects of interviews.)

We recommend that you begin with a set of questions aimed at creating a sense of trust that will help your interviewee feel comfortable. Ask factual questions about his or her personal and professional background and make him or her feel at ease and confident in talking with you. It is always helpful if the interviewer is attentive to the interviewee's responses; the more you listen with interest, the more willing they are to talk! Additionally, be sensitive to the interviewee's perceptions of the questions and, if necessary, clarify the question by rephrasing it or by adding examples for clarification (e.g., a question is not clear or its meaning is misinterpreted). Based on the interviewee's responses, you may probe or ask additional questions that you did not think about when you initially planned the interview guide.

End the interview by asking if there is another question that you should have asked or any additional information that you should know. Again, thank the interviewee for participating in the study and ask permission to follow up if you need to clarify answers or need more information. Clarify whether the interviewees would like to read a transcript of the interview and don't forget to send or e-mail a thank-you note!

After the Interview

Immediately after the interview is completed, reflect on the process and the content of the interview. We suggest that you listen carefully, several times, to the recorded interview. Ask yourself: What are the salient themes? What are the major ideas? and Which sentences should be presented verbatim and which will be paraphrased or summarized?

Next, transcribe the interview (including "hmm . . . and "ahh . . . ") and provide an accurate and authentic account of the interviewee's words. Do not edit the way the answers were phrased. Assess whether the interview yielded the information you need for the study. For example, consider whether additional questions, rephrasing the wording of a question, or changing the order of the questions will improve the next interview.

Now you are ready to complete Section II of the interview guide (Figure 5.9) focusing on the following:

▶ **The interviewee description:** Write a detailed description of the interviewee's background, sociodemographic information, physical appearance, tone of voice, and body language that are helpful in understanding his or her perspective.

▶ **Data obtained:** Based on the interview's major themes, report the information you have obtained from the interview. Insert many direct quotes!

▶ **Reflections:** Evaluate the interview process. For example, how comfortable and responsive was the interviewee? Did you ask the right questions? What could you do to improve the process?

Focus Group Interview

A useful interview technique is having a *focus group* with several individuals who come together and share among themselves their ideas, thoughts, and experiences about the topic of your study. You may convene groups of students, parents, or teachers and serve as a facilitator while the participants interact with one another. The data emerge from the conversation among the participants.

One obvious advantage of a focus group is that it allows many participants to be interviewed in a single session. Moreover, as the participants respond to each other, they introduce varied points of views, and stimulate and extend each other's thinking, which can yield a broad range of opinions. Focus groups may be particularly beneficial for interviewing children. Children often feel intimidated during individual interviews and are reluctant to speak up. In the company of their friends they feel emboldened to talk and express their views (Currie & Kelly, 2012; Morgan, 1997; Robinson, 2012).

Here are some suggestions to ensure a productive focus group interview:

1. Form a focus group of four to seven participants.
2. Create a seating arrangement so that everyone can see and hear each other.
3. Present clear and open-ended questions to the group.
4. Provide an appropriate time limit for each question.

5. Facilitate an open and free discussion; however, keep the conversation on track.

6. Ensure that all participants have an opportunity to express their views.

7. Make sure that all opinions are heard respectfully.

8. Prevent one or two participants from dominating the conversation.

9. Avoid a situation in which the majority opinion silences a contradicting point of view.

Online Interview

The use of the Internet to interview participants can be a time-saving technique. Online interviews can be organized through chat rooms when the interviewer and the interviewee are both online at the same time (synchronous interview) or it can be via e-mail (asynchronous interview). Using e-mails, you can send a set of questions to respondents and they, in turn, send their answers back. Another option is to send a series of back-and-forth exchanges, in which you expand your focus, send follow-up questions, and ask for clarifications, examples, or additional details (Kvale & Brinkmann, 2009; Salmons, 2010).

For example, Lindsey, a preservice middle school math teacher, is looking for a teaching position. She is very excited at the prospect of having her own class. However, although she is comfortable about her content knowledge and ability to put into action many creative and fun activities that will enhance student learning, she is not confident in her classroom management abilities. In fact, this was the weakest point in her practicum experience. Lindsey decides to be proactive and get suggestions from veteran teachers who are known for their ability to establish discipline while also having warm and democratic classrooms. Lindsey asks her advisor for names of three outstanding middle school math teachers. She sends each one of them a series of questions seeking their advice about their classroom management techniques. After receiving their responses, Lindsey analyzes these responses to the online interview.

There are advantages and disadvantages to online interviews. One obvious advantage is the time saved as the interview is already in a text format and there is no need to transcribe the answers. It also enables you to interview people who live far away and are not easily accessible. Additionally, the online interview allows participants to respond to the questions whenever and wherever is most convenient for them. However, the major disadvantage with the use of online interviews is that the immediacy of face-to-face verbal and nonverbal communication is lost. Although online interviewing allows for respondents' reflexivity, when you replace verbal exchange with computer-mediated communication, your ability to "read" between the lines, to gain deeper insight into the respondents' feelings and inner thoughts, and to respond spontaneously are diminished.

Figure 5.10 presents a checklist of practical suggestions and guidelines for you as you plan and carry out your interviews.

SURVEYS

Surveys are one of the most common and efficient ways to gather information. They provide large-scale responses very fast and can be utilized very efficiently and with minimal expense and can be easily and quickly analyzed. While a distinction can be made between surveys and questionnaires, in this book we use these terms interchangeably.

Surveys can be used to gather a variety of information about people's opinions, perceptions, and attitudes, and in planning and evaluating programs (Fink, 2009). Surveys can also be used to identify and assess needs; document behaviors; summarize outcomes; assess opinions, attitudes, beliefs, and perceptions; and gather information. In the field of education, survey data can help educators and other stakeholders make informed decisions. For example, you may want to assess your students' opinions after implementing a new teaching method or new curriculum materials, or survey your students' parents about their children's homework and study habits at home. If you are a school administrator, you may want to survey your teachers about their preferences for professional development days, or ask parents for feedback about the school website and the type or quality of information it provides.

There are, at times, opportunities to survey your students as part of your ongoing instruction. For example, you may quickly survey your students by asking for a show of hands in response to a simple set of questions about students' attitudes; or, you may ask the students to use a clicker to show their understanding of a new concept that you teach. These strategies allow you to obtain information easily and quickly, as a natural part of the teaching process.

One of the main problems in using surveys in action research is that often the response rate is not high and those who respond do not necessarily represent

✓	Suggestions
	1. Arrange a convenient time and place for the interview.
	2. Choose carefully who you will interview.
	3. Consider whether you would like to conduct the interview one-on-one or as a focus group, face-to-face, online, or via telephone.
	4. Plan your timetable carefully, allowing time to secure the cooperation of those you plan to interview, create the interview guide, pilot test it, administer it, and analyze the interviews.
	5. Develop an interview guide consisting of (1) interview questions, and (2) reflections on the process.
	6. Ask clearly phrased, open-ended questions.
	7. Begin with background factual questions.
	8. Group the questions by topic.
	9. Sequence the questions from simple to complex.
	10. Avoid asking leading questions.
	11. Do not combine two or more questions together.
	12. Pilot test the interview questions with several people who are similar to your target group of interviewees.
	13. Bring your recording device and test it before the interview.
	14. Take time to develop rapport with your interviewees and appear interested in what they are saying.
	15. Encourage respondents to be as specific in their answers as possible; if needed, ask for further clarification.
	16. Keep your personal opinions in check.
	17. Listen attentively to the interviewees.
	18. Transcribe the interview accurately and authentically.
	19. Reflect and evaluate the interview process.
	20. Reflect on the information shared and consider whether changes need to be made in the interview process.

FIGURE 5.10. A checklist of suggestions for planning and collecting data using interviews.

the whole group of potential respondents (Fowler, 2009; Fraenkel et al., 2011). Another major problem is that respondents may or may not be honest in their responses. They may choose those response choices that they believe are expected, rather than express their true opinions, attitudes, or beliefs. Regardless of the response rate, it's always a good idea to collect demographic information about the survey respondents and report this information along with the response rate when you present your study's results (Suskie, 2009).

Survey questions and response choices can elicit various types of responses and the data collected can be both numerical and narrative. The advantage of questionnaires is that they can be administered directly (face-to-face) or indirectly by distributing them to people and collecting them later on or by sending them to the respondent via regular or electronic mail. On the other hand, surveys and questionnaires lack the richness of personal interviews and direct observation. Using them, you will find it very difficult to form a relationship of trust with the participants and find out, in depth, how each feels about the issue you are investigating. As a compromise, you may choose to use a questionnaire and then conduct follow-up interviews with selected participants who provided written answers.

The use of the Internet to administer surveys is growing fast, as more and more people are becoming proficient and comfortable using it. When designing items to be used in e-mail, it's easy to ensure that people do not skip important items (i.e., they cannot continue with the survey if they skip and are reminded to go back and complete these items). Contingency items are also much easier to use in electronic surveys. A contingency-question format allows the researcher to establish a sequence of questions for respondents based on their selected responses to questions (Fraenkel et al., 2011). For example, respondents may be asked a question about a certain issue and if they respond "Yes," they are automatically "jumped" to another set of questions. If they respond "No" to the contingency question, they are sent to a different set of questions. Additionally, in online-administered surveys, drop-down response choices can be used, thereby limiting the amount of space required for listing multiple-response choices. For example, if you want to know the month a person was born in, the drop-down menu can list all 12 months, asking the respondents to choose one. Another advantage of electronic surveys is that the responses can be downloaded into a spreadsheet for easier tabulation and analysis.

Remember that most surveys measure respondents' perceptions or attitudes, not what they actually do or how they behave. When you interpret the survey data, do not overextend your findings or treat them as factual information or evidence. For example, if 75% of your survey respondents indicate that they differentiate their instruction regularly, you should not cite this finding as a fact and claim that the majority of teachers actually do so (i.e., regularly differentiate their instruction).

The process of constructing the survey items is based in part on your literature review and the instruments used in other studies (Andres, 2012). It also depends on your research questions and the type of data you need, as well as on your schedule and timetable, access to participants, and level of expertise.

The following guidelines and suggestions focus on written questionnaires, especially those in which respondents are asked to choose among several options, or those that require brief responses (ranging from one word to one sentence).

The Process of Conducting Surveys

In writing, administering, and analyzing surveys, we suggest that you follow these steps:

1. Clearly articulate to yourself the purpose of the survey and the research questions you hope to answer.

2. Identify the type of information you want to collect and how you would use that information to answer the research questions.

3. Decide what demographic information (e.g., gender and age) you need to gather in your study.

4. Develop a plan to administer the survey (e.g., online, hard copies, or face-to-face) and to gather the surveys.

5. Prepare a timetable for constructing, distributing, and collecting the surveys, and for coding, analyzing, and interpreting the responses.

6. Determine the sample needed for the study. If you plan to survey students, teachers, or parents, make sure that you have permission to administer the survey. Have viable and realistic plans to ensure a satisfactory response rate.

7. Give a title to your survey (e.g., "Students' Attitudes toward Extracurricular Activities," as opposed to simply calling it "A Survey").

8. Write the first draft of your survey items (questions, statements, and response choices).

9. Pilot test the survey, if possible, or consult with colleagues and classmates and ask them to review the items before you administer the survey to your sample. (This is a very important step that is often overlooked!)

10. Prepare a cover letter or a brief explanation of the survey.

11. Provide clear directions to the survey respondents at the beginning of the survey on how to complete the survey items.

12. Administer the surveys; collect the completed forms.

13. Code the data; enter the numerical data into a spreadsheet; or type the open-ended responses.

14. Analyze and interpret the results. (See the guidelines in Chapter 7.)

Writing the Survey Items: Types of Questions and Response Choices

Survey items may be divided into two general categories: structured (also called forced choice or fixed choice) and unstructured (open-ended). In structured items, the respondents have to choose from a series of responses (Mertler, 2012) usually by circling, checking off, rating, or rank ordering their response choices. The structured response choices that are presented to the respondents may be ordered (e.g., from *never* to *always*) or unordered (e.g., subject teaching or position in school). In unstructured items, a statement (or question) is followed by a blank space where the respondents are asked to record their responses. An example might be a question asking teachers to list the certifications they hold.

Writing structured items and analyzing responses from open-ended items require more time and a greater level of expertise. Computer software programs (such as Excel and SPSS) can make the task of analyzing data from structured items faster and easier by summarizing the data and visually displaying the findings. (See Chapter 7.)

Structured items are also easier for respondents to complete and require less of their time. Therefore, the response rate is usually higher for surveys using such items, compared with open-ended items, especially those that require long answers.

By providing the response choices in structured items you have more control over the responses chosen, compared with items for which respondents can write in their responses. In addition, you may find that reading people's handwriting can be challenging at times (although when the surveys are administered electronically, the handwriting issue is no longer a problem).

Even though in responding to structured items the respondent is asked to choose from a list of options, sometimes a choice of *other* is added to allow those responding to add a choice that is not on the list.

Suggestions for Writing Survey Questions

The following are some suggestions that should help you write your survey questions. These suggestions pertain to both the "stems" (e.g., questions or statements) and the response choices.

1. *Write simple, concise, clear questions.* Some experts suggest questions of no more than 10 to 20 words, with shorter and simpler wording for younger respondents.

2. *Make sure the response choices you provide are appropriate for that question.* For example, response choices of *yes* and *no* should be used with questions that ask for factual information (e.g., "Student X knows how to use the Internet"). On the other hand, response choices that are on a continuum (such as responses that range from *never* to *always,* or from *strongly disagree* to *strongly agree*) are appropriate for questions that measure attitudes, opinions, or perceptions. For example, "Most of my students like using the Internet," with response choices of *strongly disagree* to *strongly agree.*

3. *Make sure the respondents are knowledgeable about the topics of the questions you ask.* Do not ask them, for example, to reflect on how to accommodate highly gifted students in their classroom if they may not have had experience with such students. Instead, ask them first what is known as a *contingency question* (e.g., "Have you had a highly gifted student in your class?"). Those who say they have had such an experience are then asked about it.

4. *Avoid including two ideas or thoughts in the same item* (called "double-barreled" items; see Figure 5.11). For example, you may consider your instructor to be knowledgeable, but you also think that he or she does not return assignments on time.

5. *Avoid using words, such as "sometimes" or "often."* Each respondent may interpret these words differently. Figures 5.12 and 5.13 are examples of a poorly worded item and a better-worded item, respectively. For some of those responding to the question in Figure 5.12, the word *sometimes* may mean three times a *week,* whereas for others it may mean three times a *month.* Figure 5.13, by comparison, offers more precise options in place of "sometimes" or "often."

> I believe my instructor is knowledgeable and returns assignments on time.

FIGURE 5.11. Example of a "double-barreled" item.

> How often do you download a movie to watch at home?
>
> Never   Sometimes   Often   Always

FIGURE 5.12. Example of a poorly worded item.

> How often do you download a movie to watch at home?
>
> Five to seven times/week   Two to four times/week   Once a week   One to two times/month   Never

FIGURE 5.13. Example of a better-worded item.

6. *Avoid questions that can bias the respondents* (e.g., see Figure 5.14). In this example, stating that the majority of parents have a certain opinion about year-round school may lead the respondents to agree with the opinion of the majority of the other respondents, even if this does not reflect their opinion.

7. *Avoid using words or stereotypes that might be offensive to some groups of respondents, and avoid using clichés and slang words.* For example, new teachers should not be referred to as "young teachers."

8. *Avoid presumptions in writing your questions.* For example: "How often do you drink alcoholic beverages?" This question assumes that the respondent drinks alcoholic beverages.

> The majority of the parents in the district are opposed to year-round school; what is your opinion?
>
> Strongly agree   Agree   Neutral   Disagree   Strongly disagree

FIGURE 5.14. Example of a biased question.

9. *Provide clear directions for answering the survey items* (see Figure 5.15).

10. *Make sure the survey looks attractive.* (This is most important for surveys that are administered as hard copies.) The layout of the survey is important and the text should be easy to read and follow. The survey's questions and response options should be spaced properly and not appear too crowded. Figures 5.16 and 5.17 show examples of good and poor layouts, respectively. The respondents will find it easy to record their answers in the example shown in Figure 5.16. By comparison, the response choices are too crowded together in the example in Figure 5.17.

11. *Number the survey items.* Number the questions consecutively; this will help you later when you record the survey responses or enter your data on a spreadsheet for numerical (i.e., statistical) or narrative (i.e., qualitative) analysis.

12. *Order the survey items.* Group the items according to their content and the response choices provided. For example, when surveying children about their

---

- **Circle** the response that best represents your opinion.
- **Rank order** the five reasons listed below, assigning 5 to the *most* important reason and 1 to the *least* important reason.
- Circle *all* that apply.

FIGURE 5.15. Examples of good directions for answering survey items.

Questions	SD	D	A	SA
1. In my opinion, parents should be held responsible for their children's homework completion.				
2. I believe that most parents are knowledgeable about their children's homework assignments.				

FIGURE 5.16. Example of a good survey layout.

---

1. In my opinion, parents should be held responsible for their children's homework completion.
   Strongly agree Agree Disagree Strongly disagree

FIGURE 5.17. Example of a poor survey question layout.

attitudes toward school, you may want to group items that measure attitudes toward classmates, teachers, administrators, and the school in general. Within each category, items that use the same response format should be grouped together. For example, group together all the rating-scale items, or all the checklist items.

13. *Determine the length of the survey.* Depending on your respondents, some may be willing to spend more time responding to the survey, while others may not be willing to invest more than 5–10 minutes. You need to estimate and predict the amount of time your respondents may be willing to spend completing the survey. Most practitioners who are engaged in action research limit the length of surveys to no more than two to three pages.

14. *Gather relevant demographic data.* There are two main reasons for you to collect demographic data: (a) to describe your sample, and (b) for use in the analysis of your data. The demographic data collected allow you to accurately and completely describe those who responded to the survey, thus providing information about the sample and its characteristics. You can also use the demographic information in analyzing the data. For example, you may be able to compare the responses of female and male respondents, or the responses of parents, teachers, and students. The decision as to what demographic information should be gathered is up to you, as the teacher researcher, and may depend to a large extent on the nature of the study and the research questions that you are investigating.

Consider placing items designed to gather demographic data at the *end* of the survey. Such items are considered more sensitive and objectionable and most people are more likely to answer them when they are placed at the end (Salant & Dillman, 1994), after they have already completed the survey and have "gotten used" to responding to questions. Additionally, after completing the other survey questions, the respondents can better see the importance, relevancy, connection, and usefulness of providing demographic data, whereas this may not be evident at the beginning.

15. *Number each survey after it is completed, giving it an identification number (ID number).* When you enter the data into a spreadsheet or transcribe the data, it is very helpful to be able to match respondents with their survey data.

Structured Responses

The response choices to structured items are divided into several categories: Rating responses, yes/no responses, ordered responses, unordered responses, checklist, and rank-ordered responses.

Rating Responses

In this category, several (usually three to seven) graded responses are provided. The responses are ordered from one end to the other and the respondents are asked to choose the response that represents their opinion, attitude, or belief about the question or statement provided. The most common rating scales are the Likert scale and the Likert-type scale (Mertler & Charles, 2011). In a Likert scale, the responses range from *strongly agree* to *strongly disagree* or from *strongly disagree* to *strongly agree* (Fink, 2009). Likert-type, or rating-scale, response options often include those that record quality of some behavior or performance (e.g., from *excellent* to *poor*); self-perception (e.g., from *not like me at all* to *very much like me*; or *frequency* (e.g., from *never* to *always*). When the latter is used, it is helpful to clarify the middle points on the frequency choice scale. For example, while the terms *never* and *always* are self-explanatory, you may want to clarify the middle points on the scale. For example, you may indicate that *"Sometimes = one to two times per week"*, and *"Often = three to four times per week."* Figure 5.18 shows examples of Likert-scale and Likert-type questions. Following are some points you need to consider when writing rating-scale items.

THE NUMBER OF RESPONSE CHOICES. You have to decide whether you want to provide an odd or even number of response choices. The most common scale has five options: strongly agree, agree, neutral, disagree, and strongly disagree. (The same five choices can also range from strongly disagree to strongly agree.) The middle point, neutral, is provided for those who do not have a clear opinion or attitude one way or another. The disadvantage of providing a middle point is that respondents have a tendency to choose the middle category (McMillan & Schumacher,

---

1. An example of a **Likert-scale** question:

   I would be interested in spending more time being a friend to a student with special needs.

   Strongly disagree   Disagree   Uncertain   Agree   Strongly agree

2. An example of a **Likert-type** question:

   I feel that I can do my homework by myself.

   Never   1–2 times a week   3–4 times a week   Always

FIGURE 5.18. Examples of Likert-scale and Likert-type questions.

2010). Additionally, those who choose the middle category are often those who do not want to take a stand or spend too much time considering each question. When summarizing the responses, the neutral responses do not add much to our understanding of people's attitudes and opinions. Including an even number of responses (e.g., strongly disagree, disagree, agree, and strongly agree) is often referred to as *forced choice*, because you force the respondents to indicate their opinion on the *disagree* or *agree* side. When designing surveys to be administered to young children, you may want to consider providing only three choices and using graphics to indicate the response choices (Mertler, 2012). For example, you may use smiley faces to represent agree, neutral, or disagree response choices (see Figure 5.19 for a sample of response choices for young children).

THE DIRECTION OF THE WORDING OF THE ITEMS. Consider including some statements that present an opposing or negative view (Suskie, 2009). In such items, a positive attitude is indicated by choosing the response of strongly disagree (SD). This will prevent respondents from checking a certain response all the way through the survey without actually reading each statement and considering it carefully.

For example, in a survey measuring attitudes toward standardized tests, we may have the two items shown in Figure 5.20. Those opposing standardized tests

FIGURE 5.19. Sample response choices for young people.

	Strongly Agree	Agree	Disagree	Strongly Disagree
1. In my opinion, the time we spend on preparing for and taking standardized tests is a waste of time.				
2. I believe that the results from the standardized tests taken by my students accurately reflect my students' knowledge and skills.				

FIGURE 5.20. Measuring attitudes toward standardized tests.

would respond to the first question by choosing strongly agree, while their response to the second question is likely to be strongly disagree.

THE NUMBER OF POINTS ASSIGNED TO EACH RESPONSE CHOICE. When using Likert-scale items in which the response options range from strongly agree (SA) to strongly disagree (SD), or from strongly disagree to strongly agree, you may want to assign the highest number of points (e.g., 4 or 5 points) to the response choice that represents the most positive response to the items and the lowest number of points (1 point) to the response choice that represents the most negative response to the item.

For example, let's say you want to measure your students' attitudes toward the variety of extracurricular activities offered in your school. A higher score would indicate a more positive attitude and a lower score would indicate a more negative attitude (see Figure 5.21 for two samples of different directions of the scoring key). Reversing the scoring key can be done as you enter the data onto a spreadsheet or after entering the data.

Yes/No Responses

In this category, respondents are asked to indicate their responses by choosing one of two choices only: *yes* or *no*. Yes/no responses are most appropriate for gathering factual information (see Figure 5.22). Occasionally, a third choice, such as "don't know" or "not applicable" is added. You also can use *true/false* responses at times in place of the yes/no responses. However, do not force people to choose either a

---

Example 1: In this question, **4 points** would be given to the **strongly agree (SA)** response, and **1 point** to the **strongly disagree (SD)** response:

1. I believe our school offers a great choice of extracurricular activities.

    SA   A   D   SD

Example 2: In this question, you will reverse the scoring key by assigning **1 point** to **strongly agree (SA)** and **4 points** to the **strongly disagree (SD)** response:

2. I wish we had more choices of extracurricular activities at our school.

    SA   A   D   SD

FIGURE 5.21. Two examples with different directions for the scoring key.

1. I have a driver's license.	Yes	No
2. I plan to take at least one AP class next year.	Yes	No

FIGURE 5.22. Examples of yes/no response choices.

yes or no response for items for which there are likely to be in-between response options. For example, for the statement, "Student *X* plays with other students during recess," you should probably provide "frequency" options (e.g., "at least once a day" or "never"), rather than yes/no responses.

Ordered Responses

This category is used when the responses can be presented in some logical order. Figure 5.23 shows an example of choices that are ordered logically, from the lowest to the highest level of education. Student age and grade level are also examples in which the responses should be presented in a certain order. You can use categories to avoid having too many response choices. For example, when asking your colleagues in a K–12 unit school to indicate the grade level they teach, the grades may be grouped into categories such as primary, intermediate, middle, and high school.

Please put a check mark next to your highest level of education.

_____ Elementary school

_____ High school

_____ High school+

_____ BA

_____ BA+

_____ MA

_____ MA+

_____ Doctorate

FIGURE 5.23. Example of ordered response choices.

Unordered Responses

This category is used when the responses cannot be presented in any particular, predetermined order. An example of unordered responses may be the item in a survey given to school staff shown in Figure 5.24.

Checklists

Checklists are used to record or assess items, behaviors, skills, or other occurrences. Checklists are used in surveys in which respondents are asked to consider a list of choices and place a check mark next to the items they choose. The list of choices is dichotomous as opposed to the list of choices on rating scales that are on a continuum. The respondents typically are asked to choose one of more items on the checklist. An example may be the list of activities shown in Figure 5.25.

Please indicate your position/role:

_____ Classroom teacher

_____ Aide

_____ Support staff/specialist

_____ Administrator

_____ Other (please list) _____

FIGURE 5.24. Example of unordered response choices.

Check *all* the activities planned for your reading class today:

_____ Group work

_____ Worksheets

_____ Silent reading

_____ Teacher reading to the class

_____ Students reading aloud to the class

_____ Other (please specify) _____

FIGURE 5.25. Example of items on a checklist.

A variation of the checklist may be a list from which respondents are asked to choose only three items. For example, you can offer a list of adjectives and ask teachers to mark the three that best describe their school principal.

Rank Order

In items using the rank-order format, a list of choices is provided and the respondents are asked to rank order the items on the list. If you plan to use this format, do not offer too many choices, because ranking becomes a difficult task when too many choices are provided. Make sure you tell the survey takers how to rank order. Figure 5.26 shows an example in which there are seven options and the respondents are asked to assign 1 to their favorite choice and 7 to their least favorite choice.

Unstructured (Open-Ended) Responses

There are two major types of responses in this category: those that require a limited range of responses and those that require one or more sentences. Open-ended responses, especially those that are one or more sentences, can also be used to help explain why people have responded in a certain way, or to clarify answers to other questions.

Rank order your favorite school subject, writing 1 next to your *most favorite* subject and 7 next to your *least favorite* subject.

_____ Reading/language arts

_____ Math

_____ Social studies

_____ Science

_____ Physical education/gym

_____ Music

_____ Art

FIGURE 5.26. Example of a rank-order format item in a survey of sixth-grade students.

Short Write-In Responses

Figure 5.27 shows an example of an item with a short write-in response in which the survey takers are asked to respond to a question with limited response options, usually one or a few words, or a number.

Responses with One or More Sentences

In this type of item, respondents are asked to write longer responses, usually in complete sentences. The amount and quality of the responses may depend to a large extent on the writing skills of the respondents. The response rate may also suffer because most people tend to be more willing to circle or mark responses that are provided, as opposed to constructing their own narrative. These items usually ask the respondents for additional information, comments, or feedback and it is better to place these longer open-ended responses at the end of the survey (see Figure 5.28)

In a *typical school week*, how many *minutes per day* do you spend on the following activities?

Activity	Number of Minutes per Day
Homework	
Watching TV/videos on my computer	
Playing with friends or family members	
Playing electronic games	
Doing chores	

FIGURE 5.27. Example of an item with a short write-in response.

What did you like best about this professional development day and why?

_____

_____

_____

FIGURE 5.28. Example of a question requiring a response with one or more sentences.

Figure 5.29 presents suggestions and guidelines for you to consider as you plan and carry out surveys.

Official and Personal Artifacts and Documents

Artifacts are physical documents and records that allow teacher researchers to construct a layered and contextual understanding of their topics. These may include students' work, meeting minutes, school reports, and public records. These formal and informal documents provide historical, personal, and demographic information that can provide additional knowledge about individuals (e.g., students, parents, teachers, and administrators), the social and cultural life of the school, and the general characteristics of the educational process. Data sources like grades, test scores, student self-assessments, essays, portfolios, and parents or students' e-mail messages are often easily available. These are naturally occurring data in the practice of your teaching that do not require extra time or special arrangements to collect. Like many other teachers and teacher candidates, you may find that these methods of data collection are the most practical and doable for action research. This information can corroborate, expand, or challenge what you have gathered through other data collection tools (Cohen et al., 2011; Prior, 2012). For example, Joan, a fifth-grade teacher, is investigating the success of a new curriculum in social studies. She collects student-generated artifacts such as homework assignments, students' written reflections on the curriculum, and her own artifacts, such as lesson plans, communication with parents, and bulletin board postings.

Some researchers (e.g., McMillan & Schumacher, 2010) distinguish between records that have an official purpose and documents that are prepared for personal use. *Official artifacts and documents* provide an institutional perspective on persons (students, teachers, and administrators), issues, and processes. These may include school handbooks, free-lunch lists, policy statements, and standardized test scores. *Personal* or *episodic artifacts and documents* comprise personal or episodic records, such as diaries, class projects, and student artwork. (Table 5.1 shows examples of official, personal, and episodic artifacts and documents.) Other researchers differentiate between quantitative numerical data, such as graduation rates and standardized test scores, and qualitative narrative data, such as journals and diaries, notes, letters, and student projects.

✓	Suggestions
	1. Be cognizant of the amount of time that you can devote to your survey and the access you have to the respondents and plan accordingly.
	2. Plan carefully the logistics of distributing and collecting the surveys.
	3. Consider the length of your survey and ask only what you really need to know; longer surveys usually result in lower response rates.
	4. Contemplate the possibility of surveying your students as part of your ongoing instruction.
	5. Choose the appropriate formats for the questions and response choices in order to obtain the information you need.
	6. Write the items for your survey following the guidelines provided in this chapter.
	7. Share the survey with colleagues or classmates and ask for their feedback.
	8. Pilot test your survey with a few selected respondents who are similar to those you intend to survey.
	9. Make sure your questions are clear and flow well and are appropriate for the level of your respondents.
	10. Be sensitive in the way you phrase your questions so they are not perceived as too personal or invasive of the respondents' privacy.
	11. Color code the surveys for easy identification if you are distributing hard copies to different classrooms or schools.
	12. Include open-ended (unstructured) questions or follow the survey with in-depth interviews if you want to obtain responses that reflect participants' views or feelings.
	13. Plan how you will analyze the open-ended responses and how you will tally and analyze the numerical data you collect. (Several online survey services, such as SurveyMonkey, provide a data summary and charts.)
	14. Tabulate and analyze the responses to enable you to summarize the data and find answers to your research questions.
	15. Consider using electronic surveys, when possible, because they are often the easiest and most effective way for administering surveys.
	16. Look for emerging trends, patterns, similarities, or differences in the responses.
	17. Remember when interpreting the survey data that most surveys measure respondents' perceptions or attitudes, not what they actually do or how they behave.
	18. Remember that surveys do not have to be long; they can be short and quick and be a natural part of your instruction.

FIGURE 5.29. A checklist of suggestions for planning and collecting data using surveys.

TABLE 5.1. Examples of Official and Personal or Episodic Artifacts and Documents	
Official artifacts and documents	Personal or episodic artifacts and documents
• Policy statements • School handbook • Procedure statements • School board records • School improvement plans • Minutes of meetings • Evaluation reports • Attendance records • Suspension records • Retention records • Free-lunch list • Standardized test scores • School and district report cards • Curriculum guides • Media coverage • School newsletter	• Journals and diaries • Student projects and artwork • Essays and exams • Student portfolios • Bulletin board postings • Teacher lesson plans • Classroom flyers • Letters • Notes • E-mails • Communications with parents • Scrapbooks • Student self-assessments • Photographs • Videotapes

Teacher Journals

Many teacher researchers find journals to be an especially useful research method. The journal may include critical incidents, anecdotes, situations, events, insights, questions, and uncertainties that you consider relevant to your study. You will find that your journal can be helpful in documenting your behaviors and the behaviors of others in the setting that you investigate and in increasing your insight into daily classroom interactions. This documentation will reveal patterns in classroom interactions, illuminate constraints and possibilities unnoticed in your hectic classroom life, and allow you to monitor your subjectivity and be mindful of the different roles you take in the study (Guillemin & Gillam, 2004). Raising the awareness of the different roles you take in class as a practitioner and researcher will contribute to the study's ethical considerations (Rallis & Rossman, 2012). The journal entries may range from unstructured to structured formats. *Unstructured* journal entries record, from your perspective, whatever happens in class that seems valuable and important. Journal entries may be organized around key questions drawn from your research topic. For example, Ed, a reading specialist, records in his journal during lunchtime and reflects on what took place during the morning session when he met his students. *Structured* journal entries may include lists of events, particular daily activities, and specific students' behavior dated and timed. For example, Anne, a high school science teacher, wonders about ways to improve the effectiveness of group work in her class. She depicts in her journal anecdotes of students' interactions as they work in groups on a project; records the instructions she provided; describes the seating arrangements of the different groups and the ways the groups were formed; and notes questions that were raised in her mind.

You may want to consider the timing and frequency of your entries. On the basis of our experience of working with educators conducting action research, we suggest recording the unstructured journal entries as soon as practically possible after the critical incident, situation, or behavior has occurred. By comparison, the structured entries should be logged daily or weekly at designated times (A. Campbell, McNamara & Gilroy, 2004).

Figure 5.30 presents a checklist of suggestions and guidelines for gathering and using official and personal artifacts and documents.

✓	Suggestions
	1. Be purposeful in selecting the kind of information that will be useful and relevant to your own research question.
	2. Obtain permission, as necessary, to collect and use the documents form. (Follow the ethical guidelines outlined in Chapter 4.)
	3. Look for documents and records that can be easily obtained in school offices or found on school or district websites. Other documents are not available or are not accessible to teachers.
	4. Keep a journal in which you record and reflect on critical incidents, situations, and anecdotes that occurred in your class, as well as list specific events, activities, and behaviors, dated and timed.
	5. Record the unstructured entries as soon as practically possible after they occur; designate times—daily or weekly—to record the structured entries.
	6. Make copies of the original documents and be sure to label them. Include the date and context and, in the case of students' work, identify the author by name, age, and grade.
	7. Organize the artifacts in hard copy or electronic files to help you access and document the data later.

FIGURE 5.30. A checklist of suggestions for gathering artifacts and documents.

FINAL COMMENTS ABOUT DATA COLLECTION TOOLS

This chapter presents a variety of qualitative and quantitative data collection tools which are summarized in Table 5.2. As you develop your own strategies for data collection, we suggest that you keep in mind the following points regardless of the specific tools you choose for your data collection:

1. **Set specific times for data collection.** Be deliberate and practical in planning the process of gathering and storing the data. Be cognizant of how the research strategies fit within your classroom routines. Emphasize manageable data that conflicts least with your role as a teacher, and, preferably, can be gathered as part of your everyday practice.

2. **Do not rely on any single source of data.** Triangulate, corroborate, extend, or challenge your information by collecting data through multiple and complementary strategies. (See Chapter 4 for a broader discussion on *triangulation*.)

3. **Don't feel overwhelmed by the long list of data collection methods presented in this chapter.** You do not have to use all of these strategies! Depending on your research questions, probably no more than two or three well-selected strategies will provide you with the information needed for your investigation. The quality of the data you gather is more important than the number of ways you collect it.

4. **Feel free to modify your research design plans as you go.** For example, if while conducting the study in your classroom you realize that observing in a different setting would yield better results, go back to your methodology plans and make the changes that reflect this modification.

TABLE 5.2. A Summary of Qualitative and Quantitative Data Collection Tools

Tools	Qualitative	Quantitative

Observation	• Observation protocol
	  o Descriptive
	  o Reflective
	• Behavior logs
	• Photographs, videotapes, and audiotapes
		• Tally sheet
		• Checklist
		• Rating scale

Interview	• Unstructured • Semistructured • Structured • Focus group • Online interview	
Survey	• Unstructured (open-ended) responses • Short (write-in) responses • Responses with one/more sentences	• Structured responses • Rating responses • Ordered responses • Unordered responses • Checklist • Rank order
Artifacts and documents	• Official documents • Personal or episodic artifacts and documents • Teacher journals	• Assessment data • Attendance and discipline records

CHAPTER SUMMARY

1. The selection of data collection tools and strategies derives from the nature of the research questions, rather than from theoretical orientations.

2. Because of the inherent complexity of classroom life, it is hard to divide the research tools and methods into qualitative and quantitative when carrying out teacher action research. The same tool may generate qualitative or quantitative data depending on the strategy developed.

3. When developing strategies for data collection, researchers should set specific times for data collection, attempt to gather multiple sources of data, and modify their research design plans as needed.

4. *Observation* refers to looking at a setting purposely; it allows practitioners to systematically observe the activities, people, and physical aspects of their educational settings.

5. The observation strategies available to teacher researchers lie on a continuum: from qualitative to quantitative, from open-ended to closed-ended, from unstructured to structured, and from holistic to focused.

6. Action researchers should determine what their role will be during their observation; when observing their own classrooms, they should consciously look from the perspective of an outsider.

7. An *observation protocol* contains descriptive and reflective field notes that are detailed descriptions of what the researchers see, hear, and sense during the observation, and the thoughts, feelings, and understandings these observations provoked.

8. *Descriptive field notes* aim to record what is happening during the observation by describing the physical setting, the participants, activities, and events that take place, and by documenting conversations verbatim.

9. *Reflective field notes* are used to record reflections and insights about what is happening in the setting.

10. A *behavior log* is a useful observational tool for a more focused observation to help keep track of the behaviors exhibited by an individual student or a small group of students during a given situation; an *interval behavior log* is used to record what is happening at regular intervals.

11. Observational tools (like photographs, audiotapes, and videotapes) can enhance the researcher's capacity to capture student behaviors, attitudes, and social interactions through images and sounds.

12. *Structured closed-ended observations* are focused on predetermined categories and checks are made to record specific measurable behavior that results in numerical data.

13. *Quantitative observations* allow a comparison among settings, individuals, and situations, and frequencies, patterns, and trends.

14. *Tally sheets* are used to track the frequency of a target behavior or event at a specific point in time.

15. A *checklist* is made up of a predetermined list of behaviors or activities that are the focus of the observer's attention.

16. A *rating scale* is used to record the extent to which a specific behavior or situation exists.

17. An *interview* provides an understanding of the participants' experiences from their own

perspectives as it allows them to voice their ideas, opinions, values, and knowledge on issues related to the investigation.

18. The *unstructured interview* is an informal, though purposeful, conversation; the interview questions are broad and are presented in a casual style, and the interviewer lets the conversation proceed naturally on its own course.

19. The *semistructured interview* is based on open-ended questions that are prepared prior to the interview; the participants are invited to co-construct the narrative and raise and pursue additional issues that are related to the study.

20. The *structured interview* is based on prepared questions in which the interviewers frame the questions using an exact wording, replicating the order of the questions and providing identical questions to all of the participants' answers.

21. An *interview guide* contains two sections: (a) Section I is completed before the interview and contains the research question and concrete information about the interview and the interviewee; notes taken during the interview may also be recorded in this section; and (b) Section II is completed after the interview and provides a narrative description of the interviewee and the interviewer's reflections and insight gained through the interview.

22. A *focus group* is an interview technique in which several individuals come together and share among themselves their ideas, thoughts, and experiences about the topic of the study.

23. The use of the Internet to interview participants can be a time-saving technique; it can be organized through chat rooms, when the interviewer and the interviewee are both online at the same time (synchronous interview) or it can be via e-mail (asynchronous interview).

24. *Surveys* are one of the most common and efficient ways to gather information about people's opinions and attitudes, as well as factual information. Surveys can be utilized very efficiently and with minimal expense and can be easily and quickly analyzed and provide large-scale responses very quickly. While some make a distinction between surveys and questionnaires, in this book we used these terms interchangeably.

25. One of the main problems with using surveys in action research is that often the response rate may not be high enough and those who respond do not necessarily represent the whole group of potential respondents. Another major problem is that the respondents may or may not be honest in their responses and may choose those response choices that they believe are expected, rather than record their true opinions, attitudes, or beliefs.

26. Survey questions and response choices can elicit various types of responses, and the data collected can be both numerical and narrative. Questionnaires can be administered directly (face-to-face) or indirectly by distributing them to people and collecting them later on or by sending surveys to respondents via regular or electronic mail.

27. Survey items may be divided into two general categories: *structured* (also called forced choice or fixed choice) and *unstructured* (open-ended). In structured items, the respondents have to choose from a series of responses, usually by circling, checking off, rating, or rank ordering their response choices. In unstructured items, a statement (or question) is followed by a blank space where the respondents are asked to record their responses.

28. Artifacts are formal and informal documents and records that provide historical, personal, and demographic information that can provide additional perspectives on individuals, the social and cultural life of the school, and the general characteristics of the educational process.

CHAPTER EXERCISES AND ACTIVITIES

The following activities present several data collection tools. You may choose those most appropriate for your study. These activities can be done individually, with a peer, or with your research group.

1. List the types of data collection tools (observation, interview, survey, or artifacts and documents) that you plan to use in your research project and the reasons for using them. Explain how the different research tools will allow triangulation and offer different perspectives.

2. Using Figure 5.2, develop an observation protocol. Decide on the foci of the observation and what behaviors, interactions, activities, or conversations interest you about the particular situation. You may find the following steps helpful in the observation process:

   a. Find a public setting where multiple interactions take place (e.g., library, cafeteria, playground, or swimming pool).

   b. Write down detailed *descriptive notes* on what you see, hear, and sense during the observation and *reflective* notes on the thoughts, feelings, and understandings that these observations provoke.

    c. End the observation by noting your interpretation of and insight into what you have learned from the process.

    d. Assess the observation process and evaluate your descriptive and reflective field notes. You may address the following points:

- Do the field notes represent accurately the context of the observation?
- How rich and detailed is the description of the participants' actions?
- Are the "voices" of the participants "heard"?
- Are the tentative interpretations supported by the data?

      If you conduct the observation with a colleague, compare each other's account and discuss any differences between your subjective observations.

3. Using Figure 5.9, develop a 15-minute interview guide on a topic related to your research project or another issue of interest.

    a. Assess your interview guide and evaluate your questions by addressing the following points:

- How are the interview questions relevant to your research topic or issue of interest?
- Are the questions formulated clearly?
- Are the questions organized logically?
- Are the questions phrased according to the suggestions in the chapter?

    b. Pilot test the interview questions with one or more persons. (You may use a recording device.)

    c. Reflect on the interviewing experience using the following points:

- How did the interviewee(s) respond to your questions? Explain.
- How comfortable were you during the interview? Explain.
- Were there obstacles during the interview? How did you overcome them?
- What questions would you revise, rephrase, add, or omit for the next time you conduct a similar interview?

4. Using the guidelines in the chapter and the examples in Figures 5.11–5.28, develop a 5- to 10-item survey that can be used to collect data related to your research topic. Be sure to include both structured and unstructured items.

    a. Review the complete survey to ensure that it includes easy-to-understand items, appropriate response choices, and clear instructions.

     b. Administer the survey to a small group of respondents (four to eight people) and gather the following information:

- How long did it take the respondents to complete the survey?
- Were there any questions that were not clear?
- Do the respondents have any suggestions for item revision?

     c. Reflect on the data you collected and draft your summary of the responses.

     d. Revise the survey items as needed.

5. Make a list of documents, records, or artifacts that you plan to use for your study. (Table 5.1 may be helpful in making your choices.)

     a. How will you obtain these documents?

     b. Explain how these documents will contribute to your investigation.

     c. What additional information is provided by the documents that cannot be obtained in other data collection tools?

ADDITIONAL READINGS

Brown, J. D. (2001). *Using surveys in language programs.* Cambridge, UK: Cambridge University Press.

Bryant, D. (2010). *Observational measures of quality in center-based early care and education programs* (OPRE Research-to-Policy, Research-to-Practice Brief OPRE 2011-10c). Washington, DC: Office of Planning, Research and Evaluation, Administration for Children and Families, U.S. Department of Health and Human Services.

Eisner, E. W. (1998). *The enlightened eye: Qualitative inquiry and the enhancement of educational practice.* Upper Saddle River, NJ: Prentice Hall.

Geertz, C. (1973). Thick description: Towards an interpretive theory of culture. In C. Geertz (Ed.), *The interpretation of cultures* (pp. 3-32). New York: Basic Books.

Kawulich, B. (2005). Participant observation as a data collection method [81 paragraphs]. *Forum Qualitative Sozialforschung/Forum: Qualitative Social Research, 6*(2), Art. 43. Retrieved from *http://nbnresolving.de/urn:nbn:de:0114-fqs0502430.*

Olstein, J., & Gubrium, J. (Eds.). (2003). *Inside interviewing: New lenses, new concerns.* Thousand Oaks, CA: Sage.

Opdenakker, R. (2006). Advantages and disadvantages of four interview techniques in qualitative research. *Forum Qualitative Sozialforschung/Forum: Qualitative Social Research, 6*(2), Art. 11. Retrieved from *www.qualitative-research.net/index.php/fqs/article/view 175/392.*

Rea, L. M., & Parker, R. A. (2005). *Designing and conducting survey research: A comprehensive guide* (3rd ed.). San Francisco: Jossey-Bass.

Spradley, J. P. (1979). *The ethnographic interview.* New York: Holt, Rinehart & Winston.

Spradley, J. P. (1980). *Participant observation.* New York: Holt, Rinehart & Winston.

WEBSITES FOR SURVEY DESIGN

http://www.howto.gov/customer-service/collecting-feedback/basics-of-survey-and-question-design

www.surveysystem.com/sdesign.htm

http://changingminds.org/explanations/research/measurement/likert_scale.htm

www.john-uebersax.com/stat/likert.htm

http://dataguru.org/ref/survey/responseoptions.asp

CHAPTER 6

Using Assessment Data in Action Research

Assessment data are an integral part of life in schools. With the heavy emphasis on accountability, evidence-based decision making, and students' scores from standardized tests, you are surrounded by test data. Although most of these data are designed to monitor students' progress and performance, they are also used to evaluate teachers and schools.

You are probably aware of the multiple testing data available to you as an educator (e.g., state testing data, district-designed tests, unit tests, and your own teacher-designed assessment tools). Being a reflective practitioner, you routinely collect and incorporate these data into your practice. Knowledge about creating and effectively using assessment tools is an essential part of your roles as an educator and action researcher.

Assessment also plays an important role in your quest to improve your practice through action research. Assessment information can be a valuable data source as you explore the effectiveness of your practice, including examining your teaching strategies, exploring a new curriculum unit, or evaluating a schoolwide program. Therefore, in this chapter, we describe the various methods of assessment most commonly used by educational practitioners.

As part of your action research project, you may want to collect and analyze multiple assessment data, both qualitative and quantitative. These data can include scores from teacher-made or standardized tests, students' portfolios, attendance and discipline records, referrals, communication with parents, and information about your students' behaviors, attitudes, and motivation.

While you, as a practitioner, have no control over the standardized, high-stakes tests administered to your students, you are probably responsible for ongoing *formative* (during instruction) and *summative* (at the end of instruction) assessment of your students. No single assessment is sufficient in providing information to educators to guide their instructional practices; therefore, you need to know how to design and evaluate multiple assessment tools.

The types of assessments collected at your school reflect in many ways external and internal expectations. *Formal* assessments are usually dictated by local, state, or federal mandates and policies. For example, standardized student testing and data-driven decisions have moved to the forefront of education with the enactment of the No Child Left Behind (NCLB) legislation in 2001. Consequently, students, teachers, and administrators are assessed and are held accountable for their performance using a mandatory testing program that is designed and administered by the state. Similarly, the Race to the Top enacted by the Obama administration and the Common Core State Standards Initiative include standardized testing as an important component of accountability. In addition to these tests, many districts administer other standardized tests (such as Terra Nova or Iowa Test of Basic Skills), as well as district-developed tests. Thus, formal test data have an immediate and important impact on educators' practice and professional life.

Besides the multiple formal assessments administered to school children, each teacher has many opportunities to conduct *informal* assessment of students throughout the day. For example, as a classroom teacher and an action researcher you may observe your students' levels of engagement and cooperation, their enthusiasm and participation, their interaction with one another, or how they play with each other during recess. You, as an observant teacher, know that there are many opportunities for these informal assessments that can help paint a more complete picture of the students, their dispositions, progress, challenges, and areas where they need help and where they excel.

Assessment, both formal and informal, is used by teachers as pretesting before instruction starts; during instruction (formative and diagnostic assessment); and at the end of instruction (summative assessment; Gareis & Grant, 2008; Green & Johnson, 2010; Miller, Linn, & Gronlund, 2009). Classroom testing and assessment are also used to (1) determine the best placement for students to maximize their potential; (2) plan differentiated instruction to meet the needs of all students in the class; (3) assign grades; (4) comply with local, state, and federal laws; and (5) communicate with parents and other stakeholders. Assessment data shared with students allow them to participate in setting their own educational goals.

In this chapter we focus on several issues: (1) understanding standardized commercial achievement tests, (2) writing instructional objectives, (3) using teacher-made traditional assessment tools, (4) using teacher-made authentic assessment tools, (5) using rubrics to assess students' performance, (6) using portfolios to assess students, and (7) comparing the major advantages and disadvantages of these assessment tools.

UNDERSTANDING STANDARDIZED COMMERCIAL ACHIEVEMENT TESTS

As a classroom teacher, your students are likely to be tested annually by standardized tests mandated by your district or your state. These tests are constructed by professional item writers and undergo extensive pretesting prior to administering them to students across the district, state, or nation. The majority of these tests can be divided into two types: norm-referenced and criterion referenced. In the section that follows, we briefly describe these types of commercial tests.

Norm-Referenced Commercial Tests

Norm-referenced tests are used by educators to interpret scores and compare the performance of a student to the performance of similar students who previously took the same test (McMillan & Schumacher, 2010; Popham, 2013). These students comprised the norming sample that was used to derive the test norms and they represent the demographic characteristics of the future test takers, such as age group and grade level. High-stakes tests are usually norm referenced and scores obtained by K–12 students on such tests can have important consequences for students, teachers, schools, staff, and the whole community. The consequences may include failing to be admitted to a program, failing to graduate from a program or pass a course, or failing to earn certification (Shermis & Di Vesta, 2011). High-stakes tests used in education are likely to be those developed by commercial companies. Examples of high-stakes tests include (1) tests whose scores are used by school systems to determine merit pay for teachers; (2) tests that are administered by the state as part of NCLB or other state or federal mandates in which low performance may result in judging schools as "failing" if the whole school or subgroups within the school do not make enough annual yearly progress (AYP); and (3) tests to determine admission into college or other professional schools, such as medical and law schools.

Test items written for norm-referenced tests are designed to maximize differences between test takers because the goal is to create a bell-shaped distribution of scores (Ravid, 2011). Most of the items are at an average level of difficulty, to be answered correctly by 40 to 70% of the examinees. Some very difficult items are designed to differentiate between the good and excellent students, and some easy items are used to differentiate among the low-performance students. Easy items can also be placed at the beginning of the test or section to encourage all students. Test scores on norm-referenced tests are reported in terms of percentiles, stanines, and grade equivalents.

To facilitate the diagnostic value of commercial norm-referenced tests, items on these tests may be tied to specific instructional objectives. For example, on the report of a student's test results, there may be a list of objectives and how well the student or the whole class achieved these objectives.

Criterion-Referenced Commercial Tests

Criterion-referenced tests are used to compare the performance of the student to a certain predetermined criterion or standard (Boyle & Fisher, 2007; Shermis & Di Vesta, 2011). Students are not compared to one another, nor do they have to compete with other students taking the test (Popham, 2013). Instead, they have to meet certain curricular criteria that are clearly articulated and meet preset benchmark criteria. For example, they have to answer correctly at least 80% of the questions in order to demonstrate mastery of the materials and pass the test, regardless of how well their classmates performed.

Because the expectation is that all students will reach mastery overall, items written for criterion-referenced tests tend to be easier than items in norm-referenced tests and relate directly to the objectives or standards they are designed to assess (Ravid, 2011). Often, criterion-referenced tests can better inform teachers and other educators about students' progress and help plan remediation or reteaching.

The educational standards movement in the United States has contributed a great deal to the popularity of criterion-referenced tests. The standardized tests that are administered in all states to comply with state or federal mandates such as NCLB are based on standards. Usually, in order to pass the test, students have to meet or exceed state standards as measured by test items. Many districts also use their own benchmark tests that tie in test items with benchmarks that are appropriate for each grade level. Chapter or unit tests that are prepared by textbook publishers are usually criterion-referenced tests.

TABLE 6.1. Main Advantages and Disadvantages of Norm-Referenced and Criterion-Referenced Standardized Commercial Achievement Tests	
Main advantages	**Main disadvantages**
• Developed by professional test writers • Pilot tested and carefully constructed • Tests usually have high reliability • Can be standardized across different settings • Students and parents are familiar with these test formats • Can accommodate the needs of students with learning difficulties • *Norm-referenced* tests allow a comparison to other similar students across the district, state, country, or internationally • *Criterion-referenced* tests allow a comparison to preset criteria or benchmarks rather than to other students	• Cannot provide ongoing monitoring of students' progress • May not have content validity and may not match the curriculum being taught • May not be sensitive to cultural, linguistic, or ability differences • High-stakes tests can cause a great deal of test anxiety and stress • Preparation for high-stakes testing takes time away from classroom instruction • *Norm-referenced* tests may not have immediate implications for teaching • *Criterion-referenced* tests may not easily allow for a comparison across different settings

Table 6.1 summarizes the main advantages and disadvantages of norm-referenced and criterion-referenced standardized, commercially developed achievement tests.

TEACHER-MADE TESTS

As a classroom teacher, you are responsible for continuously assessing your students by using a variety of formal and informal means. These multiple approaches include quizzes, essays, homework assignments, projects, portfolios, oral presentations, paper-and-pencil tests, and performance tasks. Some of these assessments are referred to as traditional and others are considered alternative or authentic. Traditional assessments include choices such as true/false, matching, short answers, or essays. The focus of alternative (or authentic) assessments is on directly meaningful and real-life tasks.

Our discussion of teacher-made tests focuses on the following: (1) planning and writing instructional objectives, (2) writing and evaluating traditional test items, and (3) using authentic assessments tools.

Make sure that you clearly communicate with your students and explain to them why you test, how the test is formatted, how you will score the test, and how they will be graded on the basis of the test. Because teacher-made written tests are very commonly used in schools as a means for assessing students, the following section guides you through the steps of writing and assessing your own classroom tests.

WRITING INSTRUCTIONAL OBJECTIVES

Start your instructions by articulating your instructional objectives to yourself and to your students. When you are ready to assess your students, write tests that will allow you to assess the level at which these objectives have been met by the individual students in your class and the class as a whole. In writing your instructional objectives, you may want to consider the taxonomy of the cognitive domain. The taxonomy, which was developed by Benjamin Bloom in 1956 (Bloom, Engelhart, Furst, Hill, & Krathwohl, 1956), classifies cognitive–intellectual skills into six levels, going from the lowest to the most complex (see Table 6.2). When planning a test, you need to consider what levels of the taxonomy to assess and how many items to use for each level. Table 6.2 contains a list of the levels of the taxonomy. Definitions and typical verbs that can be used in writing objectives for each level are also included.

Writing instructional objectives will help you to clearly communicate the intended objectives of your instructional unit and will allow you to assess how well

TABLE 6.2. An Explanation of Bloom's Taxonomy

Level of taxonomy	Description includes	Typical verbs used
Knowledge	Knowing and memorizing facts	List, state, label
Comprehension	Understanding	Describe, restate, explain
Application	Applying new knowledge to a new, but similar situation	Construct, illustrate, use
Analysis	Logically breaking down into components	Contrast, differentiate, deduce
Synthesis	Integrating and organizing information to create something new	Compose, design, organize
Evaluation	Judging and appraising new and existing knowledge	Conclude, judge, assess

your students have accomplished these objectives. Creating a well-crafted table of specifications will greatly enhance the content validity of your test. (See our discussion of content validity later in this chapter.)

Preparing a Table of Test Specifications

After writing the instructional objectives for the unit you are going to teach (e.g., chapter, story, or semester), you can now plan the test by preparing a *table of test specifications*, or a *test blueprint*. The goals of creating a test blueprint is to help you focus on those learning goals that you consider most important (Suskie, 2009), as well as communicate your expectations to your students (Stiggins & Chappuis, 2011). In this table, you list the contents of the items as the rows, while the columns show the outcomes you choose to highlight from some of the six levels in Bloom's taxonomy. The number of points assigned to each outcome is also listed. In each cell, the number of items to be included in that category is indicated. Figure 6.1 is an example of a table of test specifications used by a teacher to plan student assessment.

Although it is important to clearly articulate your objectives and create a table of specifications, in all likelihood you will find that you do not have the time to create such a table every time you design a test. Still, you should ensure that your tests reflect the content and skills that you covered in class and write appropriate items that will allow you to assess your students. Other, less formal approaches, which include a systematic review of the materials to be tested and the construction of corresponding items, also can contribute greatly to the high content validity of your test.

	Outcomes			
Content	**Knowledge** 15 points	**Comprehension** 20 points	**Application** 15 points	**TOTAL** 50 points
Topic A	5 items	3 items	2 items	**10 items**
Topic B	5 items	3 items	2 items	**10 items**
Topic C	5 items	4 items	1 item	**10 items**
TOTAL	**15 items**	**10 items**	**5 items**	**30 items**

FIGURE 6.1. Example of a table of test specifications for planning an assessment.

CONSTRUCTING TEACHER-MADE TRADITIONAL ASSESSMENT TOOLS

Teacher-made assessment tools can be used in all stages of instruction. They may be *diagnostic* (used prior to instruction), *formative* (during instruction), or *summative* (at the end of instruction). In creating these tests, teachers can choose from a variety of item formats depending on the curriculum and their instructional goals. The following suggestions focus on the most common test formats used by classroom teachers. We start by discussing two types of assessment: *selection type* and *supply type*. In selection-type items, you ask your students to select the correct or best response from a predetermined number of options that are presented to them (Gareis & Grant, 2008). Examples of selection-type items include multiple choice, matching, and true/false (Stiggins & Chappuis, 2011). Supply-type items require your students to recall, compose, or analyze information and construct an answer to a question (Gareis & Grant, 2008). Examples of supply-type items include short answers, completion (fill in the blank), and essay.

Writing Test Items

Following are explanations, examples, and guidelines for writing *selection-* and *supply-type* items. Regardless of the type of test you develop for your class, you

✓	Suggestions
	Avoid using ambiguous, confusing, or vague wording.
	Keep the language level of your test items appropriate for your students.
	Write items that match the content of the materials that you have taught.
	Write questions that are short and to the point.
	Review the order of the items in your test to ensure that it is logical; when possible, place easier items at the beginning of the test to encourage students and reduce their anxiety.
	When possible, write items that have one correct answer (with the exception of essay questions or multiple-choice questions that have more than one correct answer).
	Ensure that your questions do not provide clues to the correct answer.
	Emphasize (e.g., underline, use boldface, or type in upper case) important words, such as *all, none,* and *don't.*

FIGURE 6.2. A checklist of suggestions for writing selection- and supply-type items.

will find these guidelines helpful. Additional guidelines and suggestions for writing good items can be found in many books on classroom assessment (e.g., Fisher & Frey, 2007; Gareis & Grant, 2008; Nitko & Brookhart, 2010; Russell & Airasian, 2012; Salend, 2011; Shermis & Di Vesta, 2011; Stiggins & Chappuis, 2011; Suskie, 2009; Van Blerkom, 2009). We start with a checklist of general suggestions for writing selection- and supply-type items (see Figure 6.2).

Selection-Type Items

In selection-type items, the student is asked to choose the correct or best answers to a series of questions (Stiggins & Chappuis, 2011). Selection-type items share several characteristics; they are easy to score and analyze, but allow students to guess the correct answer. You may want to set the task for the students by requiring them to "select the *best* answer" rather than "select the *correct* answer," especially in cases where there is a slight possibility that more than one answer is correct, but one is clearly better than the other one. The following are guidelines for constructing selection-type items.

Multiple-Choice Items

Multiple-choice items consist of two parts: the stem, which represents the problem or question, and a set of options (usually three to five) from which the students select an answer (Green & Johnson, 2010). The stem can be written as a question or an incomplete statement (Shermis & Di Vesta, 2011). In most cases, there is only one correct answer and the rest of the alternative responses, called *distractors*, are incorrect (Nitko & Brookhart, 2011). The responses should be organized logically and should sound plausible. To avoid a predictable response pattern, the location of the correct answer should vary (Nitko & Brookhart, 2011; Popham, 2013). Multiple-choice items are used extensively in achievement tests, mostly to test knowledge and comprehension. However, with practice you may be able to construct multiple-choice items to measure higher levels of the cognitive processes, such as interpretation, application, analysis, and synthesis. Recently, due to advances in software used to score multiple-choice tests, a number of multiple-choice tests include items with more than one correct answer. Figure 6.3 shows two examples of multiple-choice items; the first shows an example in which the stem is written as a question, and the second shows an example in which the stem is written as an incomplete statement. In both examples, there are four response choices.

Example 1:

Which state in the following list of states **did not** participate in the American Civil War?

   a. Alabama

   b. California

   c. Hawaii

   d. Virginia

Example 2:

The **Rhine River** is in the continent of _____ .

   a. Africa

   b. Australia

   c. Europe

   d. South America

FIGURE 6.3. Examples of multiple-choice items.

Interpretive Exercise

Multiple-choice items are often criticized for their frequent use in education to measure lower-order skills. However, selection-type items can also be used to measure higher-order skills (such as generalizing, inferring, and problem solving) by requiring students to interpret materials in order to answer a question (Russell & Airasian, 2012). The materials to be interpreted can be graphs, tables, pictures, or audiovisual materials. As in all multiple-choice items, the exercise includes a question and several responses (i.e., the correct answer and several distractors). Interpretive exercises take longer to construct and respond to and usually their number is more limited (Green & Johnson, 2010). Their greatest advantage is that they can be a more authentic representation of the materials and skills taught in class. Figure 6.4 shows an example of an interpretive item.

Matching-Format Items

This format is used to determine whether students can distinguish and match similar ideas or facts. The exercise consists of two columns; the left column is called the *stems* or *premises*, and the right one is called the *responses*. The stems are usually numbered, whereas letters are used for the responses. The whole list of premises

Study the train fare chart below which shows the costs of train tickets for one-way, 10-rides, and monthly rides.

Zone	Ticket Class	Zone A	Zone B	Zone C	Zone D
A	One-way 10-ride Monthly	$2.25 $18.20 $60.50			
B	One-way 10-ride Monthly	$2.60 $22.00 $65.25	$2.25 $18.20 $60.50		
C	One-way 10-ride Monthly	$3.50 $29.35 $88.60	$2.60 $22.00 $65.25	$2.25 $18.20 $60.50	
D	One-way 10-ride Monthly	$4.10 $35.40 $90.20	$3.50 $29.35 $88.60	$2.60 $22.00 $65.25	$2.25 $18.20 $60.50

1. Jacob has to ride the train round-trip from Zone B to Zone C every Monday for a month (a total of 4 days). Which ticket class would be the cheapest for him to buy?

   a. One-way

   b. 10-ride

   c. Monthly

FIGURE 6.4. Example of an interpretive question.

and responses should be homogeneous, dealing with only one topic or concept (Popham, 2013; Suskie, 2009; Taylor & Nolen, 2008), and each word or phrase in the left column should have only one correct answer in the right-side column. Ideally, you should have no more than 10 to 12 responses for older children to match, and about 4 to 5 responses for younger children to match (Gareis & Grant, 2008; Popham, 2013; Taylor & Nolen, 2008). The reason for this is that the student is required to deal with two sets of items (two columns of words, phrases, pictures, or graphics) at the same time, and this task can be challenging if there are too many items to match. To reduce the effect of guessing, it is recommended that the number of response choices be higher than the number of the premise items in the left-side column (Lamprianou & Athanasou, 2009: Stiggins & Chappuis, 2011). Figure 6.5 shows an example of a matching exercise in which the number of response choices (right column) is higher than the number of premises in the left-side column.

Match the books with their authors.	
Books	**Authors**
_____ 1. *Alice in Wonderland*	a. Jane Austen
_____ 2. *The Last of the Mohicans*	b. James Fenimore Cooper
_____ 3. *Gulliver's Travels*	c. Charles Dickens
_____ 4. *Pride and Prejudice*	d. Sir Walter Scott
_____ 5. *Ivanhoe*	e. Louisa May Alcott
_____ 6. *White Fang*	f. Jonathan Swift
_____ 7. *A Tale of Two Cities*	g. Jack London
_____ 8. *Little Women*	h. Daniel Defoe
_____ 9. *The Great Gatsby*	i. Ernest Hemingway
_____ 10. *Robinson Crusoe*	j. Lewis Carroll
	k. F. Scott Fitzgerald
	l. Leo Tolstoy

FIGURE 6.5. Example of a matching exercise.

Another type of matching exercises is called *category matching*. In this exercise, one column has a list of items, and the other column includes a limited number of categories. Each item should be matched to a category and each category should include at least one item (see Figure 6.6).

True/False Items

True/false items provide two response choices for each item: it is either true or false (Russell & Airasian, 2012; Stiggins & Chappuis, 2011). True/false items are relatively easy to construct and score and can be answered quickly by students. The main disadvantage of the true/false format is that students can more easily guess the answer (Popham, 2013). The true/false format is appropriate for measuring a factual statement (Taylor & Nolen, 2008) only for items that are clearly true (correct) or false (incorrect). Figure 6.7 presents two examples.

Another option that would make true/false items more challenging is to ask students to correct false items in order to make them true and thereby earn extra

Match the words in the list on the left side with their category on the right side.	
Animal	**Category**
____ 1. Fly	a. Reptile
____ 2. Turtle	b. Insect
____ 3. Bear	c. Fish
____ 4. Dog	d. Mammal
____ 5. Iguana	
____ 6. Bee	
____ 7. Salmon	
____ 8. Monkey	
____ 9. Tuna	
____ 10. Crocodile	

FIGURE 6.6. Example of a category matching exercise.

1.	True/False:	The book *Tom Sawyer* was written by Mark Twain.
2.	True/False:	The United States president during the Civil War was George Washington.

FIGURE 6.7. Examples of true/false items.

credit. For example, in item 2 in Figure 6.7, students who circle false can get extra credit for listing Lincoln instead of Washington.

Supply-Type Items

In supply-type items, the student has to provide the answer (Gareis & Grant, 2008). Supply-type items are generally easier to construct compared with selection-type items, and their use minimizes the likelihood that students will guess the correct answers. Completion items that require writing longer responses can also measure higher-order skills by asking the students to write in complete sentences, explaining and developing ideas and positions. The following is a brief description of each type of supply-type items.

Completion Items

Completion items (also called fill in the blank) require students to construct their own answers by filling in or completing a sentence from which a word or a phrase has been omitted (Russell & Airasian, 2012). Completion items are easy to score because there is usually only one correct answer. The wording of these items should provide sufficient clues to help lead students to the correct answer, yet be challenging and not simply help those who try to guess the answer. Figure 6.8 shows two examples of completion items: The first example is too vague and can have a number of correct answers. The second example specifies that the correct answer should be the year when the war started.

Short-Answer Items

The short-answer format requires the student to supply a word, phrase, name, or sentence (Popham, 2013) in response to a question. Although short-answer items are not effective at measuring higher-order cognitive abilities, they can be used to measure broad areas of knowledge, as well as specific skills, such as mathematics, in which students are asked to compute or solve a problem. These items are fairly easy to construct and decrease the likelihood of guessing. Though in most cases scoring them is fairly easy, in some cases scoring may require some subjective judgment, such as when words are not spelled correctly or the answer is not complete. Figure 6.9 shows examples of short-answer items.

---

1. A poor item (there could be many answers such as "in the fall" or "in Germany" or "in Europe"):

World War II started in _____.

2. A better item (it is clear that the answer should be a year):

World War II started in the year _____.

FIGURE 6.8. Examples of completion items.

Example 1: What was the **main reason** the United States joined the Allies in WWII?

Example 2: What does the expression "It's raining cats and dogs" mean?

FIGURE 6.9. Examples of short-answer items.

Essay Items

An *essay* item requires students to respond to a question or a prompt by composing a response that is more than one sentence, usually one or more paragraphs. Essay items provide a more authentic way for students to respond to these items, as well as the freedom to decide how to approach the task and how to structure and organize their responses. The biggest disadvantage with essay items is that they are time consuming for students. Additionally, teachers may find that it is hard to reliably score students' responses (Popham, 2013). Nonetheless, essay items provide you with a good way to assess your students' ability to organize, analyze, express, and defend their ideas (Russell & Airasian, 2012), rather than just repeat or recall facts. Be sensitive to the fact that essay items place a premium on writing skills, and therefore may penalize students whose writing skills or language ability is limited. To help your students use their time effectively, you should inform them about the approximate time they should spend on each essay item and the number of points assigned to each item. To assist you in scoring, you may want to develop a scoring guide in the form of a checklist or a rubric (Stiggins & Chappuis, 2011). (See the discussion of rubrics in this chapter.) Figure 6.10 shows an example of an essay item.

Table 6.3 summarizes the main advantages and disadvantages of teacher-made traditional assessment tools with selection-type and supply-type items.

Evaluating Traditional Teacher-Made Assessment Tools

According to the results of the test, you assign grades to students, plan your instruction, or make decisions about students' placement. Therefore, you need to be confident that the test results accurately reflect your students' knowledge and

---

Explain the main advantages of recycling and its effects on the environment.

- Describe and compare at least three different types of recycling programs.
- Explain at least three advantages and positive impacts on the environment.
- Be sure to elaborate on the general and unique benefits of each recycling approach.
- Write at least one complete paragraph.

Your responses will be assessed in terms of organization of ideas, completeness, accurate information, clarity, and language mechanics (grammar, spelling, and punctuation).

FIGURE 6.10. Example of an essay item.

TABLE 6.3. Main Advantages and Disadvantages of Teacher-Made Traditional Assessments with Selection-Type and Supply-Type Items

Main advantages	Main disadvantages
• Usually have high content validity and reflect the knowledge and skills taught in class • Teachers have control over the test content and format • Allow for frequent and ongoing assessment of students and modifying instruction accordingly • Identify students' strengths and weaknesses • Item format is familiar and used in many other contexts • Allow teachers to adapt the test to the unique needs of individual students • *Selection-type* items can be electronically and quickly scored • *Selection-type* items can cover a large amount of content • *Supply-type* items allow for assessing higher-order skills, writing skills, and creativity • *Supply-type* items can provide opportunity for nuanced and original answers	• Writing good test items requires time and expertise to construct, score, and evaluate • Tend to have lower reliability than commercial tests • Inconsistent grading system within and across settings • *Selection-type* items tend to measure lower-level skills such as recalling facts • *Selection-type* items usually have only one correct answer, unlike real life • Guessing can be a confounding factor in *selection-type* items • *Supply-type* items can be more difficult to grade objectively • *Supply-type* items may not well represent the content being tested or the curriculum objectives • Scoring *supply-type* items, such as open-ended questions and essays, may be subjective and time consuming

understanding of the material you have taught. After you administer a test to your students, you need to analyze and interpret the results of the test and their meaning. The test and its individual items should be analyzed and assessed as a whole. This is especially important if you are planning to use the test with other groups of students. In this section, we suggest several steps that you may take, including the assessment of the test validity and reliability. Several approaches to item analysis are also discussed.

Content Validity and Reliability of Tests

Every achievement test that you use, whether it is one you have created or one prepared by others, should have content validity. *Content validity* refers to the degree of match between a classroom test and the instruction, content, knowledge, and skills the test is designed to assess (Lamprianou & Athanasou, 2009).

As you write the test, be sure that the test items are a representative sample of the content and skills that were taught. Using a table of test specifications that we discussed earlier can enhance the match between the content that you taught and your test and increase the content validity of your test (Green & Johnson, 2010). For example, Joanna, a seventh-grade science teacher, is unable to fully complete the first-quarter curriculum unit about plants and animal cells. To ensure the content validity of the end-of-unit test that is provided with the textbook, she decides to exclude a few items relating to material she did not cover in class.

The question of reliability pertains to the *consistency* of the test results and the degree to which the same results will be obtained when the test is used repeatedly with the same individuals or group (Green & Johnson, 2010). Most approaches to assessing test reliability involve using statistical programs or lengthy computations. Therefore, they are of concern mostly to commercial test makers.

As a practitioner, you can affect test reliability by writing good test items. Another factor is the length of the test; shorter tests tend to have lower reliability than longer tests (Green & Johnson, 2010). The reason is that longer tests provide a more consistent sample of students' abilities and performances, whereas shorter tests allow more room for chance and guessing. Additionally, it is recommended that you write several items to measure each objective or specific area of content to reduce the chance of guessing.

In most cases, tests created by teachers cannot compete with those created by the experts in terms of reliability. On the other hand, teacher-made tests are likely to have higher content validity because they are written by the classroom teachers who know best what was taught in class and who recognize their students' culture, language, and level of understanding.

Looking at Students' Response Choices

Inherently, all tests have a certain level of error. As you develop your tests, your goal is to minimize this problem so that students' test scores will represent as closely as possible their knowledge and skills. Errors can result from several sources, including the way test items are phrased, the choice of response options, and guessing, fatigue, and conditions during testing. Therefore, you should review each individual test item and analyze student responses.

Another way to evaluate a test is to look at each selection-type item, such as multiple choice and true/false items, and tabulate the number of students who chose each response option. For example, if your test includes a multiple-choice item with four response choices, tabulate the number of students who chose each response. You will note that good items can better differentiate between those students who know the materials and those who are guessing the correct answers (Shermis & Di Vesta, 2011; Suskie, 2009).

Figures 6.11 and 6.12 present examples of a well-written multiple-choice item and a poorly written multiple-choice item, respectively.

USING TEACHER-MADE AUTHENTIC ASSESSMENT TOOLS

Authentic assessment tools were created as an alternative to standardized commercial achievement tests, as well as to the extensive use of multiple-choice or other similar items in teacher-made tests. Authentic assessments, also referred to as alternative assessments, ask students to perform real-life tasks (Suskie, 2009).

Response Choices				
	A	B*	C	D
Percent of students choosing each response option	12	65	11	12
*Note that the majority of students selected B (the correct answer). The rest of the students, who probably did not know the answer, were equally divided among the other three choices (A, C, and D); this is evidence that all three distracters were equally attractive to students who did not know the correct answer.				

FIGURE 6.11. Example of distribution of responses for a well-written multiple-choice item.

Response Choices				
	A*	B	C	D
Percent of students choosing each response option	45	7	40	8
*Note that the number of those choosing the correct response (A) was only slightly higher than the number of those who chose C, one of the distractors. Very few students chose the other two distractors (B and D). Option C was too attractive for those who did not know the correct answer.				

FIGURE 6.12. Example of a distribution of responses to a weak multiple-choice item.

These assessments have several characteristics. They (1) emphasize the practical application of the knowledge, (2) encourage open-ended thinking rather than finding one correct answer, and (3) present realistic problems drawn from everyday life.

In our discussion of authentic assessment we present two examples: performance assessment, and curriculum-based measurement (CBM). We end this section with an overview of rubrics that are typically used to evaluate students' performance on authentic assessment tools.

Performance Assessment

At times, you may feel that the traditional means of assessing your students do not fully reflect their knowledge and ability. In such cases, you may choose to use performance assessment as a formative or summative evaluation of your students. Performance tasks provide students with opportunities to demonstrate their mastery of different concepts in nontraditional ways (Fisher & Frey, 2007). In doing so, you can observe your students and directly assess their performance on a relevant task. Using performance assessment allows teachers to combine assessment with students' learning (Suskie, 2009). For example, you may ask your students to perform an experiment in the lab and assess how well they complete this task, as opposed to asking them to simply write the steps of the experiment without actually doing it. Or students may demonstrate their knowledge and skills through performance such as dance, drama, artwork, and electronic media.

Although most types of performances in the context of education relate to learning tasks, you may also wish to assess students' performance on behavior tasks, such as cooperating with other students during team sports in physical education classes or assisting students with special needs.

Many educators consider performance assessment to be authentic and more closely related to real life in comparison with traditional types of tests, such as multiple choice or fill in the blank. The assessment task usually involves more creative and higher-order thinking and can provide opportunities to students to be actively involved in their own assessment.

The tasks that you use to assess students' performance can be a part of their daily life (such as their attitudes toward peers in the lunch room or during study hall) or a specially designed situation where they know that their performance is being assessed (such as producing a play or a digital story on a specific topic). Assessing students' performance is usually done with rubrics that are shared with the students prior to their performance. (An explanation of rubrics is provided later in this chapter.)

It is important that the criteria you use to assess students' performance be clearly articulated and explained to students in advance (Taylor & Nolan, 2008). It is common to assess the *product* being created by the students as well as the *process* used to create the product. For example, Latisha, a sixth-grade language arts teacher, asks her students to work in groups to create a game that incorporates the vocabulary words from the last unit. The game is considered the product and it is assessed based on the vocabulary used, as well as the students' creativity and imagination in designing and constructing it. Students are told that they will also be assessed on the basis of their behavior and attitudes in the process of creating the game. Together, Latisha and her students develop a rubric that includes criteria such as how they relate to each other, their cooperation skills, and how well they follow classroom rules. Additionally, the quality of the game they develop is evaluated on criteria such as its structure, the instructions provided, and the vocabulary words used.

Table 6.4 summarizes the main advantages and disadvantages of teacher-made performance assessment.

TABLE 6.4. Main Advantages and Disadvantages of Teacher-Made Performance Assessment

Main advantages	Main disadvantages
• Provide opportunities for students to demonstrate their unique strengths and needs • Encourage open-ended thinking and creativity • Provide opportunities for practical application of knowledge • Allow for an authentic integration of a wide range of student abilities • Allow evaluation of complex learning tasks and real-life knowledge • Allow students to participate in the assessment process • Provide transparent assessment criteria	• Articulating clear assessment criteria may be challenging • Do not easily allow for a comparison to other students • Creating high-quality performance tasks is difficult and demands teacher expertise • May be implemented inconsistently across settings • Completing performance tasks is time consuming and may take time away from instruction • May meet with resistance from parents who are used to traditional assessment procedures • May create resistance and be difficult to implement in an environment of high-stakes testing

Curriculum-Based Measurement

CBM is another alternative approach used to assess student performance. In CBM, students' academic performance is evaluated in relation to the curriculum (Boyle & Fisher, 2007), rather than in relation to external standards or norming groups. What distinguishes CBM from other approaches is that (1) it is done often, (2) it is usually very short (1 to 5 minutes), (3) it is directly related to the materials and content taught in class, and (4) it is easy to score and grade. These key features make CBM accessible for classroom teachers and easy to implement. CBM measures are useful in (1) diagnosing students' areas of difficulty early on, (2) planning appropriate interventions, and (3) closely following students' response to the planned intervention. Using CBM is especially helpful with students who are identified as at risk or those who seem to have difficulty mastering the course material. CBM is often used to assess student progress in basic subjects such as reading, math, and spelling (Green & Johnson, 2010).

For example, Ethan, a second-grade teacher, focuses his action research project on the effectiveness of using supplementary intervention materials with three of his students who have learning disabilities. He monitors the progress of these struggling students by using short reading passages from their textbook. These 1-minute tests are administered once a week. In his CBM, he records their oral reading fluency including decoding, sight vocabulary, number of words read correctly, and comprehension.

Table 6.5 summarizes the main advantages and disadvantages of CBM.

TABLE 6.5. Main Advantages and Disadvantages of Curriculum-Based Measurement

Main advantages	Main disadvantages
• Highly related to the curriculum and classroom instruction	• Usually measure only basic skills
• Allow the assessment of individual skills and gaps in knowledge	• Lack long-range goals
• Allow for early diagnosis and interventions for students with specific learning problems	• May limit teacher's ability to provide nuanced and specific feedback
• Provide continuous monitoring of students' progress by documenting small increments in their growth over time	• Used mostly in elementary grades
• Provide immediate feedback	• Time consuming to administer frequently to a large number of students
• Inexpensive to create and easy to administer	• Require extensive recordkeeping
	• Require ongoing revisions to the assessment tool

Using Rubrics to Assess Student Performance

A rubric is an authentic scoring system that is used to assess various processes and products (Russell & Airasian, 2012), as well as students' performance on various tasks. These tasks include assignments such as artistic projects, essays, papers, projects, and behaviors. For example, you can use rubrics to assess a video that is produced by your students; a play, a poem, or a research paper that they write; a science project that they develop as a group; and their level of cooperation during group work.

Using rubrics allows you to assess these complex and multifaceted assignments that are often hard to evaluate objectively. This formative and ongoing assessment provides you with information and feedback that you can use to improve your teaching and enhance your students' learning.

To create your own rubrics, establish ahead of time a set of criteria that are linked to your learning objectives and assign a range of numerical values to these criteria. Engage your students in the task of defining and distinguishing a good-quality product from a poor-quality product (Stiggins & Chappuis, 2011). Sharing these criteria with your students has several advantages: (1) it allows you to communicate your objectives; (2) it helps your students understand what is expected of them and how they will be graded, (3) it increases their understanding of how the assignments relate to their learning, and (4) it enables your students to take control of their learning and progress.

Although in most cases you will develop your own rubrics, you may find it helpful to develop them collaboratively with your students. This approach gives your students a sense of ownership (Russell & Airasian, 2012), creates a more democratic classroom environment, and helps your students become more autonomous and self-directed. Constructing the rubric with the students also allows the students to gauge their level of progress on the project being assessed (Fisher & Frey, 2007).

Rubrics can range from a simple assessment tool to a more complex one. A simple rubric rating scale contains two elements: the performance criteria to be assessed and a rating scale of the performance proficiency levels. The more complex descriptive rubric adds a third element that includes descriptors of each performance proficiency level. The rating scale can be represented by numbers (e.g., 1–3) or words (e.g., *beginning, competent*, and *exemplary*).

To demonstrate the use of a rubric as an assessment tool, let's look at Esther, a middle school Spanish teacher. At the end of a unit on visiting a Spanish-speaking country, Esther asks her students to write a composition using the new vocabulary and grammatical structures introduced in the unit. The composition has to be at least 130 words. To assess the compositions, Esther and her students develop a scoring rubric. The criteria they develop focus on the following elements among others: vocabulary, spelling, grammar, organization, and expression of ideas.

After they develop the criteria, Esther presents two rubric framework options to her students: a rating scale and a descriptive rubric. Figure 6.13 shows excerpts from a rating scale that contains the performance criteria and the proficiency levels. Figure 6.14 shows excerpts from a descriptive rubric that provides a description of each proficiency level, in addition to the rating scale.

Table 6.6 summarizes the main advantages and disadvantages of using rubrics to assess students' performance.

Using Portfolios to Assess Students' Performance

In our discussion of assessment tools in this chapter we distinguished between various types: commercial versus teacher made, and traditional versus authentic. Portfolios can bring all these tools together to provide a more holistic way of evaluating and documenting students' learning. A *portfolio* is a systematic collection

Performance Criterion	Exemplary 4	Accomplished 3	Developing 2	Beginning 1
Vocabulary: a. Appropriate use of new vocabulary				
Vocabulary: b. Use of vocabulary learned in previous units				
Sentence structure: a. Correct order of words				
Sentence structure: b. Subject/word agreement				

FIGURE 6.13. Excerpts from a rating scale used to assess end-of-unit composition in Spanish as a second language.

Performance Criterion	Exemplary 4	Accomplished 3	Developing 2	Beginning 1
Vocabulary: a. New vocabulary	Utilizes most of the new vocabulary words	Utilizes some of the new vocabulary words	Utilizes a small number of new vocabulary words, some of which are used incorrectly	Utilizes very few new vocabulary words, most of which are used inappropriately and/or incorrectly
Vocabulary: b. Previously taught	Utilizes a wide variety of existing vocabulary including nouns, verbs, and adjectives to express ideas	Utilizes a variety of vocabulary including nouns, verbs, and adjectives to express ideas	Utilizes a small variety of vocabulary, some of which are used incorrectly	Utilizes a very limited vocabulary; most words are used inappropriately and/or incorrectly

FIGURE 6.14. Excerpts from a descriptive rubric used to assess end-of-unit composition in Spanish as a second language.

TABLE 6.6. Main Advantages and Disadvantages of Using Rubrics to Assess Students' Performance

Main advantages	Main disadvantages
<ul><li>Enable teachers to link instruction to assessment</li><li>Can assess different tasks and different levels of instructional objectives</li><li>Communicate clearly assessment criteria.</li><li>Enhance teachers' ability to communicate their expectations to their students</li><li>Provide unbiased and consistent evaluation across students</li><li>Allow students to participate in creating the rubric and in evaluating their own work</li><li>Make the scoring process clearer and faster</li><li>Provide specific feedback to students</li></ul>	<ul><li>Creating rubrics requires teacher expertise and is time consuming</li><li>Using correct language to express performance expectations can be difficult</li><li>Articulating clear rubric criteria may be challenging</li><li>May be used inconsistently across teachers</li><li>May limit teachers' ability to provide nuanced and specific feedback</li><li>May not always serve as an effective diagnostic tool</li><li>May lack credibility with some parents who are used to traditional assessment methods</li></ul>

of samples of students' work (Popham, 2013). These samples are carefully and purposely chosen by a teacher, students, or both. Portfolios may contain paper or electronic copies of materials such as assignments, formative and summative tests, student writings, art projects, videos, and audio recordings. Electronic portfolios that use digital storage processes are increasingly replacing the more traditional paper type because they are more dynamic and present sound, motion, and color better. Additionally, they do not take up as much storage space, nor are they subject to deterioration as paper portfolios are.

If you decide to assemble your students' assessment information into portfolios, you need to meet with your students and together choose artifacts that reflect the curriculum unit and your students' learning goals. These portfolio samples may represent your students' best work (Russell & Airasian, 2012), demonstrating mastery of materials taught in class. The samples can demonstrate students' growth over time through samples of their work in progress and reflections on their experience throughout the learning process. Additionally, you may ask your students to provide an explanation of the value and significance of the various artifacts that they chose to include in the portfolio.

You need to develop evaluation criteria to assess your students' work samples. These criteria are often presented in the form of a rubric and are shared with students ahead of time. As part of the process, you and your students will probably wish to hold formal and informal conferences to review their work, reflect on their achievement, and set future learning goals.

Involving your students in choosing items to include in their portfolios will promote students' ownership of their portfolios (Russell & Airasian, 2012) and encourage them to take a more active role in their own learning and in becoming self-directed learners. Portfolios assist students in assessing their own work (Van Blerkom, 2009). Using portfolios enables you to differentiate your instruction by developing goals, teaching materials, and assessment criteria to meet the unique needs of each of your students. You may find also that the use of portfolios strengthens your communication with parents by allowing you to authentically show the quality of their children's work as evidence of their growth over time.

For example, Jeanette, a kindergarten teacher, focuses her action research on developing ways to improve students' involvement and ownership in setting goals for themselves and self-directing their learning. She decides to use portfolios as one of the means to accomplish this goal. She starts by explaining the idea and process of portfolios to the whole class. She then holds a conference with each student and together they decide on the learning goals for the next week and what should be included in the portfolios to demonstrate that these goals were achieved. The items chosen by the learners are both paper and digital. Examples of paper items are students' drawings, samples of their writing of the alphabet letters, and their home phone number. Some of the digital samples include an audiotape of the student telling a story and a videotape of a play created and acted by a group of students.

At the end of the week, Jeanette meets with each student to review his or her portfolio. They go over each new item that was added that week, and she asks her students to evaluate their work and decide what they would like to improve, change, or add in the coming week. They also create goals for the coming week and plan the activities that will demonstrate these goals.

Jeanette keeps a journal about her weekly conferences with each student. She documents improvements in her students' ability to set goals for themselves and to choose appropriate activities to reflect those goals.

Table 6.7 summarizes the main advantages and disadvantages of using portfolios to assess students.

TABLE 6.7. Main Advantages and Disadvantages of Using Portfolios to Assess Students

Main advantages	Main disadvantages
• Allow teachers to differentiate their instruction to meet students' individual needs and strengths • Complement the curriculum rather than take time away from instruction • Allow for a holistic view of students • Involve multiple ways of showing students' progress • Provide teachers with continuous feedback that enables planning for future instruction • Encourage student creativity and expression of individuality • Promote students' autonomy and self-directed learning • Facilitate communication with parents by sharing tangible evidence of students' progress	• Tend to be time consuming to plan and create • Finding time for the teacher to meet regularly with each student is challenging • Require organizational skills by both teacher and students to logically present the portfolio artifacts • Scoring involves extensive use of subjective evaluations • Data gathered over time can be difficult to analyze or summarize • Expensive electronic equipment or ample storage space are required to create and maintain portfolios • Do not prepare students to take mandated standardized achievement tests

FINAL COMMENTS ABOUT CLASSROOM ASSESSMENT

Classroom teachers have many methods available to them to evaluate their students. Each of these methods provides opportunities for the teacher to evaluate aspects of their students' development, growth, accomplishments, and further needs. Each of the methods has advantages and disadvantages. Teachers should consider how each method contributes to understanding their students' achievement and use these assessments appropriately. As educators, we understand that a combination of different assessment tools will provide a richer, more holistic insight into each student's work. When it comes to researching your own practice, you may benefit from the multiple forms of assessments that are used in your classroom: standardized, commercial tests, teacher-made assessment tools, and teacher-made traditional tests, as well as authentic assessments. The richer the data you collect, the better you will be able to analyze, synthesize, and interpret the issue at the center of your study.

CHAPTER SUMMARY

1. Student assessment data are an integral part of school life and, although most data are designed to monitor students' progress and performance, they are also used to evaluate teachers and schools.

2. Assessment information can be a valuable data source for school action researchers as they explore the effectiveness of their practice, by collecting and analyzing qualitative and quantitative assessment data.

3. Because no single assessment is sufficient in providing information to educators to guide their instructional practices, educators need to know how to design and evaluate multiple assessment tools.

4. Assessment, both formal and informal, is used by teachers to assess students' readiness and dispositions; diagnose and monitor students' progress and performance; determine the best placement for students to maximize their potential; plan differentiated instruction to meet the needs of all students in the class; assign grades; comply with local, state, and federal laws; and communicate with parents and other stakeholders.

5. Sharing assessment data with students allows them to participate in setting their own learning goals and evaluating their own progress.

6. The majority of standardized commercial tests can be divided into two types: *norm-referenced* tests that are used to compare the performance of a student to the performance of a norming sample, and *criterion-referenced* tests that are used to compare the performance of the student to a certain predetermined criterion or standard.

7. Writing instructional objectives helps teachers to articulate and clearly communicate the intended objectives of their instructional unit and assess how well students have accomplished these objectives.

8. Teacher-made assessment tools can be used in all stages of instruction: *diagnostic* (used prior to instruction), *formative* (during instruction), or *summative* (at the end of instruction).

9. *Selection-type* items, in which students are asked to select the correct response from a number of options that are presented to them, are easy to score and analyze, but allow students to guess the correct answer.

10. *Supply-type* items, in which students are asked to recall, compose, or analyze information and construct an answer to a question, are fairly easy to construct and minimize the likelihood that students will guess the correct answers. However, longer response items or essays may be harder to score.

11. Every achievement test should have *content validity* that refers to the degree of match between a test and the content, knowledge, and skills it is designed to assess, and *reliability* that pertains to the *consistency* of the test results and the degree to which the same results will be obtained when the test is used repeatedly with the same individuals or group.

12. *Authentic assessment* tools emphasize the practical application of knowledge, encourage open-ended thinking rather than finding one correct answer, and present realistic problems drawn from everyday life. *Performance assessments*, which allow teachers to observe their students and assess their performance on a relevant task, should include clearly articulated criteria to evaluate the *product* being created by the students as well as the *process* used to create the product.

13. *Curriculum-based measurement* (CBM) is used to evaluate student performance in relation to the curriculum; this measurement is done often, is usually very short, is directly related to the materials and content taught in class, and is easy to score and grade.

14. A *rubric* is an authentic scoring system that is used to assess students' performance on various tasks; rubrics can range from a simple assessment tool to one that is more complex.

15. A *portfolio* is a systematic collection of samples of students' work that are carefully and purposely chosen by the teacher, the students, or both. Portfolios allow students to take a more active role in their own learning and can bring various assessment tools together to provide a more holistic way of evaluating and documenting students' learning.

16. Each assessment method has advantages and disadvantages; thus, a combination of different assessment tools can provide for richer and more holistic insight into students' work.

17. Practitioners conducting action research can utilize data obtained through different assessment tools to enrich and expand their investigations.

CHAPTER EXERCISES AND ACTIVITIES

1. List at least three assessment tools used in schools and indicate whether they are used locally, statewide, or nationally. Choose one of these three tools and examine the following: intended audience of the test, the purpose and use of the test, types of questions used, and how the results are reported.

2. List three examples in which assessment data can be used in action research projects.

3. Reflect on your own experience as a student taking tests. What test format did you like the best and why?

4. Choose and describe a topic for assessing students that you teach or plan to teach. Using the information in Table 6.2, write five to eight items on the topics of your choice, measuring knowledge, comprehension, application, synthesis, and evaluation. Each item should include one of the action verbs listed in the right column of the table.

5. Following are responses of 100 students to a multiple-choice test item. Would you consider this to be a good item? Explain.

	Response choices			
	A	B	C (correct response)	D
Number of students choosing each response	21	24	31	24

6. Choose a topic or an instructional unit, as well as a grade level, and design a performance assessment task. Be sure to include instructions for the students about completing the task, and an explanation of how they will be assessed.

7. Plan a curriculum-based measurement that may be used by a first-grade teacher or a special education teacher. Explain the reasons for your choice.

8. Create a rubric that you can use to evaluate your students' learning on a unit of your choice. (You may want to consult Figures 6.13 and 6.14 in creating the rubric.)

9. Choose a grade level and a subject and develop a list of five to ten items that may be included in a portfolio. Indicate the purpose of the portfolio and the reasons for including these particular items.

ADDITIONAL READINGS

Chappuis, J., Stiggins, R. S., Chappuis, S., & Arter, J. A. (2011). *Classroom assessment for student learning: Doing it right—using it well* (2nd ed.). Upper Saddle River, NJ: Pearson.

Gardner, J. R. (Ed.). (2012). *Assessment and learning* (2nd ed.). Thousand Oaks, CA: Sage.

Hosp, M. K., Hosp, J. L., & Howell, K. W. (2006). *The ABCs of CBM: A practical guide to curriculum-based measurement.* New York: Guilford Press.

Johnson, J., Mims-Cox, S., & Doyle-Nichols, A. R. (2009). *Developing portfolios in education: A guide to reflection, inquiry, and assessment* (2nd ed.). Thousand Oaks, CA: Sage

Popham, W. J. (2008). *Transformative assessment.* Alexandria, VA: Association for Supervision and Curriculum Development.

Tovani, C. (2011). *So what do they really know? Assessment that informs teaching.* Portland, ME: Stenhouse.

CHAPTER 7

Data Analysis and Interpretation

By now, using various strategies, you have collected data from different sources. Standing before the mass of raw data, you, like many action researchers, probably feel a bit overwhelmed. You may be asking yourself: How should I proceed from here in making sense of all the information I have gathered? What steps will allow me to turn the data into research findings? and What strategies will enable me to use my data to answer my research questions?

Data analysis is a crucial stage in the action research process. Like many other practitioners engaged in research, you may find this phase to be the most challenging, as well as the most rewarding. At last you are about to discover, buried within the raw data, the answers to your research questions, and satisfy the curiosity that launched your inquiry journey.

Teachers and other school practitioners are constantly and intuitively analyzing and interpreting information as they make spontaneous decisions throughout the daily routine of school life. However, action researchers' data analysis is a systematic and deliberate process that results in trustworthy and reliable findings. These findings are transformed into dependable new understandings, assertions, explanations, and conclusions about the issues at the center of their investigations. Educators' new research-based knowledge can now lead to a plan of action and have direct implications for their practice.

The process of *analysis* is defined as breaking down the whole into elements in order to discover its essential features. *Interpretation* means providing a description or explanation of the meaning of the study. The research questions and the nature of the data—whether narrative, numerical, or mixed—dictate the strategies that might be appropriate for the analysis and interpretation process.

In this chapter we describe common methods that we have found most useful for analyzing and interpreting the data collected in action research. We review the process of organizing, analyzing, interpreting, and presenting the data. These steps are similar in both qualitative and quantitative research (Creswell & Plano Clark, 2011). We describe the methods most often used for qualitative analysis and interpretation followed by a discussion of several of the most commonly used quantitative strategies. Next, we offer ways to combine both in mixed-methods research. We end this chapter with suggestions for writing the study's conclusions and implications.

As we have suggested previously, receiving feedback on your writing from a critical friend, colleague, or research group member as you plan, design, and carry out your investigation is very helpful (Samaras, 2011). To facilitate the feedback process, this chapter includes checklists that will enable you and your group to critically read and assess the section of your report that includes your data analysis, interpretation, and conclusions. The questions listed serve as a guide for writing specific comments, offer ideas for revisions, and provide suggestions for improvement. You may, of course, adapt the questions to fit your own particular study and your own specific needs.

QUALITATIVE DATA ANALYSIS

The goal of qualitative data analysis is to bring meaning and order to the mass of collected data by looking for recurring themes, categories, and patterns (Hatch, 2002; Shank, 2006). This insight allows you to discover the significant connections and relationships among the parts in order to build a coherent interpretation and present logically structured findings. The new gained understanding will enable you to answer your research questions and consider the implications of the newly gained knowledge for your practice (Marshall & Rossman, 2011; Miles & Huberman, 1994; Shank, 2006).

In qualitative studies, analysis often goes hand in hand with data collection (Glesne, 2010; Merriam, 2009; Miles & Huberman, 1994). The researcher begins analyzing data as they are collected, and the emerging preliminary understandings help shape, revise, and refine the investigation throughout the data collection process. For example, Jonathan, a sixth-grade reading specialist, wants to investigate the value of homework and its contributions to his students' learning. For this purpose, he plans to interview the school principal, teachers, and parents to obtain their perspectives. Jonathan starts the inquiry by interviewing the principal. After he analyzes the information from the interview, he gains a better understanding of the school's policy regarding homework. As a result, when he develops the interview guide for the sixth-grade classroom teachers and parents, he adds several questions based on the new knowledge gained from the interview with the principal.

The strategies for data analysis that you can use during and after data collection are mostly the same. Unlike in quantitative data analysis in which data analysis and data interpretation are two separate phases, in qualitative data analysis the procedures are often integrated and recursive (Gibson & Brown, 2009; Marshall & Rossman, 2011). In the following sections, though, we focus on the final phase of the study, after all data are collected and you are analyzing the data to answer your research questions. For clarity purposes, we present the procedures linearly. We first describe the steps in data analysis followed by a discussion of the process of synthesizing and interpreting the data. We conclude by outlining ways to present the findings of your data analysis and their meaning.

Although there are many approaches to qualitative analysis, they all share an inductive process, which means that the analysis moves from analysis of parts to a whole, or from analysis of specifics to a general understanding (Hatch, 2002; Merriam, 2009). The analysis process begins by examining a myriad amount of information and organizing it into codes, themes, and categories. This is followed by an identification of the connections, relationships, and patterns in the data, and pulling them together into a significant whole that describes and explains the issue at the heart of the investigation. The data analysis process follows these steps:

1. Preparation for analysis
2. Analysis of the data
3. Synthesis and interpretation of the data
4. Presentation of data analysis and interpretation

Qualitative analysis and interpretation are very dynamic and subjective processes (Corbin & Strauss, 2007). Using the guideposts we outlined above may assist you in gaining trustworthy and dependable insights. We hope it will also allow you to assert the implications of your findings and achieve a coherent understanding that will guide your actions. However, it is important to remember that these guidelines should not be perceived as a recipe but rather as a set of suggestions to be adapted to your own individual project and inquiry (Patton, 2002).

Preparation for Analysis

Transforming Data into Readable Text

The first step in the data analysis process is to organize the data so they can be easily retrieved for analysis. This means transcribing the audiotapes, videotapes, observation field notes, and open-ended survey items into typed text, and using a computer scanner to transform visual images, pictures, and documents into digital copies. We recommend housing the data electronically in a database, though you also may want to keep a set of hard-copy files (Gibson & Brown, 2009; Richards, 2009).

Sorting the Data into Files

Next, sort and organize the data into specific files (Richards, 2009). For example, you may create separate files by sorting the data according to participants or data sources. Let's say you explored through interviews and open-ended survey questions the perspectives of reading specialists, parents, and students on the value of using drama in a language arts class. You may arrange the data into three files according to the participants: a file dedicated to the parents, a file dedicated to the students, and a file dedicated to the reading specialist. Another option is to file the data according to the method of data collection: all the interviews in one file, all the observations in another file, and all the documentations in a third file. Breaking down the data into smaller units will help later as you read through the text and code responses.

Creating a Data File Organizer

Another helpful step in preparing data for analysis is to create a table for the data you collected and the files you created to organize it. Record helpful information like the name, role, age, or grade of the participant, as well as the methods used to collect the data, the date and place where the data were collected, and any other information you deem appropriate. This will provide an organizing framework, allow efficient retrieval of the data, and keep a paper trail of useful identifying details (Richards, 2009). Figure 7.1 is an example of a data file organizer.

Immersing Yourself in the Data

Before you separate the data into particular elements, categories, and patterns, immerse yourself in the transcribed data: read and reread the data in their entirety.

File I: Parents' Perspectives on Using Drama in Language Arts							
Name of parent	Age	Demographic information	Source of data	Date	Location	Name of student	Student's level of reading

FIGURE 7.1. Data file organizer.

The purpose is to get an overall sense of the information and become familiar with the ideas and views being expressed. You may want to jot down initial comments, questions, or ideas. At the same time, avoid making judgments or engaging in premature guessing of what the information means (Patton, 2002).

Analysis of the Data

The process of analyzing data is based on categorizing and coding procedures that identify units of meaning within the data. Then these units of meaning can be organized into thematic clusters so patterns can be discovered (Boyatzis, 1998; Marshall & Rossman, 2011; Miles & Huberman, 1994; Shank, 2006). As mentioned above, qualitative data analysis is an open-ended inductive process of moving from particular categories to general patterns. These categories may be predetermined or emerging from the text. Next, we outline the procedures for analyzing data using both kinds of categories.

Using Predetermined Categories

Identifying the Predetermined Categories

Start this process by identifying the categories that will serve as a guide for grouping the data. These categories may be drawn from your research question(s) or they may emerge from your literature review or another source (Boyatzis, 1998; Hatch, 2002).

List the categories and make sure that they accurately express the issues that you are concerned about and that they do not overlap. For example, Sharon, a middle school social studies teacher, chairs a committee that is charged with the responsibility of developing a new integrated literature and social studies unit that will emphasize moral values. Before developing the unit, the committee decides to conduct a preliminary study to find out how values currently are being taught formally and informally during social studies and literature classes. Sharon and her committee decide to observe two social studies and two literature teachers and interview them. Based on their reading of existing literature, Sharon and the committee members identify the following eight categories and apply them in the data analysis:

1. Values are integrated within the teaching (content).
2. Values are reflected in classroom interactions and relationships.
3. Connections are made between classroom discussion and student's actions, behaviors, and relationships in and outside of class.
4. Values are transmitted from one point of view or diverse perspectives are encouraged.
5. Links are made between values discussed and current events that include controversial issues.
6. The nature of classroom management style (e.g., democratic, acceptance of differences, caring, autocratic) is explored.
7. Sharing of students' family and community values is encouraged.
8. There is recognition of the influence of peers and social networks on students' points of view.

Dividing the Data According to Predetermined Categories

Once you create the list of categories, comb through the transcript closely and look for segments in the data that belong to each category. As you find a segment that fits a category, mark it to make it easy to retrieve later. Repeat this process for each category. You probably will find that parts of the data you collected are irrelevant to the chosen categories, whereas some segments are contained in several categories.

There are several methods for dividing the segments and separating the data by categories; choose the one you feel most comfortable with. If you prefer the method of sorting the data manually, color code the segments or use symbols, numbers, or abbreviations to identify these entries and aggregate them (Hatch, 2002). Word processing programs perform this function quickly and easily. Another option is to use special computer software programs, such as NVivo, for organizing, sorting, and analyzing qualitative data (Bazeley, 2007; Flick, 2009; Lewins & Silver, 2007).

As you separate sections of data from the complete dataset and group data into categories, the segments are taken out of their original place and become decontextualized. Be sure that you have one intact version of the complete dataset that serves as a master copy, and that each entry is marked and identified to indicate the source of data and page number. Reread the sections you have inserted in each category. You may want to modify and refine the categories by merging or by adding new categories to the list (Richards, 2009).

Looking for Themes within Each Category

Once you formulate the categories, they become units of analysis. Within each individual unit, look for central themes that describe the theme and arrange them in a logical order. Themes are ideas, points of view, or experiences that run through the category (Boyatzis, 1998; Miles & Huberman, 1994; Shank, 2006).

To discover the themes, read and reread your units of analysis. During this process, it can be helpful to ask questions such as What is important here? What are the critical incidents? and What are the key elements and issues? In the margin, label the main element(s) and highlight quotation(s) that illustrate them. For each unit of analysis, compile the labeled elements that you discovered. You also may add a succinct description of the content of each element.

Now look for similarities among these elements and how they are connected. For example, look for recurring concepts, incidents, and issues and the common threads that connect them. The connected elements that are threaded throughout the units of analysis are the category themes.

Organize these themes in a logical order. Using a table or other organizers, record the categories and choose the quotes that capture the essence of each category. For example, Sharon and her committee identify several themes in their predetermined category 4: Links are made between values discussed and current events that include controversial issues. They first arrange these themes logically and then insert the quotes that reflect them (see Figure 7.2).

Category 4:	
Links are made between values discussed and current events that include controversial issues.	

Identified Theme	Selected Quotes from the Data
a. Making a Link	• "It is important to raise the moral questions the text presents because at some point in their lives, they will face these challenging questions." (Ms. A., SS, p. 41) • "I want the students to make the connection between the text and their lives. However, they just want to talk about themselves." (Ms. B., Lit., p. 29)
b. Linking to Current Events	
• Classroom	"At times, a tense situation in the story we read reminds students of something similar that happened in our class." (Ms. B., Lit., p. 31)
• Schoolwide	"Last week we talked about the waves of immigration during the turn of the 20th century and Joan cried out: 'Do we treat the immigrant students among us any better than they did then?'" (Ms. A., SS, p. 39)
• Social and political events	"Often in our class conversations, students connect events we discuss to something they just watched on the news. I like that." (Mr. F., SS, p. 57)
c. Linking to Controversial Issues	
• Open debate	"For me, when students discover that social and political issues are morally complex I do not care if we do not cover all that I have planned for this lesson. For me, this is education." (Mr. G., SS, p. 36)
• Limited debate	"As a teacher, I need to make a decision if the students want to discuss the moral issue because it is meaningful to them or they want to avoid the challenging content of the text." (Ms. L., Lit., p. 48)
• Debate discouraged	"Frankly, I do not think that many of the fuzzy issues that the students want to discuss are relevant to the subject matter or to a classroom. I am not a psychologist!" (Ms. B., Lit., p. 30)

FIGURE 7.2. Example of Sharon's theme organizer with selected quotes.

Using Emerging Categories

Unlike the process of using predetermined categories, in which the categories are identified *before* the data analysis process begins, identifying emerging categories is something you do from the ground up (Charmaz, 2006). This process begins by developing codes from the data and organizing them into categories.

Coding the Data

To develop a set of codes, read the data slowly and carefully and divide them into topics. The topic may appear in different segments within the data. These segments can vary from a phrase, a sentence, a paragraph, or even several pages (Gibson & Brown, 2009). Bogdan and Biklen (2006) offer questions to help action researchers scrutinize the data to discover meaningful topics. You may want to consider some of these:

▶ Events   What is going on here?
                 How is the event perceived by the participants?

▶ Behavior   What action(s) led to a particular behavior?
                 What is the response to this behavior?

▶ Perspectives   How do the participants perceive the investigated issue?
                 Are there differences and similarities of opinions among the participants?

▶ Relationship   How do the participants feel about each other?
                 What are the relationships between the participants?

▶ Strategies   What strategies are used by the participants?
                 How useful are these strategies from the participants' perspectives?

Once you identify a segment to be coded, mark and assign a coding label that properly depicts its meaning (Bogdan & Biklen, 2006). You may choose an abbreviation of key concepts, actual words used by the participants, or standard educational terms as your coding labels. Record the coded label in the margin of the segment page. You may also want to note your insight in the other margin. Repeat this coding process, transcript by transcript, identifying codes that were already noted, while at the same time looking for new ones. After all the transcripts have been reviewed and coded, make a list of the codes. Review the codes to be sure that you understand their meaning, and combine codes with duplicating or overlapping meaning.

Your choice of codes depends on your research question and the purpose of your research (Marshall & Rossman, 2011). As a rule, try to reduce the codes to a manageable number. As you explore the transcripts you will probably realize that a considerable amount of data is irrelevant or peripheral to your study (Maxwell, 2013). Get rid of the excess! On the other hand, be careful not to overlook important issues that contribute to your understanding of the data, although they may appear infrequently in the transcript.

To illustrate the process of identifying emerging codes, let's follow Jesse, a sixth-grade student teacher. Jesse is concerned about the challenges of classroom management. For his action research project, Jesse decides to explore the issue of classroom management styles. He conducts semistructured interviews with four sixth-grade teachers and with the school principal. He also administers an open-ended survey to one sixth-grade class. Figure 7.3 shows the codes assigned by Jesse to teachers' responses to one of his interview questions: "What is your opinion about punishing students for their misbehavior in your class?" The figure also contains Jesse's insight.

Moving from Codes to Emerging Categories

You are ready now to proceed to the next step of data analysis: organizing the codes into emerging categories. Review the list of codes that represent topics you identified in the data and cluster codes (that are close in content) into emerging categories. Each category represents a theme around which similar topics are grouped (Charmaz, 2006). For example, under the category of "The goals of classroom management" (shown in Figure 7.3) Jesse lists the following topics:

▶ Enhancing learning

▶ Respecting others

▶ Scaffolding behavior

▶ Recognizing consequences for one's behavior

▶ Developing personal responsibility

▶ Making good choices

Insight and Reflections	Quotes	Abbreviated Codes*
Can be used as a quote?	**Transcript A:** Teacher I (29, F, 2 yrs' experience) [I feel that *punishment is a failure*. I feel that when I punish a student *I fail myself and my students*.]	**P as failure**
Reminds me of Glasser's theory	[My goal is to help my students learn to make *good choices* that lead to good behavior.] [My job is to help my students examine their behavior, understand the reasons for their misconduct and what can they do about it. Class meetings are an essential element in addressing behavior problems.] [Punishments *emphasize teacher control*; I prefer to *empower* my students.]	**G: good choice**
Potential theme: goals of classroom management		**Impl.**
		Power S
Potential theme: implementation of chosen technique	**Transcript B:** Teacher II (46, M, 11 yrs' experience) [Basically, I prefer incentives and *positive rewards* over punishment. *Rewarding good behavior* is more effective in *scaffolding my students' behavior. Immediate feedback, consistency, and positive reinforcement* of good behavior can change troublesome behavior.] [However, I do use *punishment as a last resort* to discourage inappropriate actions. Students should know that every act has *consequences*, good or bad.]	**Impl.**
		G: scaffolding behavior
Seems like behavior modification		**Impl.**
		P as consequence
Possible theme: extrinsic vs. intrinsic rewards	**Transcript C:** Teacher III (28, F, 2 yrs' experience) [I do not think that classroom management should focus on punishment.] [My goal is developing my students' *personal responsibility*.] [This can be done by sharing responsibility in establishing together class rules.] [Punishments and rewards assert *teacher control, but* I want to *empower my students*.] [I have to admit that sometimes I am *not consistent* in my response and resort to punishments and rewards. But I am working on myself to be less dependent on *external control* and more on guiding students to develop *self-discipline from within.*]	**G: personal responsibility**
		Impl.
Seems like a democratic classroom approach		**P as teacher control**
		Power S
		Consistent impl.
		Ext/Int
Reminds me of Lee Canter's assertive learning approach	**Transcript D:** Teacher IV (53, F, 28 yrs' experience) [Rather than punishment, I prefer to call it *consequences*.] [I define what an unacceptable behavior is and *I firmly apply appropriate consequences* when a student exhibits	**P as consequence**
		Impl.

(continued)

FIGURE 7.3. Coding of responses and insights by Jesse to one interview question.

	objectionable behavior.] [Without *proper control* no teacher can have an effective classroom.] [Classroom management that is based on firmness, kindness, and *consistent reinforcing* of	**Power T**
		Consistent
Possible quote?	rules results in effective learning.]	**G: effective learning**

*Abbreviated Codes:	
P = Punishment as . . .	**Consistent** = Following one's method
Impl. = Implementation of classroom management	**G** = Goal of punishment
Power T/S = Whose power is emphasized: teacher or student	**Ext/Int** = Extrinsic/intrinsic

FIGURE 7.3. *(continued)*

Similarity in a theme does not mean that it embodies a single point of view. On the contrary, a category should comprise converging perspectives agreed on by many educators, as well as divergent points of view held by few (Gibson & Brown, 2009). For example, in Jesse's study about classroom management, the theme of "management as power" presents the point of view of two of the teachers who believe that the teacher needs to have the power to enforce the proper regulations and rules. The remaining two teachers want to empower the students and believe that the emphasis on control does little to teach students to make good choices.

The process of identifying emerging categories can be facilitated by computer software programs. Their capabilities for storing data, assigning codes, and locating and retrieving coded materials are particularly effective (Bazeley, 2007; Flick, 2009; Gibson & Brown, 2009; Lewins & Silver, 2007). The software packages are especially useful for managing a large database.

Now you should revisit and refine your emerging categories (Bogdan & Biklen, 2006). First, examine the data represented by each category and ensure congruency between the data and the category. Next, reflect on how the topics within the category relate to each other and arrange them hierarchically according to a logical order. Last, using a table, record the categories and add quotations that demonstrate their content (see Figure 7.2).

In qualitative analysis, the way you classify the predetermined, as well as the emerging categories, is subjective and is done in a manner that makes sense to you, the researcher (Charmaz, 2006). Nevertheless, you are expected to be consistent, reliable, and systematic. You may want to go back to your research group or a trusted friend and share with them your categorization system and the rationale that underlies your analysis.

The process of using predetermined and emerging categories to analyze data is summarized in Figure 7.4.

Synthesis and Interpretation of the Data

You are ready now to move to the next phase of the analysis process: the synthesis and interpretation of data. The strategies we discuss apply to both predetermined and emerging categories, and from this point on we make no distinction between the two. Regardless of whether you used predetermined or emerging categories during the analysis process, you have taken the data apart, sorted the data into themes and categories, and analyzed each category separately. Now, as the synthesis and interpretation phase begins, you put the parts together, examine how they relate to each other, and identify patterns (Miles & Huberman, 1994). The aim is to build on these patterns to develop a holistic story and interpret the data's meaning (Patton, 2002). This requires an ability to see the "big picture" while carefully attending to the particulars. Looking at the overall picture without getting lost in the details allows you to discover what the data tell and the significance of the story for your research question (Bogdan & Biklen, 2006; Charmaz, 2006).

As mentioned before, in qualitative research often the analysis and interpretation of the data are not distinct or separate phases. The process of analyzing data and interpreting findings is not linear and may take place simultaneously. Nevertheless, for purposes of clarity, we present the process sequentially, and in the following section we focus on the interpretation phase only. We outline four steps in the interpretation process: (1) identifying patterns, (2) creating a concept map, (3) supporting the findings with evidence from the data, and (4) validating a trustworthy interpretation.

Identifying Patterns

In your interpretation of the data, present your insights and understandings that are based on the analyzed data and that relate to your research questions. Such a holistic understanding can be gained by connecting the categories and identifying patterns and relationships among them (Corbin & Strauss, 2007; Shank, 2006).

You may begin the process by examining the categories (either predetermined or emerging) that you have obtained in the analysis phase. Next, group similar or duplicated categories together into larger, more general, and encompassing categories (Charmaz, 2006; Hatch, 2002). For example, in the study on how values are taught in school during social studies and literature classes, Sharon and her committee decided to cluster the eight categories they identified into the following

USING PREDETERMINED CATEGORIES	USING EMERGING CATEGORIES
1. Identifying categories before the analysis begins: Drawing the predetermined categories from the research questions, literature review, or other sources	**1. Coding the data:** Breaking the data into segments according to topics Assigning coding labels that depict the meaning of the identified segments Developing a list of codes

2. Dividing the data according to the predetermined categories: Finding and identifying segments in the data that belong to each category	**2. Organizing the codes into emerging categories:** Identifying themes around which similar topics are grouped Identifying emerging categories that comprise the identified themes

3. Organizing the predetermined categories: Looking for themes that comprise each of the categories Arranging the themes within each category in a logical order Ordering the categories according to how they relate to each other	**3. Organizing the emerging categories:** Reflecting how the themes within each category relate to each other Arranging the themes within each category in a logical order Ordering the categories according to how they relate to each other

4. Recording the categories and adding quotations that represent each category	**4. Recording the categories and adding quotations that represent each category**

FIGURE 7.4. The process of using predetermined and emerging categories to analyze data.

four major categories: (1) teaching values through discipline content; (2) teaching values through relationships; (3) teaching values through classroom management; and (4) relating classroom discussion to familial, cultural, and political life outside of school.

The new major categories may enhance your ability to identify patterns within the data. To discover the patterns, we suggest that you examine how the categories are related to each other in terms of the following domains: context, frequency, sequence, cause and effect, and rationality. Throughout the process, be mindful of your research questions. For example, Sharon and her committee, who examine how values are taught through social studies and literature classes, realize that there is a pattern that connects the four major categories that the group identified. The pattern is the influence of the teachers' personal beliefs and of the values of the community on how moral values are taught in class. Another example is the study by Jesse as he examines the categories that he formed around the question "How should I manage my classroom environment?" Jesse realizes that there is a pattern that appears among the different categories that emerged in the data analysis phase: Good behavior is a result of discipline that is either enforced from outside or is emerging from within.

Some of the questions in Table 7.1 (Hatch, 2002; Spradley, 1979) may facilitate the pattern-seeking process and help highlight the relationships between two

TABLE 7.1. An Example of Domains and Questions for the Pattern-Seeking Process

Domains	Questions
Context	• What are the contexts in which the categories are embedded? • What are the conditions that give rise to these categories? • How do issues of race, ethnicity, gender, and ability impact the categories?
Frequency	• How often do particular things occur? • Do certain things happen more often than others?
Sequence	• In what order do things occur? • Do things happen in sequence? What is it? • Which situations, actions, or behaviors happen first? At the same time?
Cause and effect	• What are the possible causes for what happened? • What are the possible consequences or outcomes?
Rationality	• What are the reasons for the occurrence? • How is the occurrence explained by participants?

or more categories. Keep in mind that this is not an exhaustive or prescriptive list of domains or questions; you should adapt the list to your own research.

Creating a Concept Map

You may find that making a visual representation of the categories will help you in the pattern-seeking process (Miles & Huberman, 1994; Stringer, 2007). Doing so allows you to cluster them differently and to consider the interconnections among them. It also helps you visualize how the categories and patterns are related to your research question(s). Finally, like an outline, the visual device assists in writing up your findings and interpretation and communicating these to others.

There are different types of visual displays of categories including concept maps, diagrams, hierarchical trees, and flowcharts. To allow the patterns and links to emerge, write your research question(s) and use lines, arrows, and shapes to show how the categories and subcategories are related to each other. (See examples of concept maps in Figures 7.5 and 7.6.) To facilitate this process, we suggest using the statements and tables you drafted previously to describe the categories and subcategories (see Figure 7.2). Record your hunches about the emerging patterns. These notes can form the basis for generating your research findings, explanations, and tentative conclusions.

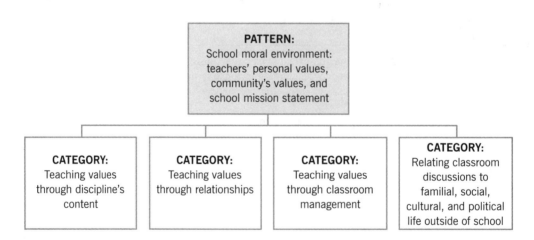

FIGURE 7.5. An example of a concept map created by Sharon and her committee while exploring how values are taught during literature and social studies classes.

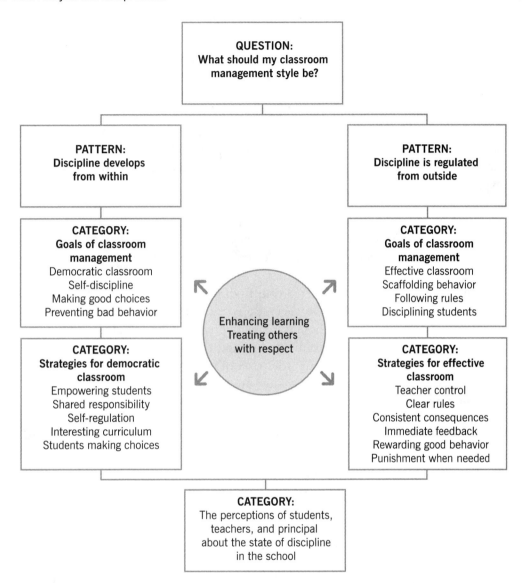

FIGURE 7.6. An example of a concept map created by Jesse in his investigation of classroom management styles.

Supporting the Findings with Evidence

Now, go back to and comb the data to test your hunches. Check your patterns against the data and seek segments in the transcript that may serve as evidence to support your insights and explanations. *Evidence* means that many segments in the data support your insight and a plausible alternative interpretation cannot be found (Hatch, 2002). This process requires moving back and forth between the categories, patterns, and data for confirmation or repudiation of your assertions. Remember, your hunches become trustworthy research findings or meaningful explanations only if the data support them.

Next, use your patterns and insights to formulate your findings and to generate answers to your research questions. The patterns may suggest plausible explanations and conclusions about your research questions. They may also guide you in considering future actions based on lessons learned from the study (Corbin & Strauss, 2007).

Finally, after you have supported your findings with the data, draft statements that summarize what you have learned as a result of the analysis process (Hatch, 2002; H. F. Wolcott, 2008). These statements present your overall interpretation and holistic understanding of your findings and their significance for your practice. They also serve as the basis for your overall story, impose order and structure on your account of the meanings you have drawn from your study, and enable you to communicate your insights and new knowledge to others.

Validating the Interpretation

Keep in mind that there is no one right or best way to arrive at the study's conclusions. Moreover, your aim in the analysis process is not to produce definitive results nor prove anything. Qualitative data analysis is not set up for that purpose; rather it is a personal process that allows subjective and tentative interpretation. However, being subjective does not mean being less rigorous or settling for findings that are not trustworthy or valid (Marshall & Rossman, 2011). You should critically examine your assertions and interpretation to ensure their credibility. Here are some strategies that may allow you to do this.

Searching for Alternative Interpretations

You ensure the trustworthiness of your findings by searching the data for discrepancies and counterevidence that may refute your assertions or provide alternative interpretations (Gibson & Brown, 2009). For example, let's look again at Jesse, the student teacher, whose research focused on classroom management. As he returned to his data looking for support for the patterns he identified, Jesse realized that the teachers and students he interviewed overwhelmingly named disrespect among the students and toward their teachers as a major problem in the school. To his surprise, the principal, on the other hand, did not mention this phenomenon even once. Jesse has to explore the reasons for this discrepancy. He considers several possible explanations: (1) although the students and teachers are routinely disrespectful toward each other, they are respectful toward the principal; (2) the principal has a different perception of what constitutes disrespectful behavior; or (3) the principal is overwhelmed with other concerns, such as declining test scores, inadequate school funding, or issues related to school safety. Similarly, if your findings are supported by your data but there are still some discrepancies, you should point to the inconsistencies and offer possible reasons without providing a definitive explanation.

Triangulating the Findings

You may want to triangulate different data sources to validate the accuracy of your patterns and findings. To corroborate your intuitive insights, cross-check different sources, situations, or points of view to see if the same patterns keep occurring (Hendricks, 2012; Lincoln & Guba, 1985). For example, after constructing his concept map, Jesse has a hunch that teachers' trust in their ability to influence students' behavior leads to a classroom management approach that is based on students' internal control rather than fear of external consequences. To confirm his hunch he returns to the data to verify whether these ideas were expressed by different participants.

Contextualizing the Findings within a Theoretical Framework

Another strategy is to link the findings to a theoretical framework. Interpret your assertions and explanations in the context of theories and research discussed in your literature review. This lends support and depth to your interpretation (Marshall & Rossman, 2011; Richards, 2009). Thus, Jesse, for example, interprets his own findings about different classroom management styles used by the teachers in his school within the context of different theoretical approaches reported in the literature.

Practicing Self-Reflexivity

Another way to lend trustworthiness to your interpretation is to practice reflexivity and openly discuss how your personal experience, biases, and subjective judgment shape your interpretations. You need to ensure that your interpretations are drawn from participants' words, behaviors, and interactions, rather than from your own personal beliefs and biases (Glesne, 2010; Rallis & Rossman, 2012). For example, Jesse deeply believes in democratic classroom management style. However, when interpreting the different styles of the teachers in the school, he consistently reminds himself to present and analyze the teachers' perspectives without judging them or projecting his own values.

Presentation of Data Analysis and Interpretation

Through the process of analysis and interpretation you have constructed meaning and newly gained knowledge out of the raw data that you have collected. All that remains now is to put into words your findings and their implications. For many, writing is an anxiety-provoking task. However, through the analysis and interpretation processes you may have already created a visual presentation of the categories and patterns that can easily be transformed into an outline for your final report. Additionally, you have drafted general statements that represent what you have learned as a result of the analysis. Together, the visual presentation and the general statements serve as the basis for your written report. To complete the process, from the excerpts you identified before, choose those that best represent and support your assertions.

In the following sections we offer some practical tips and helpful hints for proceeding with the writing process. Our suggestions are focused on reporting on the analysis process and the research findings and their meaning. As always, we suggest that you adapt these suggestions to your own personal needs, research focus, and writing style.

Reporting on the Analysis Process

You may begin writing your report on the analysis and interpretation section by describing the methods of analysis you have used (Marshall & Rossman, 2011). You want to demonstrate how these strategies involved multiple sources and multiple perspectives and how you dealt with your own research biases. You also want to show that these strategies lead to accurate and trustworthy findings. Additionally, we recommend that you report whether you used a computer software program and, if so, how it was used.

You may want to end this section by outlining the themes, categories, and patterns you have identified as a result of the analysis. This is also a place where you can display the visual formats you have developed to illustrate how you analyzed the data.

Reporting the Findings and Their Meanings

There are different formats for presenting your findings. The most common are the thematic format and the chronological format (McMillan & Schumacher, 2010).

Using a Thematic Format

In this format, research findings are organized thematically around the categories, themes, and patterns that were identified. The action researcher may start with an advanced organizer that outlines the major themes that emerged from the data and explain how each finding is supported by excerpts from the data. For each finding, start by introducing the theme, followed by a presentation of the chosen quotation(s) as evidence, and ending with an explanation of the meaning of the quotations. The study of classroom management conducted by Jesse and the study of teaching values in literature and social studies are both examples of the thematic format.

Using a Chronological Format

In this format, the findings are organized around a chronological description of the investigated topic. The action researcher starts with a description of the broader context of the study and then narrows the focus to specific events or actions that are at the heart of the investigation. For example, Nora, a third-grade teacher in an inner-city school wants to strengthen her relationships with parents and encourage them to be more involved in their children's learning. She institutes several strategies of ongoing communication, home visits, and an open invitation for face-to-face conversation. For 6 weeks Nora records the implementation of these strategies and their impact on parents' involvement. In reporting her findings, she first describes the school and classroom contexts. Then, chronologically, she relates the strategies that she implemented to promote stronger relationships and the gradual changes that occurred.

Choosing a Style of Writing

In writing your report, you may want to consider the style of writing you will use (H. F. Wolcott, 2008). Typically, action researchers report their findings in the third person. Some practitioners, though, prefer a narrative that is told from their own personal perspective. These writers share their challenges, discoveries, failures, and epiphanies during the process of analysis and interpretation. This personal style of writing is most appropriate when the practitioners are interested in illuminating significant insights about their experience in educational settings and about themselves as educators. The danger is that with this format the researcher may become self-indulgent and focus more on the self than on the issue being investigated. If you are interested in this style of narrative, you need to work hard to balance the personal and the professional. For example, Antonio, a middle school counselor, conducts research on the phenomenon of bullying in his school. In reporting his findings he reveals how saddened he was by the impact of cyberbullying on several students. In his report he reveals, "I felt extremely angry thinking about the shame and helplessness these students must feel. I visualized Simona finding out, to her horror, the vicious rumors about her that were posted for everyone to read. What can I do to remedy the situation?"

Your choice of writing style and format for your report derives from the nature of your study and your own personal preference. Nonetheless, in qualitative research, certain elements are essential. Dominant among them are providing a "thick" description that is rich, detailed, and concrete. Quoting participants' voices also contributes to the readers' sense of being present in the setting.

Using a "Thick" Description

Qualitative research reporting of the analysis outcome depends on rich, detailed description. Your vivid narrative should make the setting come alive, the participants seem familiar, and their emotions understood. The "thick"—textured and detailed —descriptions should allow the reader to see, hear, and feel what you saw, heard, and felt during the data collection, analysis, and interpretation (Patton, 2002; H. F. Wolcott, 2008). Therefore, you don't state that "The students misbehaved in class," rather, vividly illustrate how their destructive behavior manifested itself. For example, "The students whispered to each other, clearly not paying attention to the teacher. Samantha was giggling out loud as she was reading a note sent to her by a classmate. While the teacher was writing on the board with her back to the students, the class was in chaos!"

Quoting the Participants' Voices

It is important in qualitative action research to allow participants' voices to come through clearly. Use participants' words and expressions, as well as dialects and slang. If there are diverse participants in your study, make sure you represent the range of voices (Patton, 2002; H. F. Wolcott, 2008). Quotes may be a few significant words, short sentences, paragraphs, or even a dialogue. For example, on the basis of the findings from his study on classroom management, Jesse asserts that in some cases external rewards for good behavior can encourage students to follow the teacher's instruction for the wrong reasons. To provide support for his claim, Jesse chooses to include the following dialogue between two fourth-grade male students (with the initials of N and T), who are working on worksheets:

STUDENT N: Why are you not paying attention?

STUDENT T: I hate this boring handout.

STUDENT N: Because of you, we will not have the extra 10 minutes for recess that Ms. Marvell promised us.

STUDENT T: Ms. Marvell is bribing us, but she can't buy me off ...

STUDENT N: Don't be stupid. Just behave as if you are working on the handout. In 8 minutes the bell will ring and it will be all over.

The participants' voices constitute your study data. Nevertheless, data do not speak for themselves and quotes that are strung together without any explanation are meaningless. You need to make the connection between the quotes and your interpretive comments and show how the quotes support your claims.

At the end of your interpretation and data analysis section you present the conclusions of your study. This section is similar in all three research approaches: qualitative, quantitative, and mixed-methods. Therefore, we present suggestions for writing this section at the end of this chapter.

Figure 7.7 illustrates the different steps in qualitative data analysis. Step 1 is the preparation for data analysis, Step 2 highlights the two alternatives for data analysis—using predetermined or emerging categories, Step 3 is the synthesis and interpretation of the data, and Step 4 is the presentation of data analysis and interpretation.

Figure 7.8 provides a checklist with suggested questions that you can use for the analysis and interpretation of qualitative data.

STEP 1: PREPARATION FOR DATA ANALYSIS

Transcribing data

Organizing data into (computer) files

Creating a data file organizer

Immersing in the data to get a sense of the whole

STEP 2: ANALYSIS OF THE DATA: PREDETERMINED CATEGORIES

Identifying the predetermined categories

Finding segments in the data that fit each category

Looking for themes within each category

Arranging the categories and themes in a logical order

Recording the categories and selecting quotes that illustrate their essence

---

STEP 2: ANALYSIS OF THE DATA: EMERGING CATEGORIES

Generating topics from the data and assigning them codes

Organizing quotes with similar content into categories

Ensuring congruency between data and category

Arranging topics logically within each category

Recording the categories and selecting quotes that illustrate their essence

---

STEP 3: SYNTHESIS AND INTERPRETATION OF DATA

Identifying patterns in the data by finding relationships among categories

Creating a visual display of the categories and patterns

Formulating findings and supporting them with evidence from the data

Validating the findings

STEP 4: PRESENTATION OF DATA ANALYSIS AND INTERPRETATION

Reporting the analysis process

Reporting the findings and their meaning

Choosing the format and style of writing

FIGURE 7.7. The process of qualitative data analysis, synthesis, presentation, and interpretation.

✓	Feedback Checklist for Reviewing the Analysis and Interpretation of Qualitative Data	Comments
	1. Are the procedures for data analysis clearly and explicitly outlined?	
	2. Is the analysis logically and systematically developed?	
	3. Are the analysis and interpretation processes linked to the research question(s)?	
	4. Did the analysis and interpretation include a description of the search for patterns and relationships within and across categories?	
	5. Is it stated whether computer software was used to assist with the data analysis?	
	6. Are there other visual displays that could enhance understanding of the data analysis and interpretation?	
	7. Are issues of validity and trustworthiness directly addressed?	
	8. Are the subjectivity, preconceptions, and biases of the action researcher recognized?	
	9. Is there a rich description of the people, places, and events involved in the study?	
	10. Can the reader get a holistic understanding of the meaning of the data from the narrative description of the findings?	
	11. Are multiple perspectives offered?	
	12. Are the participants' words and statements quoted? Are the contexts and meanings of the quotations offered?	
	13. Are interpretations supported by appropriate excerpts from the data?	
	14. Are the findings linked or compared to theory and research discussed in the literature review?	
	15. Are the interpretations logically structured and the findings systematically presented?	

FIGURE 7.8. A checklist for reviewing the analysis and interpretation of qualitative data.

QUANTITATIVE DATA ANALYSIS

The goal of quantitative data analysis is to answer research questions posed before the start of the study. Many studies are also conducted to test hypotheses; statistical tests are applied to the data collected to determine whether the hypotheses can be supported. Statistical procedures can help you further reflect on and study your numerical findings by looking for trends, presenting the data visually, studying relationships between variables, and comparing groups on selected characteristics. The decision as to which statistical test you will use in a given situation is determined by your research question and the type of data that you have collected.

In many ways, analyzing quantitative data is easier than qualitative data. Most researchers can agree on the types of statistical tests that should be used to analyze numerical data. For example, if both you and your colleague want to study the relationship between your students' scores on two tests, you would probably agree on a correlation procedure. If you analyze the same data, you also should come up with the same results and interpret your findings in the same way. There is no subjectivity or personal interpretation in this process. Quantitative data analysis is also made easier by the availability and ease of use of computer software programs (such as Excel). These computer software programs can help you organize, graph, and analyze your data.

Quantitative research, in contrast to qualitative research, is mostly a deductive process. This means that you start with a general principle or premise and proceed to a specific conclusion (McMillan & Schumacher, 2010). Stated in another way, we can state that "If X (a more general rule or theory) is true, then we can expect Y (a more specific case or phenomenon) to be true as well." Let's say, for example, that you believe in the theory of behaviorism and in the idea that rewarding students will have a positive effect on their behavior. You may put this into practice in your classroom management. For instance, you can try to reduce the disruptive off-task behavior of Mark, one of your students, by promising him some sort of reward (such as points for a pizza party or extra time for recess) for his on-task behavior.

The numerical data that you collect are likely to be a series of numbers that are not ordered or summarized. To let patterns emerge, start by exploring your data. Your first step is to examine each of the variables, then proceed to studying the relationships among the variables (Moore, 2009). To do this you will need to prepare your data for analysis. This process may involve coding data, labeling variables, sorting the data, and using a computer program or another aid to organize the data.

The discussion that follows begins with suggestions for *entering, organizing, graphing*, and *tabulating* data, followed by procedures for describing distributions by examining their *centers* and *spread*. We continue with measures of *association* between variables and conclude with approaches to studying *differences* between groups or means. In discussing these approaches to quantitative data analysis, we define each concept, explain its use, and give an example to illustrate how it can be applied. The following steps are explained:

1. Entering, organizing, graphing, and tabulating data
2. Computing measures of distribution centers
3. Computing measures of distribution variability
4. Analyzing the data
5. Evaluating the statistical findings
6. Presenting the findings

In the discussion that follows, we start by offering suggestions for preparing your data for analysis, focusing on some of the most popular and practical techniques and statistical tests for analyzing quantitative data. Clearly, though, presenting *all* the statistical tests and approaches that can be used by researchers to create and analyze quantitative data is beyond the scope of this book. Your role as an action researcher is to choose and apply the right methods to analyze your numerical data and to interpret your findings appropriately.

Entering, Organizing, Graphing, and Tabulating Data

Coding and Entering Data in Preparation for Data Analysis

After collecting your data, you need to prepare for data analysis. In most cases, you start this process by inspecting the data you collected to determine whether you need to code any variables, assign them a numerical value, or compute new variables. For example, let's say that you want to analyze results from a survey measuring students' attitudes toward school. The survey includes eight items with response choices ranging from strongly disagree (1 point) to strongly agree (4 points). After entering your data into a spreadsheet, check and verify that you entered the data correctly and that all the information is complete and accurate. You may want to compare the data in your spreadsheet to the raw data you collected, noting any numbers that are out of range (e.g., a score of 7 on a Likert scale question with four response choices), missing data, or any other irregularities.

Creating Frequency Distributions

When you order and tally the scores, you create a *frequency distribution* (Ravid, 2011). For example, Larry, a seventh-grade math teacher, investigates a new teaching strategy and as part of his investigation, he wants to examine his students' test scores. After finishing the new math unit, Larry's 36 students take a test. Larry then creates a frequency distribution (see Table 7.2).

Graphing Data

Following are some ways you can graph your data. Keep in mind that, although there are many graphs readily available to you that are easy to create, you still need to choose the most appropriate graph to present your particular data.

Using the frequency distribution of his students' test scores, Larry can examine their performance in relation to each other and assign grades. The frequency distribution will also allow him to focus on specific students who are of concern to him. Displaying the test scores graphically would also be helpful for Larry. Two graphs may be used to depict frequency distributions: *histogram* and *frequency polygon*. A histogram is a series of bars, each representing a score or group of scores. A frequency polygon is used to display similar data using a line that connects the different data points. When there are many scores in the distribution, the polygon usually gets smoother and resembles a bell shape.

TABLE 7.2. A Frequency Distribution of Larry's Students' Math Test Scores

Test scores	Frequency	Test scores	Frequency
12	1	25	2
17	1	26	1
20	1	27	4
21	1	28	6
22	2	29	9
23	3	30	2
24	3		

Larry chooses a histogram to display the scores of his students on the math test. Inspecting the graph (Figure 7.9), Larry can see that there are slightly more students at the upper end of the distribution, which is to be expected, because the test was given right after finishing the unit, when most students knew the material. The graph also shows that there are two students with low scores.

Larry is mostly concerned about his two lowest-scoring students, Mike and Shannon. Mike, who obtained a score of 12, is an ELL student, who joined the class at the beginning of the year. Shannon, whose score was 17, is a B student who usually gets average scores on math tests. However, she missed several classes prior to taking the test due to illness. To better understand the reasons for some of his students' lower-than-average scores, Larry can examine which questions were missed by Mike and Shannon and plan his instruction accordingly. Additionally, Larry may want to examine the test questions to determine why more students did not obtain high scores on the test, because usually the number of students who get all or almost all the items correct is higher.

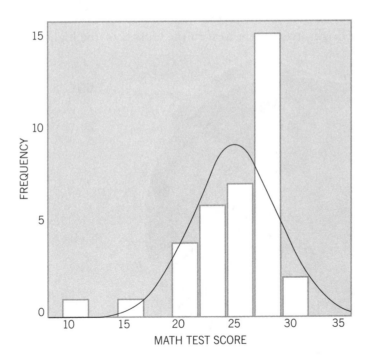

FIGURE 7.9. A histogram showing Larry's students' math scores.

Another graph you may use to display your data is the *pie graph*. The pie graph is a circle divided into wedges in which each wedge represents a certain defined category or subgroup (Ravid, 2011), and the size of the wedges indicates which one represents the largest group or set of data. The pie graph is an effective tool to display segments of data that add up to 100%. For example, Dr. Mayer, the principal of Jefferson High School, wants to examine how well her high school prepares students for college. As part of her action research, she conducts a survey of the students regarding their postsecondary plans. She found that 41% of the students plan to go to public universities, 23% plan to go to private universities, 18% plan to go to community colleges, 9% of the students indicated that they do not plan to go to college, and 9% were unsure of their plans. Dr. Mayer constructed a pie graph to depict her findings (see Figure 7.10). Using the findings depicted in the pie chart, she decides to focus on the students who do not plan to go to college or those who are unsure of their plans so that the school can provide them guidance in making informed choices about their future plans.

Another choice for you to display numerical findings is a *bar graph*. It comprises a series of bars that do not touch (unlike the histogram that is used for data on a continuum, where the bars do touch). The bars represent discrete data and are organized by height (from the lowest to the highest or the highest to the lowest).

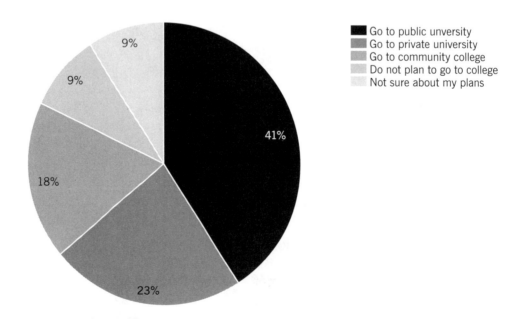

FIGURE 7.10. A pie graph showing students' postsecondary plans.

For example, Ron, the librarian of a middle school, and the school library committee, which includes other teachers and parents, decide to investigate the types of books read by the students. They also want to examine the choice of books by gender. Ron and the committee plan to use this information to decide which books to purchase in the future. They also plan to use this information to find ways to encourage students to expand their choices. Using the library book checkout information, the committee creates a joint bar graph (Figure 7.11). Depicting the information by gender allows the committee to further understand students' reading choices.

Now Ron and the library committee can examine the students' reading habits and preferences and decide whether they need to plan activities to encourage students to expand their reading choices. They can also determine whether the library's current holdings match the students' reading preferences.

The *line graph* is another available option when you want to show your data visually. It consists of one or more horizontal lines that can be used to show trends or progression over time. The graph has two axes: the *vertical* axis is used to show data points on the variable being measured, such as test scores; the *horizontal* axis is used for data that are on a continuum, such as age and calendar years. For example, Lorna, a science coordinator in the district, wants to evaluate the new curriculum that her district implemented last year. As part of her action research, she compares science test scores of fifth-grade students in the three schools in the district over the last 4 years. After tabulating the numerical results, Lorna graphs the data to get a better picture of the trends in students' performance over time (see Figure 7.12).

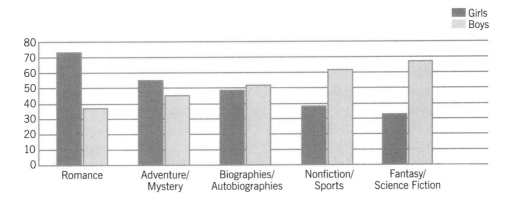

FIGURE 7.11. A joint bar graph showing the comparison of book genres read by middle school girls and boys during the academic year.

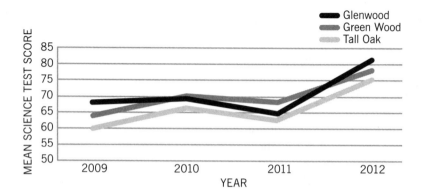

FIGURE 7.12. Line graph showing science test scores of three schools, 2009–2012.

Inspecting the graph, Lorna is gratified to see a clear gain in students' science scores between 2011 and 2012 in the three schools. This may indicate that the new curriculum, implemented in 2011, is effective. Of course, other factors may have contributed to the increase in students' science test scores. These include changes in instructional practices, a growing emphasis on science education, and implementation of enrichment programs in the district.

Remember that although it's true that a "picture is worth a thousand words," graphs rarely speak for themselves (Pearson, 2010). Additional information, such as narrative explanation and interpretation of the graphs, as well as other statistical information, present a more complete story.

Tabulating Data

Another way to organize and display data is to tally and summarize them into cross-tabulation tables (also called *crosstab* tables). Individual responses are recorded, added up, and presented as raw numbers or percentages. For example, if you administer a survey with four response choices (*strongly agree, agree, disagree,* and *strongly disagree*), you can record the questions as your rows and the responses as your columns. To illustrate, let's look at a study conducted by Jeanette, a high school geometry teacher. Jeanette is trying to implement more group work in her teaching and decides to have her students spend half of each class working in mixed-ability groups. After a month, Jeanette uses a 15-item survey to assess her students' attitudes toward working in groups. Table 7.3 shows the responses of her 37 students on the first four questions of the survey. This table

TABLE 7.3. Partial Results from the Survey Administered by Jeanette to Measure Her Students' Attitudes toward Working in Groups

Question	Strongly agree		Agree		Disagree		Strongly disagree	
	n	%	n	%	n	%	n	%
1. I like working in groups.	21	57	5	14	6	16	5	14
2. I prefer working by myself.	1	3	4	11	23	62	9	24
3. I learn better when I work with my group.	22	59	7	19	6	16	2	5
4. It is fun helping each other learn while working in groups.	24	65	8	22	4	11	1	3

Note. n = 37.

summarizes the individual responses of Jeanette's students in raw numbers and in percentages, so she can more easily determine her students' attitudes toward this instructional approach.

Inspecting the responses of her students, Jeanette can see that the majority support working in groups. She also can see that there are a few students who do not like working in groups, preferring to work by themselves. She may want to find out why those students do not like working in groups and modify her teaching to accommodate these students.

Computing Measures of Distribution Centers

Besides depicting your data visually using graphs, you can also study your data by computing measures of central tendency. These measures can be viewed as typical scores that are used to represent and summarize a set of scores. There are three such measures that are most frequently used in education: *mode, median,* and *mean* (Coladarci, Cobb, Minium, & Clarke, 2010).

Mode

The *mode* is the score that occurs with the greatest frequency in a set of scores. You can use it with any type of data. To find the mode, you first have to tally the scores in order to determine which score(s) occur with the greatest frequency. The mode is used for descriptive purposes only and is much less useful than the median and the mean.

Median

The *median* is the score or point that divides the set of scores into the top 50% and the bottom 50%. To be able to compute the median, you need to first rank order all the scores and then find their midpoint.

Mean

The *mean*, also known as the arithmetic mean, is calculated by adding up the scores and dividing the sum by the number of scores. The mean is by far the most commonly used measure of central tendency and the one that you are probably most familiar with. You can use means to describe sets of scores and to compare two or more distributions of scores, such as the performance of two classes on the same test, or pretest and posttest scores of students on some test or survey.

To illustrate the use of mode, median, and mean, let's use the spelling test scores obtained by seven students in Blake's special education class: 9, 13, 5, 14, 10, 6, and 14 (see Figure 7.13). Although Blake does not need to order the scores in order to find the mode and the mean, it is necessary to do so in order to find the median. Therefore, Blake's first step is to order the scores.

The mode of the spelling scores is 14, because there are two scores with the value of 14; no other score repeats more than one time. The median is 10; there are three scores above it and three below it. To calculate the mean, Blake needs to add up all the scores and divide the sum by 7, the number of scores. Blake finds that the sum of the scores is 71; dividing it by 7 gives him a mean of 10.14.

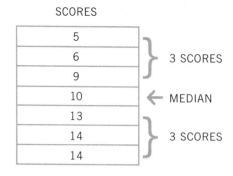

FIGURE 7.13. Distribution of seven test scores.

Outliers

Even though the mean is the most commonly used measure of a central tendency, it may provide misleading information when it is calculated for a set of scores that includes outliers. *Outliers* are extreme scores—either very high or very low—that are outside the distribution of the rest of the scores and thus they are viewed as special cases that need attention (Fraenkel et al., 2011). For example, suppose we use the same set of scores as that in Figure 7.13 from Blake's class, but change the last score from 14 to 50. The sum of the scores will be 109 and the mean will be 15.57. This new mean is higher than six of the seven scores and clearly cannot serve as their representative score. The effect of outliers can also be seen in an index that we are all familiar with in everyday life. As we all know, the "average" housing prices and salaries are reported as medians, not means (Mertler & Charles, 2011). This is done for the same reason as discussed above, namely, there are outliers in salaries and housing prices and if the mean is used, it would provide inaccurate information.

Thus, different measures of a central tendency each have advantages and disadvantages (Triola, 2006). Remember that while the mode, median, and mean provide summary information about a group of scores, these measures do not reveal information about the performance of individual students *within* that group. For example, although Blake knows the mean of his students on the test, this mean does not provide him specific information about the performance of particular students in the class.

Computing Measures of Distribution Variability

In addition to describing the center of a distribution of scores, it is also helpful to be able to describe the spread (i.e., variability or dispersion) of the scores. For example, let's say that two eighth-grade classes—Joey's and Elena's classes—took the same Constitution test. Both classes had the same mean on the test, but, as you can see in Figure 7.14, Joey's class has a wider range of scores. When combined with the mean, a measure of spread would allow us to better describe the scores.

Range

The *range* is the distance between the highest and lowest score; it is the simplest measure of spread, and the easiest to calculate and understand. In the set of scores of Blake's students (in Figure 7.13), the range is 9 (14 − 5 = 9). You must remember,

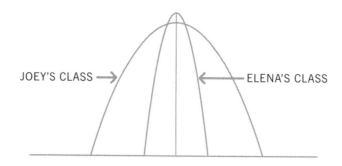

FIGURE 7.14. A graph showing scores from the classes taught by Joey and Elena.

though, that the range can be misleading because it does not provide information about the scores *within* the distribution. If the students in Blake's class had the scores of 5, 12, 13, 13, 13, 14, and 14, the range would have been the same as the range of scores in Figure 7.13. As was the case with the mean, extreme high or low scores can also inflate and skew the range.

Standard Deviation

The *standard deviation* indicates the average (i.e., the mean) distance of scores around their mean. Some scores are above the mean and some are below the mean; some are close to the mean and some are farther away from the mean. The standard deviation can be conceptualized as the average of all these distances. Because the standard deviation is an average (i.e., mean) of all the distances, extreme scores would inflate the standard deviation (Ravid, 2011). For instance, when the same test is taken by two classes with a similar number of students, and one class has a higher standard deviation on the test, it shows that there is a greater spread of scores in the class with the higher standard deviation compared with the other class with the smaller standard deviation.

As an example, Alice, a language arts teacher, believes that her morning class has a greater diversity of learning styles, ability levels, and needs compared with her afternoon class. Before starting a new unit, Alice administers the unit's pretest to her two classes and computes the means and standard deviations of both classes on this test. She finds that the standard deviation of her morning class is higher than that of her afternoon class although the means of both classes are very similar. This confirms that indeed there is greater variability in the scores between her classes. (Alice may also want to create a histogram to help her get a better visual picture of her students' test scores.) Alice decides to incorporate into her teaching additional strategies that will accommodate different learning styles and needs with a focus on her low-scoring students. At the end of the unit, Alice administers the posttest to both classes and examines the scores to determine the effect of her new teaching strategies. A smaller standard deviation in the scores of her morning class resulting from higher scores by her lower-ability students would indicate that her new teaching strategies are effective. Of course, Alice expects both classes to have a higher mean on the posttest compared with the pretest to indicate growth and increased knowledge by all students.

Analyzing the Data

In this section we introduce you to two main approaches to analyzing numerical data. The first focuses on measuring *association and relationship between variables*; the second explains how to analyze *differences between means or groups*.

Measures of Association

Correlation

To measure the relationship or association between two or more pairs of quantitative variables we use a statistical test called *correlation*. An example would be a study to investigate the correlation between students' scores on a teacher-made test and a standardized test or between students' achievement and motivation. Remember that correlation does not imply causation; the fact that two variables correlate does not mean that one *caused* the other. To compute the correlation, you would need to have two scores for each student.

Correlation Coefficient

The extent of the correlation and its direction (positive or negative) are expressed by a *correlation coefficient*, which can range from –1.00 (perfect negative) to 0.00 (no correlation) to +1.00 (perfect positive). The most commonly used correlation was developed by Pearson and the symbol used for the coefficient is *r*. A *positive* correlation means that *high* values in one variable are associated with *high* values in the other variable; a *negative* correlation implies inverted relationships in which *high* values in one variable are associated with *low* values in the other variable

(Moore, McCabe, & Craig, 2010). Correlations closer to 0.00 are defined as very low or negligible.

Keep in mind that a high negative correlation shows stronger association between the variables compared with a lower positive correlation. Figure 7.15 shows how to assess the correlation coefficient.

For example, using this chart, a correlation of $r = .75$ would be considered high positive, whereas a correlation of $r = -.20$ would be defined as low negative.

To illustrate the use of correlation, let's examine a study conducted by Simone, a third-grade teacher. Simone wants to study the relationship between her students' homework completion rate and their scores on a math test administered by the district to all third-grade students at the end of the first semester. She correlates students' homework completion rate and their math scores on the district test using Pearson correlation and obtains a correlation coefficient of $r = .65$. This is considered a moderate-to-high correlation. What can Simone conclude about the relationship between her students' homework completion rate and their performance on the district math test? Although there is a positive relationship between the two measures, it is not necessarily a *causal* relationship. In other words, Simone cannot be sure that students who complete their homework regularly would score higher on the district test, or, alternatively, that increasing students' math test scores will increase their homework completion rate. Only an experimental study can document causal relationship between these two variables.

Scattergram

Correlation can be depicted visually with the use of a *scattergram* (also called a *scatterplot*). Each dot on the scattergram represents the intersection of the two scores for each student. The pattern of the dots and their direction can indicate the strength of the correlation (high, moderate, low, or negligible) and whether it

Perfect Negative			No Correlation			Perfect Positive
−1.00 −.66	−.33	.00	+.33	+.66	+1.00	
	High Negative	Moderate Negative	Low Negative	Low Positive	Moderate Positive	High Positive	

FIGURE 7.15. Guidelines for interpreting correlation coefficients.

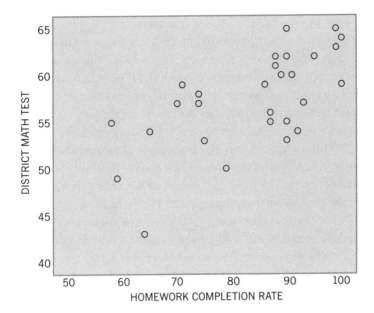

FIGURE 7.16. A scattergram depicting the relationship between students' homework completion rate and their scores on a district math test.

is positive or negative. Figure 7.16 shows a scattergram depicting the relationship between Simone's students' homework completion rate and their scores on the district math test.

Measures of Differences

Many research studies are conducted to compare two or more means to see if they are different. Here we discuss two such commonly used tests: (1) *t*-test that is used to analyze two means, and (2) analysis of variance (ANOVA) that is used to analyze two or more means.

t-Test

The *t-test* is used to compare two mean values to determine if they are different (McMillan & Schumacher, 2010). The test statistic that is computed is called the *t* value. Following is a brief discussion of the two often-used types of *t*-test: independent samples *t*-test and paired samples *t*-test.

The *t-test for independent samples* is used when the two means being compared come from two separate groups, such as boys and girls, or experimental and control group. The difference between the two means, as well as the groups' standard deviations and size (number of people), all play a role in the computation of the *t* value. For example, Nelson, a second-grade teacher of ELLs wants to test the efficacy of a new and creative way to teach vocabulary to his students. This new approach uses educational software that demonstrates the vocabulary words with the help of visuals (e.g., pictures, cartoons, and videos). Nelson is testing this new approach by teaching the traditional district curriculum for one of his classes for 4 weeks, while using the new approach in his other second-grade class. Nelson tests the two groups of students prior to the start of the study to ensure that the two groups are comparable in terms of their vocabulary knowledge. Students in both classes are tested at the end of the 4-week study. Nelson uses a *t*-test for independent samples to compare the vocabulary test scores from the two groups. If the mean score of students in the first group using the new teaching approach is higher, this higher score would provide evidence for the advantage of using visuals for teaching English vocabulary to ELL students.

The *t-test for paired samples* is used when the two means belong to the same group. An example would be pretest and posttest scores on the same or similar test obtained for the same students. For example, Halina, a middle school student teacher, wants to increase students' awareness of environment protection. As part of this effort, Halina shows students a video about the benefits of composting. Before and after viewing the video, Halina administers a questionnaire to students to assess their knowledge and willingness to participate in a composting program in school and at home. She uses a *t*-test for paired samples to compare students' scores on the questionnaire. A significant increase in students' scores would indicate the effectiveness of the video presentation.

Analysis of Variance

When researchers compare two or more means, a statistical test called *analysis of variance (ANOVA)* is used (McMillan, 2011). The test statistic computed in ANOVA is called the *F-ratio*. Similar to the *t* value, the *F*-ratio is also based on the means, standard deviations, and sample sizes. Computer programs can easily do the computations and provide the results for you. For example, let's say that Nelson, the ELL teacher mentioned above, wants to compare three instructional approaches to teach vocabulary: a traditional approach, an approach using visuals, and a combination of the two. Nelson teaches three different ELL second-grade classes and can use a different method in each class. The three classrooms are similar to each other in the level of student ability. After 4 weeks of using the three instructional methods, Nelson compares the vocabulary scores of the students in the three classes using ANOVA to ascertain which teaching approach resulted in higher student performance.

Evaluating the Statistical Findings

As an action researcher, you will analyze your data often for the purpose of *describing* existing conditions in the educational setting that you are studying. For example, if you test your students before and after implementing a new method, you can compute the means and standard deviations on the pretest and posttest or compare scores from a test, after using the new method, to typical test scores using the existing method. The difference between the two means will reveal whether your students performed better using the new approach. The standard deviation will provide a measure of dispersion; besides your desire to raise the scores of the whole group, you may want to *decrease* the standard deviation by raising the scores of the lower-ability students in your class. You can compare the two means—pretest and posttest—and decide whether the new method is effective. Or, let's say you want to know whether students' attendance is related to their reading test scores. You can use Pearson correlational analysis to study the relationship between these two variables (attendance and reading test scores). Examining the correlation coefficient can determine whether these two measures are related and the direction of the correlation (positive or negative).

When the numerical data are collected and the test statistic is computed, that statistic is evaluated to determine if it is *statistically* significant or could have happened by chance. Using the p value in such cases helps us determine the statistical significance of our results (Mertler, 2012). In most educational studies, researchers use a p value of .05 as a cutoff point in determining whether the results are statistically significant. If our p value is equal to or less than .05 ($p < .05$), the results are reported as statistically significant, which means that there is a 5% or less probability that the results were obtained purely by chance (Lauer, 2006).

Statistical Significance

In reading published research studies in which quantitative data were collected, you will often come across the concept of *statistical significance*, expressed as *probability*, or *p values*. This concept is used in studies that use samples to draw inferences about a population from which they were selected (Mertler & Charles, 2011). For example, Samira, the Assistant Superintendent, wants to survey parents about their attitudes toward extracurricular activities in the district, using a 5-point Likert scale. The district has a high number of parents, so she chooses a sample of 200 parents who represent all grade levels in the school and surveys them by phone. Next, she analyzes the results to determine parents' attitudes. In this example, the responses of the 200 parents she surveys are thought to represent the attitudes of *all* parents in the district, because her sample was carefully chosen to be representative of the entire parent population.)

Hypothesis Testing

As was discussed in Chapter 2, quantitative studies are often conducted to test hypotheses. Hypotheses are formalized predictions about the relationship between two or more variables (Slavin, 2007). There are two main types of hypotheses: *null* hypothesis and *alternative (research)* hypothesis (Schreiber & Anser-Self, 2011). The null hypothesis states that there would be no correlation between variables (when running a correlation analysis) or no difference between means (when conducting a *t*-test or ANOVA). For example, we can predict that there will be no statistically significant difference between the mean scores of girls and boys on our math test. The alternative hypothesis reflects the prediction of the researcher and states that there will be a significant correlation between variables (for correlational analysis) or that there will be a significant difference between the means (for *t*-test and ANOVA). For example, Antonio, the middle chool counselor, predicts that students will report fewer incidents of bullying after the implementation of an anti-bullying program in his school, compared with the number of incidences reported prior to program implementation. In other words, Antonio's research hypothesis is that the posttest mean will be lower than the pretest mean. The null hypothesis is that there will be no significant difference between the pretest and posttest means, or between the number of bullying incidents before and after the implementation of the anti-bullying program.

When $p < .05$, the null hypothesis is rejected, and we conclude that there is a statistically significant relationship, beyond what might be expected by chance alone, between the variables (in correlation) or a significant difference between the means (for a *t*-test or ANOVA).

For example, in our study above about the anti-bullying curriculum, we gathered pretest and posttest data before and after implementing the curriculum. We use a *t*-test for paired samples to compare the two means and use a computer program, such as Excel or SPSS, to calculate the *p* value (Abbott, 2011). Suppose we find that the *p* value is .009 ($p < .01$), which means that the differences between the pretest and posttest means could have happened by chance alone less than 1% of the time. We are fairly sure that the two means are indeed different from each other beyond what might be expected by chance alone.

When the p value is *higher* than .05 (written as $p > .05$), we *retain* the null hypothesis and conclude that the difference could have happened by chance more than 5% of the time. In such cases, the *alternative* hypothesis is not supported. For example, we may wish to correlate the math and science test scores of the students in our class. Using a computer program, we find that the correlation is low and the p value is higher than .05 ($p > .05$). Therefore, we have to retain the null hypothesis and conclude that there is no statistically significant correlation between math and science scores of our students beyond what might be observed purely by chance.

Practical Significance

Statistical significance should not be confused with *practical significance.* Just because the results are *statistically* significant, does not mean that they are *important* or *practically* significant. With large sample sizes, many correlations coefficients, t-values, or other statistical indexes are likely to be statistically significant. Conversely, with experimental studies using very small samples, the effect of the treatment may not be detected (Lauer, 2006). For example, a correlation of $r = .20$ would be reported as statistically significant ($p < .05$) when the sample size is 100, but it is still a low correlation that does not show a strong relationship between the two variables being correlated. Similarly, a gain of 2 points from pretest to posttest on a 50-item test might yield a statistically significant t-value ($p < .05$), but you will have to ask yourself if a gain of 2 points is sufficient or practically important. You, as the practitioner, will have to make this determination. Deciding about the *statistical* significance is simple and is usually done by computer programs, whereas the decision about the *practical* significance is more subjective (Mertler, 2012).

Effect Size

In experimental studies, in addition to reporting the statistical significance, researchers can also evaluate the practical significance of the intervention using an index called *effect size*. The effect size is a measure of the difference between the means of the experimental and control groups; higher effect sizes indicate larger effects of the treatment (Lauer, 2006). To compute the effect size in experimental studies, the difference in the means of the two groups is divided by the standard deviation of the control group (Slavin, 2007). Effect size is not affected by the sample size or the measures used to obtain the data and can be computed even if the results are not statistically significant (Ravid, 2011).

Remember, though, that conclusions based on numerical data are expressed in terms of probability, not certainty. As statisticians like to say, "In statistics, you never have to say you are certain. . . . "

Presenting the Findings

When you carry out quantitative studies, your findings are presented objectively and systematically in the results section. Some of your results are likely to be descriptive, such as the number of parents who came to a parent–teacher conference, or the number of students who agreed or strongly agreed with a certain statement on a survey. Your results may also be depicted visually. Therefore, tables and graphs are often found in this section.

The numerical results that you obtain may be used to answer your research questions or to test your hypotheses. For example, you may state that, as predicted, more parents came to parent–teacher conferences held in the evening compared with the number of parents who came to conferences held during the day. In another example, you may state that the hypothesis that predicted that the majority of students would disagree or strongly disagree with a particular statement was not confirmed. In writing this section, do not include any value judgments. For example, do not use words such as "I was disappointed to find out that. . . . "; or "We were pleased to see that the findings supported all our hypotheses." Such statements may be included in the discussion section, but not in the results section.

When presenting tables and graphs, or embedding statistical results in the narrative, make sure your writing is clear and easy to follow. It is always a good idea to "walk" the reader through your results and explain what they are and what they mean (Ravid, 2011). Make sure you refer in your writing to every table and graph, and that they are clearly identified and labeled. You are also expected to highlight patterns, trends, or other results that relate to your research questions and hypotheses. For example, Carina, a school board member, administers a 10-item survey to students in her school to measure their attitudes toward school uniforms. After collecting the data, she tabulates the results, broken down by gender and grade level. In her presentation of the data, she explains the structure of the tables that contain the results and points to differences or similarities between boys and girls and among the different grade levels.

Figure 7.17 provides a checklist with suggested questions that you can use for the analysis and interpretation of quantitative data.

✓	A Feedback Checklist for Reviewing the Analysis and Interpretation of Quantitative Data	Comments
	1. Are the procedures for data analysis clearly explained?	
	2. Is it stated whether and which computer software package was used to enter and analyze the data?	
	3. Are there codes or other means that were used to represent the numerical information when entering the data for analysis?	
	4. Were the data used for analysis proofed and checked to ensure their accuracy?	
	5. Were the data analysis procedures appropriately chosen to provide answers to the study's *research questions*?	
	6. Were the data analysis procedures appropriately chosen to provide information to test the study's *research hypotheses?*	
	7. Are the study's findings clearly presented in a way that is easy for others to understand?	
	8. Are the findings summarized and presented in tables or graphs? Are the tables and graphs clearly labeled?	
	9. Are references made to the tables and graphs in the narrative description of the results?	
	10. Does the narrative in the results section "walk" the reader through the findings, explaining the meaning and significance of each finding?	
	11. Is the interpretation of the findings justified based on the data that were collected?	
	12. Are the explanations of the results presented objectively and factually?	

FIGURE 7.17. A checklist for reviewing the analysis and interpretation of quantitative data.

MIXED-METHODS DATA ANALYSIS

Three of the most commonly used types of mixed-methods designs that combine both qualitative and quantitative approaches are (1) the embedded design, (2) the two-phase design, and (3) the triangulation design. The procedures of data analysis vary among the three and the differences are based on three elements: (1) whether the data are analyzed concurrently or sequentially, (2) when and how the integration of the qualitative and quantitative data occurs, and (3) whether the qualitative or quantitative approach is given priority in the study or the two approaches are equal (Creswell, 2009). Because the procedures for analyzing qualitative and quantitative data were already discussed in this chapter, in this section we provide a definition of each mixed-methods design, an example of how each design is used by the practitioner, and suggestions for how to present the analysis and interpretation of each design in the research report.

Embedded Design

In this design, one type of data (qualitative or quantitative) is embedded within a study that is dominated by the other (quantitative or qualitative) types of data (see Figure 7.18). The analysis of the two research methods is done separately. The priority throughout the analysis process is given to the primary form of data, while

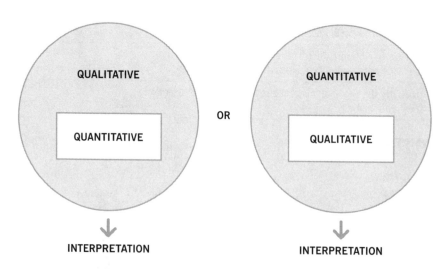

FIGURE 7.18. A diagram of embedded mixed-methods design.

the second source of data serves in a supportive role (Creswell & Plano Clark, 2011; Teddlie & Tashakkori, 2009).

For example, a middle school institutes a mentoring program in which the eighth-grade students mentor the fourth-grade students in a nearby school. Two parents conduct action research based on embedded mixed-methods design to assess the impact of the program from the perspective of participating students. In the parents' study, the majority of the data obtained comprises two qualitative sources: field observations and semistructured interviews. A limited amount of quantitative data is gathered using an observation checklist. As the parents analyze the data their primary focus is on the qualitative data, whereas the information gained from the quantitative data serves as a support to augment the findings from the primary qualitative data analysis. As the parent researchers report the results of the study, the quantitative and the qualitative data analyses are discussed separately.

Two-Phase Design

In this design, the data analysis of one research method (qualitative or quantitative) is used to build the second phase (quantitative or qualitative) of data collection and analysis. The purpose of the second phase is to expand, extend, or refine the results from the previous one (Creswell & Plano Clark, 2011; Teddlie & Tashakkori, 2009). Figure 7.19 is a diagram of the two options in the two-phase mixed-methods design.

An example of a *quantitative* study followed by a *qualitative* approach is a study conducted by Larry, the seventh-grade math teacher, that we discussed above. As you remember, Larry used students' math test scores at the end of a unit to evaluate a new teaching strategy. As he was examining his students' numerical test scores, he realized that two of his students scored far below their classmates. Larry decides to conduct a follow-up interview with the two students and their parents to gain insights into why they fell so far behind their peers and what, from their perspectives, can be done to help them.

An example of a first-phase *qualitative* study that is followed by a second-phase *quantitative* study is an investigation conducted by Pam, the assistant principal of a small rural high school. Pam wants to understand the reasons for a drop in the number of students who participate in the after-school programs offered by the school. The qualitative data that she obtains from interviewing several students in the first phase of the study are analyzed by coding and categorizing the factors that have contributed to the recent decline in student participation in after-school

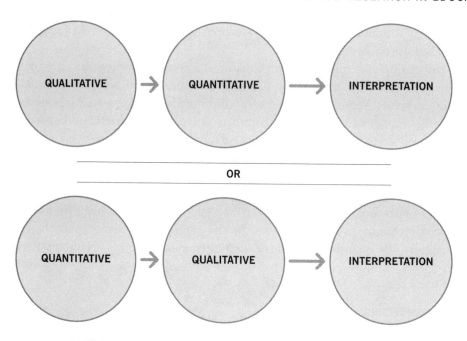

FIGURE 7.19. A diagram of two-phased mixed-methods design.

programs. The categories that emerge from the first phase of the study are used by Pam to develop a Likert-scale survey to be used in the second phase of the study. In this second phase, this schoolwide survey yields numerical data that she analyzes using graphs and descriptive statistics.

The presentation of the data analysis in a two-phase design is organized into qualitative (or quantitative) analysis followed by quantitative (or qualitative) analysis. As the action researchers interpret the study's findings, they contemplate how the findings from the second phase of the study helped them to explain or extend their understanding of the results from the first phase of the study.

Triangulation Design

In this approach, the qualitative and quantitative databases are given equal priority. Qualitative and quantitative data are collected and analyzed at the same time, but separately. The findings of both forms of data are compared and contrasted to determine whether they yield similar results (Creswell & Plano Clark, 2011;

Teddlie & Tashakkori, 2009). The triangulation mixed-methods design is illustrated in Figure 7.20.

For example, Audrey, a second-grade teacher, conducts action research to assess the impact of a new computer software program on her students' level of acquisition of new vocabulary and their opinions of the new program. For her study, Audrey collects both qualitative and quantitative data. For her qualitative data, she conducts classroom observations and interviews five students of different achievement levels to gain insight into their perceptions of the program. She also collects quantitative data from a questionnaire given to the whole class and from the students' scores on several weekly vocabulary tests. Audrey compares the qualitative themes, categories, and patterns that emerge from her qualitative data analysis with the quantitative results. In her interpretation of her findings, Audrey discusses the value of combining the two methods of research for a deeper understanding of the impact of the program. She also highlights how the qualitative and quantitative findings complement each other.

In a mixed-methods triangulation design, the analyses of the qualitative and quantitative data are presented separately. However, in the interpretation and

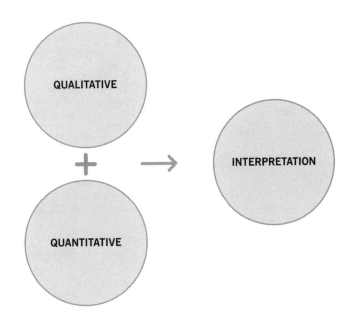

FIGURE 7.20. A diagram of triangulation mixed-methods design.

conclusions phases—when Audrey discusses the meaning of the findings in relation to each research question—the approaches are integrated (Hesse-Biber, 2010).

Content analysis is a strategy that may be used also in triangulation design to enhance the comparison between quantitative and qualitative data (Krippendorff & Bock, 2009). The comparison is achieved by transforming the qualitative data into numerical form. This conversion starts by analyzing the data inductively by generating codes and categories. Predetermined categories may also be used. After calculating the number of times these categories appear in the transcript, they are counted and tabulated. The numerical results are then compared to those obtained through the quantitative method. For example, Rhoda, a high school AP history teacher, wants to assess the efficacy of using group work in her teaching. She divides the students into groups of four for the first month of the school year to get them used to working in groups. During the first week in October, she asks the students to fill in an exit slip at the end of each class reflecting on and assessing their experience working in groups. Each slip starts with the prompt "Working in groups . . . " Rhoda then reads all the slips and marks each comment as either positive (+) or negative (–), and as pertaining to several categories that emerge from her data: social aspect of working as a group (social), learning and understanding the material taught in class (learning), comparing working in groups to other traditional classroom structure (comparison to traditional), and general comments (general). Next, Rhoda can tabulate the comments in terms of the number of positive and negative comments in each category using Figure 7.21.

Category	+	–	Total
Social			
Academic			
Comparison to Traditional			
General			

FIGURE 7.21. An example of a content analysis table used by Rhoda to tabulate her findings.

✓	A Feedback Checklist for Reviewing the Analysis and Interpretation of Mixed-Methods Data	Comments
	1. Is there a clear explanation of the rationale for using a mixed-methods analysis to answer the research questions?	
	2. Are the procedures for combining qualitative and quantitative approaches that were used in the analysis and interpretation clearly outlined?	
	3. Is it indicated whether the analysis occurred concurrently or sequentially?	
	4. Is there a description of when and how the integration of the two approaches occurred and which approach was given priority?	
	5. Is there a discussion of the value of combining the two approaches?	

FIGURE 7.22. A checklist for reviewing the analysis and interpretation of mixed-methods data.

Figure 7.22 provides a checklist with suggested questions that you can use for the analysis and interpretation of mixed-methods data.

REPORTING THE STUDY'S RESULTS, CONCLUSIONS, AND IMPLICATIONS

You are now ready to complete your study by reporting its conclusion or implications based on the analysis and interpretation of your data. Writing your conclusion allows you to present what you have learned through the long and challenging process of analyzing your data and interpreting the meaning of your findings. In this section we offer suggestions for reporting the results, drawing conclusions, and assessing the implications of your study. In many ways, in action research, reporting the study's conclusions does not differ a great deal for qualitative, quantitative, or mixed-methods studies. All action research studies emphasize the usefulness of the inquiry results to one's own practice rather than seeking to generalize the results and make them applicable to different educational settings (Hendricks, 2012; A. P. Johnson, 2011).

In writing your conclusion, you provide a short reiteration of the major findings and insights from your data. Additionally, you present your interpretation and explain your findings. In writing this section, don't overstate or understate your assertions, and any conclusion you put forward should be grounded in the data. Following the action research tradition that does not aim to generalize or find conclusive answers, be tentative in pronouncing the study's outcomes. Use phrases such as "The data suggest . . . ," "Based on my study, it seems that . . . ," or "It is reasonable to assume that. . . . "

Be sure to address all of your research questions and hypotheses in your discussion. If you feel that your questions were not properly answered, reflect on the reasons for this and offer possible explanations (Mills, 2011). For example, were there difficulties in implementing the data collection methods that you planned for the study when designing it? Did you change the focus of your research questions as the study evolved? Have your professional responsibilities limited your ability to conduct the study as you originally planned? Similarly, if your study's hypotheses were not confirmed, there can be several possible explanations, such as Was the duration of your study too short? Were the participants in your study dishonest in their responses to your survey questions? Or, alternatively, Was your hypothesis simply incorrect? Limitations of your study should be acknowledged and discussed.

To strengthen your study's interpretations and conclusions, connect your findings with other theories and studies that were reported in your literature review. Comparing and contrasting the results of your study with the knowledge gained from previous research on your topic adds trustworthiness and validity to your findings (Ravid, 2011).

In your conclusion, carefully assess the implications of your study. You may ask yourself questions such as How might my action research contribute to my practice? What changes will I make as a result of my newly gained knowledge? How can the new information be helpful to others? and Are there additional questions that were brought up in my study that I might pursue in the future? Additionally, you may want to reflect on your journey as an action researcher. Questions that you may ask yourself include What might I change or do differently next time I launch an action research project? How did the experience of action research affect my perception of my work? and How did it affect my professional development?

The checklist in Figure 7.23 includes questions that can help you review and evaluate your study's conclusion.

✓	A Feedback Checklist for Reviewing the Study's Conclusions for Qualitative, Quantitative, and Mixed-Methods Studies	Comments
	1. Is a summary of the major results of the study offered?	
	2. Are the interpretations and conclusions consistent with the findings?	
	3. Are all the assertions, explanations, and claims supported by evidence?	
	4. Do the conclusions and interpretation relate to the research questions and hypotheses?	
	5. Are the limitations of the study acknowledged?	
	6. Are the findings linked to or compared with theory and research discussed in the literature review?	
	7. Are the implications of the study discussed and explicated?	
	8. Are there personal reflections on the study's results and its effects on you as a practitioner?	
	9. Are there suggestions for directions for future research?	

FIGURE 7.23. A checklist for reviewing the study's conclusions.

CHAPTER SUMMARY

1. Although teachers and other school practitioners are constantly and intuitively analyzing and interpreting information, action researcher's data analysis is a systematic and deliberate process that results in trustworthy and reliable findings.

2. The process of *analysis* is defined as breaking down the whole into elements in order to discover its essential features. *Interpretation* is referred to as providing a description or explanation of the meaning of the study.

3. The research questions and the nature of the data—whether narrative, numerical, or mixed—dictate the strategies that might be appropriate for data analysis and interpretation.

4. There are many qualitative analysis approaches, and they all share an inductive process in which the analysis moves from individual parts to a whole and from specifics to a general understanding.

5. Preparing for data analysis involves several steps: transforming the data into readable text, sorting the data into files, creating a data file organizer, and immersing yourself in the data.

6. Predetermined or emerging categories can be used to analyze the data.

7. The predetermined categories serve as a guide for grouping the data into units of analysis and may be drawn from the research questions or the literature review.

8. The emerging categories are created from the ground up. This process involves developing a set of codes that are grouped together and organized into categories.

9. In the phase of synthesis and interpretation of data, researchers put the parts together, examine how they relate to each other, and identify patterns.

10. Four steps of data interpretation are described: identifying patterns, creating a concept map, supporting findings with evidence from the data, and validating a trustworthy interpretation.

11. The report on the analysis and interpretation section may start by describing the methods of analysis that were used, how these strategies involved multiple sources and perspectives, and how the researchers dealt with their own research biases.

12. The written report on the analysis and interpretation section can start by describing the methods of analysis used in the study, the study's multiple sources and perspectives, how the researcher's biases were addressed, and how accurate and trustworthy were the findings obtained.

13. In qualitative studies, a thematic or a chronological format may be used to present the findings; "thick" description and quoting the participants' voices are common writing styles.

14. The goal of *quantitative* data analysis is to answer research questions posed before the start of the study. Studies may also be conducted to test hypotheses; statistical tests are applied to the data collected to determine whether the hypotheses can be supported.

15. Quantitative data analysis, in contrast to qualitative data analysis, is a deductive process, starting with a general principle or premise, and hypothesizing that certain predictable things will happen as a result of that principle or premise.

16. The process of analyzing numerical data may involve coding data, labeling variables, sorting the data, and using a computer program or another aid to organize the data.

17. Data can be depicted visually using graphs; measures of central tendency (e.g., mean) and dispersion (e.g., standard deviation) are often used to describe distributions of scores.

18. Correlation is a statistical test used to measure the relationship or association between two or more pairs of variables; *t*-test and analysis of variance (ANOVA) are statistical tests that are used to compare different means.

19. When analyzing results, researchers want to know whether they are statistically significant or could have happened by chance. Using the *p* value in such cases helps determine the statistical significance of our results.

20. When carrying out quantitative studies, findings are presented objectively and systematically in the results section.

21. The numerical results that you obtain may be used to answer your research questions or to test your hypotheses.

22. When presenting tables and graphs, or embedding statistical results in the narrative, the results should be presented and explained by highlighting patterns, trends, or other results that relate to the research questions.

23. The three most common types of mixed-methods designs that combine both qualitative and quantitative approaches are the embedded design, the two-phase design, and the triangulation design.

24. The procedures of data analysis vary among the three mixed-methods designs based on three elements: (a) whether the data are analyzed concurrently or sequentially, (b) when and how the integration of the qualitative and quantitative data occurs, and (c) if the qualitative or quantitative approach is given priority in the study or the two approaches are equal.

25. In the *embedded* design, one type of data (qualitative or quantitative) is embedded within the larger action research that is dominated by the other (quantitative or qualitative) type of data and the analysis of the two research methods is done separately.

26. In the *two-phase* design, the data analysis of one research method (qualitative or quantitative) is used to build the second phase (quantitative or qualitative) of data collection and analysis and the purpose of the second phase is to expand, extend, or refine the results from the previous one.

27. In the *triangulation* design, the qualitative and quantitative databases are given equal priority and both types of data are collected and analyzed at the same time, but separately. The findings from both forms of data are compared and contrasted to determine whether they yield similar results.

28. The conclusion section should provide a short reiteration of major findings and insights from the data and present an interpretation and explanation of the findings. Assertions and conclusions should not be overstated but rather grounded in the data.

29. The study's research questions and hypotheses should be addressed in the discussion section, and possible explanations should be provided in cases where the outcomes are different from those expected.

30. Connecting and comparing the study's findings with other theories and studies that were reported in the literature review strengthen the study's interpretations and conclusions and adds trustworthiness and validity to the findings. Implications and limitations of the study should also be noted.

CHAPTER EXERCISES AND ACTIVITIES

1. On the basis of the literature that you have read, list two to five possible themes that you expect to emerge from the data you have collected.

2. At the end of an action research class, students were asked to reflect on the contribution of action research to their current or future practice by responding to a survey that included open-ended questions. In the box that follows are responses of 14 of these students to one of the questions. Read carefully the students' responses and look for themes and subthemes. Note that there are negative and positive responses and different reasons are given for each one. If you are working with a peer, colleague, or a group, compare and contrast the themes that were generated. Write a short summary of your findings.

**Students' responses to the question
"What are the contributions of action research to you as a teacher?"**

#1 I think that teachers constantly do research in their classrooms and it is important to understand what they are looking at. Additionally, learning about action research helps teachers understand and evaluate published research.

#2 Action research helps me evaluate whether or not I am effective as a teacher.

#3 I feel confident in my ability to conduct research, and it does make for more informed decisions in the classroom. However, it is difficult to conduct the research correctly when in the middle of teaching . . . it is a bit like changing a tire while the bus is still in motion.

#4 Conducting research helps me to effectively gauge published research and criticize more objectively any conclusions that the research is telling me.

#5 It helps you learn from your students and reflect on your actions in the classroom.

#6 I believe that one can be a very effective teacher by reading current educational research and not actually conducting action research. However, if an educator wants to grow in his or her practice and evolve to the next level, conducting action research is a logical step.

#7 Conducting research is a lot of work. I would like to be engaged in research but I am not sure I can actually do it in my practice.

#8 Research does a few things for teachers. First, it affirms what you are doing in the classroom. Second, it might change what you do in the classroom. Third, it allows you to explore concepts you might find an interest in.

#9 I believe that action research allows me to better understand what is going on in my class. It forces me to look at my students and what I do in a systematic way. It is a lot of work but it is worth it.

#10 Because I conduct action research I can present before the parents and school administration evidence of what is done in my class. I feel more appreciated as a professional.

#11 I think that action research helps you to become aware of how you teach and helps you to continue to improve and become a better teacher.

#12 There are more important aspects in being an effective teacher than conducting research.

#13 The human brain is constantly doing research whether we're aware of it or not. It is human nature. Why not channel it into something beneficial to others?

#14 After conducting action research in my class, I view education completely differently. I am not ready just to follow instruction given from above but rather I examine what works for my students. I am not sure my administrators appreciate this, but I am certainly enjoying my work more.

3. Select the data obtained for your research project from one or two sources that you collected.

   a. With the help of analysis guidelines presented in the chapter indicate three to four emerging categories.

   b. Summarize the categories indicating the central aspects of each one.

   c. Exchange your narrative with a researcher colleague and reflect in writing what you have noticed in each other's categories. Discuss your insights.

4. Examine the emerging or predetermined categories that you obtained from your analysis and write a preliminary interpretation. The following steps may help you in the analysis process:

   a. Create a visual display of the patterns and categories identified in your data using a concept map (see examples in Figures 7.5 and 7.6).

   b. Consider the logical order of the themes and the patterns.

c. Triangulate your findings with evidence from at least two sources. Show how you presented the different opinions and attitudes expressed by the research participants.

d. Create an outline of your analysis report and note what quotations and supportive evidence you will use.

5. The correlation of a teacher-made math assessment test with the standardized math test administered by the state in the spring is $r = .82$. What are your conclusions about the relationship between the teacher-made test and the state test?

6. Compare two bar graphs in Figures 1 and 2 that show responses to two survey questions. How are the responses different or similar?

Figure 1. Responses to Question 1

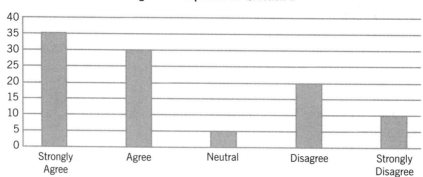

Figure 2. Responses to Question 2

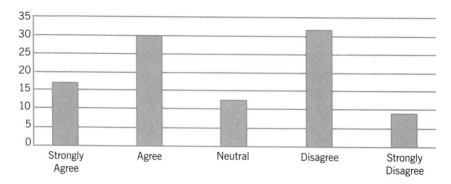

7. Results of a study to assess attitudes toward reading of 35 second-grade students from two different classrooms in the school are given. Students were administered

a survey measuring attitudes toward reading at the beginning of the year (pretest) and again at the end of the year (posttest). During the year, the teachers of both classes designed a series of weekly activities designed to enhance students' attitudes toward reading. The scores of the students from the beginning and end of year were compared using a paired-samples t-test. The mean on the pretest was 34.31; the mean on the posttest was 36.77. There was an increase of 2.457 points from pretest to posttest. The statistical significance was $p < .01$ level. Was the gain from pretest to posttest *statistically* significant? Was it *practically* significant? Explain your answers.

8. Organize and tabulate the numerical data that you collected, using graphs and tables (see examples of tables and figures in the chapter.) Write your preliminary interpretation, sharing, when possible, with a peer or classmate. Use the checklist in Figure 7.17 to help you reflect on your report.

9. Read your analysis and interpretation using the checklists for qualitative data (Figure 7.8), quantitative data (Figure 7.17), or mixed-methods data (Figure 7.22). If you are working with research partner(s), assess each other's work and provide constructive feedback.

10. List the main findings or conclusions of your study. How are your findings related to theories or studies you reported in the literature review? Do your findings confirm or disagree with them or do they add another perspective? Do your study's findings reaffirm or differ from your educational experience (as a student, student teacher, parent, teacher, or other roles as a school practitioner)?

ADDITIONAL READINGS

Ary, D., Jacobs, L. C., Razavieh, A., & Sorensen, C. K. (2009). *Introduction to research in education* (8th ed.). Belmont, CA: Wadsworth.

Creswell, J. W. (2011). *Educational research: Planning, conducting, and evaluating quantitative and qualitative research* (4th ed.). Boston: Addison Wesley.

Dane, F. C. (2011). *Evaluating research: Methodology for people who need to read research.* Thousand Oaks, CA: Sage.

Dicks, B., Mason, B., & Coffey, A. J. (2005). *Qualitative research and hypermedia: Ethnography for the digital age.* London: Sage.

Gay, L. R., Mills, G. E., & Airasian, P. W. (2011). *Educational research: Competencies for analysis and applications* (10th ed.). Boston: Addison Wesley.

Gibbs, G. R. (2002). *Qualitative data analysis: Explorations with NVivo.* Buckingham, UK: Open University Press.

Glass, G. V., & Hopkins, K. D. (2008). *Statistical methods in education and psychology* (3rd ed.). Boston: Allyn & Bacon.

Grbich, C. (2007). *Qualitative data analysis: An introduction.* London: Sage.

Greene, J. C. (2007). *Mixed methods in social inquiry.* San Francisco: Jossey-Bass.

Holstein, J. A., & Gubrium, J. G. (2011). *Varieties of narrative analysis.* Thousand Oaks, CA: Sage.

Hoy, W. K. (2010). *Quantitative research in education: A primer.* Thousand Oaks, CA: Sage.

Huck, S. W. (2012). *Reading statistics and research* (6th ed.). Boston: Pearson.

Kering, P. K., & Baucom, D. H. (Eds.). (2004). *Couple observational coding systems.* Mahwah, NJ: Erlbaum.

Krippendorff, K. (2012). *Content analysis: An introduction to its methodology* (3rd ed.). Thousand Oaks, CA: Sage.

Muijs, D. (2010). *Doing quantitative research in education with SPSS.* Thousand Oaks, CA: Sage.

Neundorf, K. A. (2002). *The content analysis guidebook.* Thousand Oaks, CA: Sage.

Ryan, G. W., & Bernard, H. R. (2000). Data management and analysis methods. In N. K. Denzin & Y. S. Lincoln (Eds.), *Handbook of qualitative research* (2nd ed., pp. 769–802). Thousand Oaks, CA: Sage.

Stake, R. E. (2005). *Multiple case study analysis.* New York: Guilford Press.

Tanner, D. E. (2011). *Using statistics to make educational decisions.* Thousand Oaks, CA: Sage.

Tashakkori, A., & Teddlie, C. (Eds.). (2003). *Handbook of mixed methods in social and behavior research.* Thousand Oaks, CA: Sage.

Wolcott, H. (1994). *Transforming qualitative data: Descriptions, analysis and interpretation.* London: Sage.

CHAPTER 8

Writing, Sharing, and Implementing the Research Findings

Y ou have reached the final phase of your investigation and are probably excited to put into action what you have learned about your research topic. Nevertheless, there is one more important thing left to be done: to produce a report that tells the story of your research journey and its implications for your practice and make public your newly gained knowledge (Altrichter et al., 2008).

You may feel that there is no need to share your study results with others because you are the only one to act on your findings. Still, we believe that all practitioners involved in action research need to document their study.

Reflecting and reporting on the full cycle of inquiry, from shaping a research question to reaching the study's conclusions, has several benefits. First, the very act of writing the report allows you to stand back and think holistically about what you have seen, heard, experienced, and learned from the process. This self-reflection enhances your ability to organize your thoughts, crystallizes your understanding of the study's results, and presents clearly and convincingly your newly gained knowledge (Hinchey, 2008; H. F. Wolcott, 2008). Second, the written account serves as tangible evidence of your personal achievement, documents your professional accomplishments, and contributes to your career portfolio (Mills, 2011; Phillips & Carr, 2010). Third, producing a report of your inquiry allows you to expand your circle of influence by sharing your findings with your colleagues and a wider audience (Mertler, 2012). Finally, making your research accessible to others helps you connect with a community of learners who share your desire for school improvement and personal growth through action research (Holly et al., 2009).

In this chapter we discuss different aspects of writing and sharing your research project. We also reflect on how doing research can become an integral part of your professional growth as an individual and as a member of a community dedicated to improving practice through action research.

We divide our discussion into four parts: (1) writing a formal action research report, (2) developing alternative formats for reporting on action research, (3) sharing the research findings, and (4) implementing the research findings.

WRITING A FORMAL ACTION RESEARCH REPORT

There are different ways to report action research studies, although most of them follow a similar structure. In this section, we highlight the different parts of a formal research report. While different publication writing styles can be used for describing your research, we focus here on APA (2010) style because it is the preferred format in education.

A formal report usually includes the following sections: *introduction, literature review, methodology, findings and results, discussion and implications*, and *references* (McMillan & Schumacher, 2010). As you recall, we have elaborated on each of these sections in the previous chapters. Therefore, in the discussion that follows, we review only various report sections. Some reports also have an *appendix*. Published reports may also include an *abstract* that summarizes the study and appears at the beginning, before the formal Introduction.

Introduction

In the *introduction*, you describe the study's background and state the purpose of the study (Huck, 2012). Here you present the topic of the study and the questions you explored, including your hypotheses, if any. The statement of the problem that you investigated can be phrased as a question or in a declarative form. You also articulate the rationale for the inquiry and its significance and how it will contribute to your educational practice. In this section, define terms that are at the heart of your study and that may have more than one definition (Fraenkel et al., 2011). For example, you may choose to define terms such as *gifted*, *RTI*, or *cyberbullying*.

Literature Review

The *literature review* section provides a summary of existing research on your topic (Slavin, 2007). Remember to analyze and synthesize the studies that you reviewed and highlight controversies or points of agreement between researchers, as well as conflicting findings or any gaps in knowledge. To avoid plagiarism and to maintain the integrity of your report, cite carefully the information you gleaned from other authors and properly indicate what was quoted.

Methodology

In the *methodology* section, describe the procedures you used in conducting your study. There are usually several subsections in the methodology: *site and participants, data collection procedures, researcher role*, and *data analysis*. The order and headings of these subsections may differ from one report to the next, but this section is designed to provide clear, detailed information about how you conducted the study.

Researcher Role

Here you explain your role as the researcher. For example, describe your biases and subjectivity, or how the subject of your research related to you personally.

Site and Participants

In this subsection, describe those who participated in your study. Include relevant demographic information about the participants (APA, 2010) such as the students' grade level, gender, ethnic/race distribution, or eligibility for free or reduced-price lunch. Also include a description of how the participants were selected (Dane, 2011). At the same time, be sensitive to issues of confidentiality. Consult with your supervisor (e.g., department chair or principal) about these issues. When in doubt, use general demographic information about the school that is available to the public. You may have included several samples in your study, such as parents, other teachers in the school, or students. Make sure you describe each one of these groups of participants.

Data Collection Procedures

In this subsection, describe how you collected your data and the tools (qualitative, quantitative, or mixed methods) that you used. For example, if you collected observation data, explain *what* you observed and *how* you recorded your observations. Or, if you gathered interview data, report information such as the interview protocol and the questions you asked. Similarly, describe how you collected your quantitative data. For example, if you used a Likert-scale survey, provide information about it including the number of questions, sample questions, and other demographic questions that you may have included. Also, convey how you distributed and collected the surveys. You can place samples of the qualitative and quantitative data in the report's appendix.

In this subsection you should also describe how the study was carried out. It should be detailed enough for a reader to understand how you conducted the study and collected your data. Include information such as the process for obtaining permission for your study, enlisting participants' cooperation, and length of the study.

Data Analysis

This subsection is designed to explain how you analyzed the data you collected. For qualitative studies, describe how you transcribed the data and developed the codes, categories, and patterns. For quantitative studies, describe how the numerical information is displayed, and what—if any—statistical tests were calculated. You may want to mention your research questions and explain how you analyzed the data to address each of your research questions. If you used computer software packages to analyze your data, report this information in this subsection.

Findings and Results

The results of your study are reported in this section. For qualitative data, describe how you discovered the themes and organized them around categories and patterns. On the basis of your evidence, provide a plausible explanation for your findings, draw conclusions, and answer your research questions. You may find that tables and graphs would enhance the presentation of your findings (Huck, 2012). If your data are quantitative, report your findings as they relate to your research questions and hypotheses. Present your results objectively without interpreting them or expressing any value judgments. If you identify the real names of the participants or educational setting, or if you use pictures or other artifacts, you need to obtain permission to do so.

Discussion and Implications

In this section you revisit your own study by looking at the research questions (and hypotheses, if you had any) and examining the data you collected and analyzed. You should explain the implications of your findings for your practice and suggest changes and modifications that may take place as a result of your study. Also, explain your findings in a broader context (Fraenkel et al., 2011), describe where your findings confirm or contradict those reported by others, and give possible explanations for these discrepancies. You should acknowledge your study's limitations and offer suggestions for future research.

References

In this section, you list all the references you cited or quoted in your study (Dane, 2011). The exact order of the list may depend on the publication style that you use. For example, in APA style, which is commonly used in educational research, the references are listed in alphabetical order according to the author's last name. There should be a complete match between the text citations and the reference list. This means that all the studies that you cited in the text should be listed in your reference list, and that all the sources listed in the reference list should have been cited in your text.

Appendix

The appendix often contains information that is distracting or inappropriate to include in the body of the report (APA, 2010), or information that is too detailed or too long to be included in the report itself. For example, samples of interview transcripts, observation field notes, artifacts, permission letters, classroom seating charts, student work, and copies of tests—all of this material can be included in the appendix. All the items in the appendix should be ordered and labeled clearly and referred to in your report.

Table 8.1 offers a summary of the structure of a formal action research report.

TABLE 8.1. Structure of a Formal Action Research Report

Section	Content
Abstract (a summary of the study, optional)	Overview of the study
Introduction	Presentation of the topic of the study and the questions you explored
Literature review	Summary of existing research on your topic
Methodology	Explanation of how the study was conducted and the data collection methods
Findings and results	Presentation of the study's findings with relevant evidence
Discussion	Explanation of the results in relation to the study's questions and to other research on your topic, implications for practitioners, suggestions for future studies
References	A list of the references cited or quoted in the report
Appendix	Additional documentation (that is too detailed to include in the report itself)

DEVELOPING ALTERNATIVE FORMATS FOR REPORTING ON ACTION RESEARCH

While the traditional account of communicating your findings is the most common format for presenting action research, there are other options available. As long as the procedures of collecting, analyzing, and interpreting the data are valid, trustworthy, and transparent, you may choose other ways of reporting your findings. Some of these include poster presentations, portfolios, electronic media, and artistic or dramatic performances. You may find that using one of these presentation formats can communicate your study more effectively and be more engaging and accessible to your audience than other methods. Additionally, these presentation options are more visually appealing and allow for the integration of sight, sound, and technology to complement or substitute for the narrative report. Several books discuss the advantages and procedures of alternative research presentations (e.g., Phillips & Carr, 2010; Stringer, 2008). There are also a number of online resources for creating posters, research portfolios, and multimedia presentations. We include links to several of these websites at the end of the chapter.

Poster Presentation

In a poster presentation, the essential elements of the study are summarized and written text is kept to a minimum. The action researcher stands next to the poster and verbally presents the study and responds to audience questions. The poster format usually contains the following components:

- ▶ Title of the research project
- ▶ The research question(s) you address
- ▶ Major findings from the literature review
- ▶ The context of the study: participants, setting, and research methodology
- ▶ Carefully selected data representations, such as quotations and pictures
- ▶ The study's findings and recommendations

If you choose this mode of presentation, be sure that your report is focused, succinct, and contains only the essentials. Key findings should be clearly displayed and the most representative and provocative quotes should be conveyed. It is a good idea to make the poster aesthetically appealing by using pictures, charts, and other visual displays that effectively tell your study's story (T. G. Wolcott, 1997).

Research Portfolio

Portfolios can be constructed by organizing materials in a binder or in digital formats. They are distinguished by a display of rich and varied data that include students' work, lesson plans, selected excerpts of interviews, and field notes. Portfolios often contain visual displays, such as pictures, charts, and other illustrations that capture the participants' world and the complex environment of the educational setting. The variety of authentic documents allows the reader to interact with the data and to engage in the interpretation of its meanings. The data are accompanied by the action researcher's reflections, explanations, and insights. To help the reader navigate the intricacies of your portfolio, you should organize its many elements clearly and skillfully. A table of contents and a list of the documents, figures, and artifacts will also be helpful (R. S. Johnson, 2009; Schär, 2002). Portfolios usually include:

- ▶ An overview of the research project, including the research question and its significance
- ▶ The procedures for collecting and analyzing the data
- ▶ A display of a variety of data, such as artifacts, excerpts, pictures, and charts
- ▶ Commentaries on the findings and conclusions
- ▶ Reflections on the potential impact of your study on your practice

Digital portfolios are becoming more prevalent with the advance and versatility of technology. A variety of electronic formats like DVD, CD, video, digital photography, and hypertext navigation make this format a very suitable and stimulating way to present your research. Make sure that this exciting format does not detract from the substance of your study (Abrami & Barrett, 2005).

Electronic Media

The amazing and fast-moving advancement in technology makes it possible to tell the story of your study using a dynamic integration of audio and visual presentations. The new video and electronic media production that includes a variety of tools such as video, YouTube, streaming video, and DVD allows the action researcher to create an exciting presentation of his or her findings. Through the sound and images you present, the experiences of your study's participants are brought to life in a vivid and evocative way. While this is a very powerful method for reporting your findings, it is time consuming and requires expertise in matching the research with the technology in a meaningful way. Some researchers also prepare a written summary of the key points of the study to accompany their presentation (Mayer & Moreno, 2002).

Performance Presentation

Another creative format for presenting your findings is through art or dramatic performance. Through drawing, dance, song, drama, or other artistic means you portray the insights that you discovered through the analysis of the data. Using the actual events revealed in the study and participants' own words, you illustrate your insights and understanding. This format invites the audience members into the participants' world and allows them to see through participants' eyes. If you consider using this format, be aware that it requires a great deal of imagination, creativity, and hard work (Delamont, 2012; Denzin, 2003; Glesne, 2010; Holmes, 2012; Sikes, 2012).

As you can see, there are a variety of formats you can choose to present your action research study. Your choice depends on the purpose of your presentation, your audience, your own inclination and level of comfort, and time constraints. If you conducted your research project as part of course or workshop requirements, consult the guidelines given to you by your instructor.

The following is a brief description of the presentation formats chosen by several action researchers who were introduced to you earlier: Simone, Sharon, Jeanette, Jesse, Audrey, and Antonio.

> During the year-end review, Simone, the third-grade teacher who explored the relationship between her students' homework completion rate and their scores on a math test, presented a *formal research report* as evidence of her professional growth.
>
> A *poster* presentation was the choice of Sharon, a middle school teacher, and her committee, for their presentation to the school board on how moral values were taught in school. Since there was a short amount of time given for their presentation, they felt that a poster would be the most appropriate means to present their findings clearly and succinctly.
>
> Jeanette, a kindergarten teacher, focused her research on developing ways to improve students' ability to set goals for themselves and become self-directed learners. During a Parent Teacher Association (PTA) meeting in the spring, she presented the results of her research that focused on documenting her students' growth. Her evidence included a *portfolio binder* that contained items from the students' own portfolios.
>
> While interviewing for a new teaching position, Jesse, the student teacher who studied different styles of classroom management, used a *digital portfolio* to present his findings in order to highlight his qualifications for the job.
>
> Audrey, a second-grade teacher, studied the efficacy of a new computer software program designed to help students learn vocabulary. To document the effectiveness of the new software, Audrey used *electronic media*. She maintained a wiki during the year where she embedded videos of students

using the new software, interviews with students, and students' weekly vocabulary test scores. Audrey presented this ongoing research project on the school website and invited feedback and comments from colleagues, students, and parents.

Antonio is the middle school counselor who conducted a study on the phenomenon of bullying in his school. He chose *performance presentation* to maximize the impact of his findings. He wrote a student play based on his data that was presented to the school community.

Clearly, there are multiple options for you to present your research. In this chapter, we introduced you to some of the most popular ways. These are summarized in Table 8.2.

SHARING THE RESEARCH FINDINGS

One of the greatest contributions of action research is that it encourages educators to learn from each other by sharing and advancing their experience-based knowledge. Sharing practice-oriented research allows educators to speak in their own

TABLE 8.2. Research Presentation Options

Presentation format	Brief description
Formal research report	A written report following a traditional structure and order of sections and content, similar to that found in published articles and reports
Poster	A visual display of the study that allows the action researcher to stand beside it and verbally explain the study to the audience
Research portfolio	A collection of rich data (such as students' work, lesson plans, and field notes), accompanied by the researcher's reflections, explanations, and insights
Electronic media	A means to tell the story of the study using a dynamic integration of audio and visual presentations
Performance presentation	A means of presenting the study through art or other dynamic performance (such as dance, song, or drama)

voice, take control of their work, and contribute to the creation of a vital body of knowledge (Altrichter et al., 2008).

Traditionally, educational inquiry was perceived as research conducted by outside authoritative experts for the purpose of generalizing knowledge that can be transmitted top-down to multiple settings. By comparison, action research is conducted by educators in their own settings. Acknowledging the complexity and uniqueness of each educational setting, these practitioners do not seek generalized solutions nor offer prescriptions for others to follow.

Like many other novice action researchers, you may not consider your study to be "real research" and feel reluctant to expose your investigation to a peer review. Nevertheless, action researchers like you have recognized the benefits of sharing their research and learning from one another. It is important to note that action research conducted by school practitioners has resulted in a shift in how educational research is viewed.

Problems and questions that initiated your study may resonate with issues that other practitioners face. Making your study available to others can help your colleagues gain new insights into their own practice. Your study may allow them to think about their work taking a multifaceted perspective and present new directions for future action (Hopkins, 2008).

For all these reasons we strongly encourage you to share your study with many different audiences so that colleagues in your local educational setting and beyond can learn from your work. As a first step to disseminating your study, you can build your confidence by talking to your close colleagues, students, and parents about your research project and what you have learned. You may also want to share the results of your investigation with those who participated in your study. Then, take a small step forward and consider presenting the study in a more formal mode. Professional development days organized by your school or district may be good venues for sharing your findings within the local community. Another option is to offer a workshop or to exhibit your study in a local teacher center. Local events and presentations such as these allow you to advance the issue you investigate and perhaps encourage some of your colleagues in collaboratively expanding and exploring the issue in the future (Holly et al., 2009).

Armed with these experiences, you are now ready to move beyond the local community and present your research project to a larger educational audience of professional colleagues in state, regional, or even national conferences. Presenting your findings at a conference (organized by a professional association around a specific subject that is related to your study topic) would be a good next step. You will probably feel more comfortable sharing your inquiry with colleagues, who, like you, are interested in finding ways to improve their practice through action research. Many national professional associations also sponsor regional and state conferences. You may find it less stressful to present in these familiar venues, and you will probably have a better chance of getting your proposal accepted. In most cases you will be required to submit a proposal in which you highlight the purpose of your study, its significance, and its contributions to your field.

If you want to enhance the impact of your research agenda and increase your reach to wider audiences, consider publishing your study. The options for disseminating your written report electronically include publishing in a newsletter, newspaper, or journal. As you prepare your study for publication, bear in mind that these outlets expose your writing to different audiences; you will want to choose the appropriate style, length, and depth for your writing (Mills, 2011; Stringer, 2008).

Again, in order to gain experience and increase the chance of getting your paper published, we suggest that you submit your writing first to a small local publication. Excellent places to start are parent newsletters, local papers, or district or school websites. Another option is newsletters published by professional associations at a local or regional level.

At some point you may want to publish your study in a peer-reviewed journal. You need to target a journal that is suited for your topic. Check the websites of national professional organizations, as well as their regional affiliates, to find journals that specialize in the topic of your study. Once you have identified several potential publications find out as much as possible about each. Familiarize yourself with the content and style of previous articles published in that publication (Klingner, Scanlon, & Pressley, 2005). Additionally, there are several journals in print and online that are devoted to publishing action research that may be good outlets for your study. Furthermore, if you are interested in publishing in the journal of a professional organization, be aware that their rate of acceptance is usually lower than for those journals published at the state or regional level. Table 8.3 contains a list of journals, with a brief description of each journal as well as the journals' website information.

Once you have identified the publication outlet most suited for your report, scrutinize its manuscript submission guidelines. These guidelines can often be found on the journal's website. We advise you to follow these closely.

Ideas discussed in this chapter for various venues for sharing your action research are summarized in Table 8.4.

TABLE 8.3. Journals with a Focus on Action Research in Education		
Name	Description	Website URL
Print journals		
Action Research	An international, interdisciplinary, peer-reviewed quarterly that provides a forum for the development of the theory and practice of action research	*http://arj.sagepub.com*
ALARA Journal	Contains project reports, reflections on seminars and conferences, articles related to the theory and practice of action learning, action research, and related approaches	*www.alara.net.au/publications/ journal*
International Journal of Action Research	A forum for discussions about action research, from both its present and future perspectives. A refereed journal, appearing three times a year.	*www.ctu.edu.vn/institutes/mdi/ ntth/VN/PRA/PRA-013.pdf*
Electronic (online) journals		
Networks: An Online Journal for Teacher Research	An online journal for sharing reports of action research in which teachers at all levels, kindergarten to postgraduate, reflect on classroom practice	*http://journals.library.wisc.edu/ index.php/networks*
Wisdom of Practice: An Online Journal of Action Research	Online journal dedicated to sharing action research conducted in K–12 educational settings	*http://research.vancouver.wsu.edu/ journal-of-action-research*
Educational Action Research	A free, peer-reviewed journal for elementary, secondary, and university teachers exploring the unity between educational research and practice	*www.tandf.co.uk/journals/ titles/09650792.asp*

TABLE 8.4. Ideas for Sharing Your Action Research

Means	Advantage
Share within your local community (e.g., colleagues, students, and parents)	Informal; allows you to build your confidence
Present at professional development days or workshops	Semiformal; allows you to advance your topic and encourage others to pursue this or similar topics
Present at local, state, or national conferences	Formal; allows you to share your research with interested colleagues outside your school setting
Publish your research in a local newsletter or publication	Formal; contributes to your career and allows you to be active in your professional community
Publish your research in peer-reviewed professional literature, following the guidelines of the publication	Very formal; helps you gain recognition for being published and earn a highly prestigious and rewarding professional status

IMPLEMENTING THE RESEARCH FINDINGS

While it is of great importance to disseminate your study to other professionals, ultimately the purpose of action research is to take action in your own classroom or school. For action researchers the linkage between one's research and practice is vital. The knowledge and information generated through your investigation should not be confined to reflections and communications. Findings from your study that point to aspects of your practice that need to be changed or modified, as well as recommendations generated by your inquiry that propose ways to improve your work, should inform the decisions you make about your practice (Altrichter et al., 2008).

As the cycle of action research ends—with the implementation of the study's findings—a new cycle of inquiry begins, with more questions to pursue and additional issues to explore. This is because as you put your research conclusions into action you need to monitor the impact of these actions. It is possible that your intended objectives will not be fully achieved or that new, unforeseen problems will present themselves. In these cases, some modifications will be required.

For example, Jesse, who investigated classroom management styles as a student teacher, was excited to implement his action research findings in his new position as a sixth-grade teacher. Because his study led him to the conclusion that a democratic classroom reflects his educational values and objectives, he enthusiastically implemented the classroom management methods and procedures advocated by this approach. However, in reality, things turned out to be more complicated than Jesse expected. Several of his students mistook the democratic sharing of responsibilities as a sign of his weakness and inexperience and interrupted the class. Worried about his declining effectiveness, yet not willing to compromise his belief in the value of a democratic classroom, Jesse initiated a new action research project. The focus of the new cycle of inquiry is on finding additional methods of classroom management to enforce students' discipline and respect for classroom rules within a democratic and civil environment.

In other cases, when the question that served as the impetus for the inquiry was satisfactorily answered, the action researcher may embark on a new study that builds on the information and understanding generated by the previous investigation. For example, Sharon and her committee completed their inquiry into the values that are taught in their school through language arts and social studies classes. On the basis of their findings and conclusions, the team launched a follow-up study that focused on developing a revised curriculum to improve how values are taught. This curriculum also includes methods and benchmarks to assess and monitor its effectiveness. Similarly, a new study may be initiated as the original action research is completed, and as a consequence of what you have learned while conducting the study, new, unexpected questions have risen that lead to a different focus.

Another possibility is that as you reach the conclusion of your action research you realize that the journey is not complete; in fact, it is just beginning. You may, for example, finish a research project as part of your course requirements and realize that because of time constraints or the short duration of the course, your research questions were not fully answered. However, you are so intrigued about the topic that you decide to continue to pursue it on your own.

Thus, though the reasons differ, action research tends to continue from one study to the next, as the answer to one research question leads to new questions. This cyclical process is, in fact, an ongoing looping of learning. By taking ownership of the improvement of your practice, you construct and reconstruct the questions you want to explore and the inquiries you intend to pursue. These questions guide your personal and professional growth as you incrementally extend your skills, experiment with new ideas, and critically reflect on and learn from your failures and successes. Empowered by ever-growing knowledge, action research provides you with a framework for authentic change that is tailored to your students' growth and to your own particular setting. Action research, then, is a form of autonomous, self-directed professional development (Hopkins, 2008; Stringer, 2008)

COMPLETING THE ACTION RESEARCH PROJECT

You may want to celebrate the end of this research journey by reflecting with a friend or a research colleague on the following questions:

1. What were the most important insights and knowledge you gained in your investigation?
2. What questions were not answered or were answered only partially in your study? What new questions emerged?
3. How will the research project impact your practice?
4. What have you learned about yourself, your students, your colleagues, and your school as a result of the research experience?
5. What lessons have you learned that will enable you to plan more effective action research in the future?
6. What are some of the ways you can share your study with others?
7. Will you continue conducting action research? Why? Why not?

BECOMING A PART OF THE RESEARCH COMMUNITY

Throughout the book, as we discussed each stage of the action research process, we highlighted the value of working in research groups and sharing your research with colleagues. Being part of an action research community will provide you with opportunities to talk about your experiences openly and candidly, share your successes as well as disappointments and doubts, raise questions, discuss possibilities, refine ideas, and exchange suggestions and advice. Collaborating with like-minded action researchers can reenergize you when you're in doubt, support and encourage you when you need it, and challenge you to extend yourself and to continue developing as an action researcher!

You can be a part of multiple research groups, each serving a different purpose. You may form or join a research group within your school and together develop a common research focus that will serve as an engine for moving forward in bringing about a change and improvement within your school setting. Another option is to become part of a research group comprising colleagues in your school, district, or university. While each member may have a different research agenda, all share your commitment and interest in research (Holly et al., 2009). A third possibility is to create dialogues with action researchers outside of your immediate circle. This can be accomplished through the use of technology to converse about the challenges, rewards, and enticing opportunities that action research offers (Lee & Gregory, 2008).

We have come to the end of the guided research journey. In the future, using the skills you have acquired, you will be able to navigate the action research cycle on your own. You must be proud of your accomplishments: mastering the skills of planning a study, collecting and interpreting data, and putting into action the knowledge you have gained. We hope that action research becomes an integral part of your professional life as a school practitioner. We trust that it will lead you to become a change agent and a leader within your school community.

CHAPTER SUMMARY

1. Practitioners involved in action research need to document their study and produce a research report; this self-reflection enhances their ability to organize their thoughts, crystallizes their understanding of the study's results, and presents clearly and convincingly their newly gained knowledge.

2. The *introduction* to a formal written report presents the topic of the study, the questions explored in the study, and the rationale for the inquiry and its significance.

3. The *literature review* section provides a summary of existing research on the study's topic; it includes an analysis and synthesis of the studies that were reviewed, highlighting controversies or points of agreement between researchers, as well as gaps in knowledge.

4. The *methodology* section describes the procedures for conducting the study and usually includes several subsections: site and participants, data collection procedures, researcher role, and data analysis.

5. The *findings and results* section reports the study's qualitative and quantitative results, as they relate to the study's questions (and hypotheses, if any).

6. In the *discussion and implications* section, researchers revisit their research questions and hypotheses, examine the data they collected and analyzed, explain the implications of their findings for their practice, explain where their findings confirm or contradict

those reported by others, acknowledge the study's limitations, and offer suggestions for future research.

7. In the *references*, list all the sources that were cited or quoted in the study; that is, all the studies that were cited in the text should be listed in the reference list, and all the sources listed in the reference list should have been cited in the text.

8. The *appendix* often includes parts of the report that are too detailed or too long to be included in the report itself, clearly ordered and labeled.

9. Besides using the common traditional written report of the findings, action researchers can use other means to communicate their findings, such as poster presentations, portfolios, electronic media, and artistic or dramatic performances.

10. One of the greatest contributions of action research is that it encourages educators to learn from one another by sharing and advancing their experience-based knowledge.

11. Practitioners who conduct action research may want to publish their complete study in a peer-reviewed journal; there are several print and online journals that are devoted to publishing action research that may be good outlets for their studies.

12. For action researchers the linkage between one's research and one's practice is vital, and the ultimate purpose of this research is to enable practitioners to take action in their own classrooms or schools.

13. As the cycle of action research ends with the implementation of the study's findings, a new cycle of inquiry may begin, with more questions to pursue.

14. Being part of an action research community provides educators with opportunities to talk about their experiences openly and candidly, share their successes as well as disappointments and doubts, raise questions, discuss possibilities, refine ideas, and exchange suggestions and advice.

CHAPTER EXERCISES AND ACTIVITIES

1. Develop an outline for your action research report. Write a few sentences to describe what you will include in each section.

2. Deliberate on the possible significance of your research study. How does it contribute to your own practice and professional growth? What are some ways that you think your study may contribute to your students' learning or to your colleagues' practice?

3. As you conclude the research journey, reflect on how you can implement the findings in your practice. Consider some of the steps required to put your findings into action.

4. If you had a chance to continue studying the same topic or designing a new research project, what changes might you make that will enable you to conduct more effective action research in the future?

5. Using the ideas for sharing your research project with other practitioners (see Table 8.4), choose one or two possible ideas and explain the reasons for your choice. In making your choice, consider a format for your research presentation that will best reflect the nature of the study and your target audience.

ADDITIONAL READINGS

McNiff, S. (1998). *Art-based research.* London: Kingsley.

Norris, J. (2009). *Playbuilding as qualitative research: A participatory art-based performance.* Walnut Creek, CA: Left Coast Press.

Theron, L., Mitchell, C., & Smith, A. (Eds.). (2011). *Picturing research: Drawing on visual methodology.* Rotterdam, The Netherlands: Sense.

WEBSITES FOR PRESENTING ACTION RESEARCH

Poster Presentation

Adventures in poster making:

Poster presentations (University of Buffalo Libraries):
http://library.buffalo.edu/asl/guides/bio/posters.html

Creating effective poster presentation (North Carolina State University):
www.ncsu.edu/project/posters/NewSite

Poster session tips (Pennsylvania State University):
www.personal.psu.edu/drs18/postershow

Providing poster session (UMDNJ Center for Teaching Excellence):
http://cte.umdnj.edu/career_development/career_posters.cfm

Portfolio Research Presentation

Directions for research and development on electronic portfolio:
www.cjlt.ca/index.php/cjlt/article/view/92/86

Research Portfolio—Faculty Web Pages

http://faculty.tamu-commerce.edu/scarter/research_portfolio.htm

Multimedia Presentation

Multimedia presentation (EduTech Wiki)

Designer eLearning:
http://designerelearning.blogspot.co.il/2005/09/mayers-principles-for-design-of-html

References

Abbott, M. L. (2011). *Understanding educational statistics using Microsoft Excel and SPSS*. San Francisco: Wiley.

Abrami, P. C., & Barrett, H. (2005). Directions for research and development on electronic portfolios. *Canadian Journal of Learning and Technology, 31*(3), 1–15.

Allen, L. (2012) School in focus: Photo methods in education research. In S. Delamont (Ed.), *Handbook of qualitative research in education* (pp. 241–251). Cheltenham, UK: Elgar.

Alsup, J. (2006). *Teacher identity discourses: Negotiating personal and professional spaces*. Mahwah, NJ: Erlbaum.

Altrichter, H., Feldman, A., Posch, P., & Somekh, B. (2008). *Teachers investigate their work: An introduction to action research across the professions*. New York: Routledge.

American Psychological Association. (2010). *Publication manual of the American Psychological Association* (6th ed.). Washington, DC: Author.

Andres, L. (2012). *Designing and doing survey research*. Los Angeles: Sage.

Andrew, M., Squire, C., & Tamboukou, M. (2008). *Doing narrative research*. London: Sage.

Angrosino, M. V. (2007). *Naturalistic observation: Qualitative essentials*. Long Grove, IL: Waveland Press.

Anyon, J., Dumas, M., Dumas, M., Linville, D., Nolan, K., Perez, M., et al. (2009). *Theory and educational research: Toward critical social explanation*. New York: Routledge.

Apple, M., & Beane, J. A. (2007). *Democratic schools: Lessons in powerful education*. Portsmouth, NH: Heinemann.

Atweh, B., Kemmis, S., & Weeks, P. (1998). *Action research in practice: Partnership for social justice in education.* New York: Routledge.

Ayers, W. (2004). *Teaching the personal and the political: Essays on hope and justice.* New York: Teachers College Press.

Banks, J. A., Banks, C. A. M., Cortes, C. E., Hahn, C. L., Merryfield, M. M., Moodley, K. A., et al. (2005). *Democracy and diversity: Principles and concepts for educating citizens in a global age.* Seattle: Center for Multicultural Education, University of Washington.

Bauer, S. C., & Brazer, D. (2012). *Using research to lead school improvement: Turning evidence into action.* Thousand Oaks, CA: Sage.

Baumfield, V., Hall, E., & Wall, K. (2008). *Action research in the classroom.* London: Sage.

Bazeley, P. (2007). *Qualitative data analysis with NVivo.* Thousand Oaks, CA: Sage.

Bloom, B., Engelhart, M. D., Furst, E. J., Hill, W. H., & Krathwohl, D. R. (1956). *Taxonomy of educational objectives: The classification of educational goals. Handbook I: Cognitive domain.* White Plains, NY: Longman.

Bogdan, R. C., & Biklen, S. K. (2006). *Qualitative research in education: An introduction to theory and methods* (5th ed.). Needham Heights, MA: Allyn & Bacon.

Booth, W. C., Colomb, G. G., & Williams, J. M. (2008). *The craft of research* (3rd ed.). Chicago: University of Chicago Press.

Bouma, G. D., & Ling R. (2004). *The research process.* Victoria, Australia: Oxford University Press.

Boyatzis, R. E. (1998). *Transforming qualitative information: Thematic analysis and code development.* Thousand Oaks, CA: Sage.

Boyle, J., & Fisher, S. (2007). *Educational testing: A competence-based approach.* Malden, MA: Blackwell.

Brisk, M. E. (2011). Learning to write in the second language: K–5. In E. Hinkel (Ed.), *Handbook of research in second language teaching and learning* (pp. 40–56). New York: Routledge.

Brookfield, S. D. (2005). *The power of critical theory for adult learning and teaching.* Berkshire, UK: Open University Press.

Brown, E. L. (2004). What precipitates change in cultural diversity awareness during a multicultural course: The message or the method? *Journal of Teacher Education, 55*(4), 325–340.

Burns, D. (2007). *Systematic action research: A strategy for whole system change.* Bristol, UK: Policy Press.

Burton, D. M., & Bartlett, S. (2005). *Practitioner research for teachers.* London: Chapman.

Burton, N., Brundett, M., & Jones, M. (2008). *Doing your education research project.* London: Sage.

Campbell, A., McNamara, O., & Gilroy, P. (2004). *Practitioner research and professional development in education.* London: Chapman.

Campbell, E. (2003). Moral lessons: The ethical role of teachers. *Educational Research and Evaluation: An International Journal on Theory and Practice, 9*(1), 25–50.

Campbell, E. (2008). The ethics of teaching as a moral profession. *Curriculum Inquiry, 38*(4), 357–383.

Carr, W., & Kemmis, S. (2009). Educational action research: A critical approach. In S. Noffke & B. Somekh (Eds.), *Handbook of educational action research* (pp. 74–84). London: Sage.

Chappuis, J., Stiggins, R, J., Chappuis, S., & Arter, J. A. (2011). *Classroom assessment for student learning: Doing it right—using it well* (2nd ed.). Upper Saddle River, NJ: Pearson.

Charmaz, K. C. (2006). *Constructing grounded theory: A practical guide through qualitative analysis: Methods for the 21st century.* London: Sage.

Check, R., & Schutt, R. K. (2011). *Research methods in education.* Thousand Oaks, CA: Sage.

Clandinin, D. J. (2006). *Handbook of narrative inquiry: Mapping a methodology.* Thousand Oaks, CA: Sage.

Clandinin, D. J., & Connelly, F. (2000). *Narrative inquiry: Experience and story in qualitative research.* San Francisco: Jossey-Bass.

Cochran-Smith, M., & Lytle, S. L. (1993). *Inside/outside: Teacher research and knowledge.* New York: Teachers College Press.

Cochran-Smith, M., & Lytle, S. L. (1999). The teacher research movement: A decade later. *Educational Researcher, 28,* 15–25.

Cochran-Smith, M., & Lytle, S. L. (2009). *Inquiry as stance: Practitioner research for the next generation.* New York: Teachers College Press.

Cohen, L., Manion, L., & Morrison, K. (2011). *Research methods in education* (7th ed.). New York: Routledge.

Coladarci, T., Cobb, C. D., Minium, E. W., & Clarke, R. C. (2010). *Fundamentals of statistical reasoning in education* (3rd ed.). Hoboken, NJ: Wiley.

Corbin, J. A., & Strauss, A. (2007). *Basics of qualitative research: Techniques and procedures for developing grounded theory* (3rd ed.). Thousand Oaks, CA: Sage.

Corey, S. (1953). *Action research to improve school practice.* New York: Teachers College Press.

Creswell, J. W. (2009). *Research design: Qualitative, quantitative, and mixed methods approaches* (3rd ed.). Thousand Oaks, CA: Sage.

Creswell, J. W. (2011). *Educational research: Planning, conducting and evaluating quantitative and qualitative research* (4th ed.). Upper Saddle River, NJ: Prentice Hall.

Creswell, J. W., & Plano Clark, V. L. (2011). *Designing and conducting mixed methods research* (2nd ed.). Thousand Oaks, CA: Sage.

Currie, D., & Kelly, D. M. (2012). Group interviews: Understanding shared meaning and meaning making. In S. Delamont (Ed.), *Handbook of qualitative research in education* (pp. 415–425). Cheltenham, UK: Elgar.

Dana, N. F., & Yendol-Hoppey, D. (2009). *The reflective educator's guide to classroom research: Learning to teach and teaching to learn through practitioner research* (2nd ed.). Thousand Oaks, CA: Corwin Press.

Dane, F. C. (2011). *Evaluating research: Methodology for people who need to read research.* Thousand Oaks, CA: Sage.

Delamont, S. (2012). Performance findings: Tales of the theatrical self. In S. Delamont (Ed.), *Handbook of qualitative research in education* (pp. 550–561). Cheltenham, UK: Elgar.

Denzin, N. K. (1997). *Interpretative ethnography: Ethnographic practice for the 21st century.* Thousand Oaks: Sage.

Denzin, N. K. (2003). The call to performance. *Symbolic Interaction, 26*(1), 187–207.

Denzin, N. K. (2009). *Qualitative research under fire: Toward a new paradigm dialogue.* Walnut Creek, CA: Left Coast Press.

Denzin, N. K., Lincoln, Y. S., & Smith, L. T. (2008). *Handbook of critical and indigenous methodologies.* Thousand Oaks, CA: Sage.

DeWalt, K. M., & DeWalt, B. R. (2010). *Participant observation: A guide for fieldworkers* (2nd ed.). Walnut Creek, CA: AltaMira Press.

Dewey, J. (1916). *Democracy and education: An introduction to the philosophy of education.* New York: Macmillan.

Dewey, J. (1929/1984). The sources of a science of education. In J. A. Boydston (Ed.), *The later works: Vol. 5. 1929–1930* (pp. 3–40). Carbondale: Southern Illinois University Press.

Edelstein, W. (2011). Education for democracy: Reasons and strategies. *European Journal of Education, 46*(1), 127–137.

Efron, S., & Joseph, P. B. (2001). Reflections in a mirror: Metaphors of teachers and teaching. In P. B. Joseph & G. Farrell (Eds.), *Images of school teachers* (2nd ed., pp. 75–92). New York: St. Martin's Press.

Eisenhart, M. (2001). Changing conceptions of culture and ethnographic methodology: Recent thematic shifts and their implications for research on teaching. In V. Richardson (Ed.). *Handbook of research on teaching* (4th ed., pp. 209–225). Washington, DC: American Educational Research Association.

Eliot, J. (1991/2002). *Action research of educational change.* London: Open University Press.

Elliott, J., & Norris, N. (2012). *Curriculum, pedagogy and educational research.* New York: Routledge.

Fink, A. (2009). *How to conduct surveys: A step-by-step guide* (4th ed.). Thousand Oaks, CA: Sage.

Firmin, M. W., & Brewer, P. R. (2006). *Ethnographic and qualitative research in education* (Vol. II). London: Cambridge Scholars.

Fisher, D., & Frey, N. (2007). *Checking for understanding: Formative assessment techniques for your classroom.* Alexandria, VA: Association for Supervision and Curriculum Development.

Flick, U. (2009). *An introduction to qualitative research* (4th ed.). London: Sage.

Foddy, W. (1993). *Constructing questions for interviews.* Cambridge, UK: Cambridge University Press.

Fowler, F. J. (2009). *Survey research methods* (4th ed.). Thousand Oaks, CA: Sage.

Fox, M., Martin, P., & Green, G. (2007). *Doing practitioner research.* London: Sage.

Fraenkel, J., Wallen, N., & Hyun, H. (2011). *How to design and evaluate research in education* (8th ed.). New York: McGraw-Hill.

Frank, C. (1999). *Ethnographic eyes: A teacher's guide to classroom observation.* Portsmouth, NH: Heinemann.

Frank, C. (2011). *Ethnographic interviewing for teacher preparation and staff development: A field guide.* New York: Teachers College Press.

Frank, S., & Huddleston, T. (2009). *Schools for society. Learning democracy in Europe: A handbook of ideas for action.* London: Alliance Publishing Trust.

Freire, P. (1970). *Pedagogy of the oppressed* (M. B. Ramos, Trans.). New York: Seabury.

Gall, M. D., Gall, J. P., & Borg, W. R. (2006). *Educational research: An introduction* (8th ed.). White Plains, NY: Longman.

Gareis, C. R., & Grant, L. W. (2008). *Teacher-made assessments: How to connect curriculum, instruction, and student learning.* Larchmont, NY: Eye on Education.

Gay, L. R., Mills, G. E., & Airasian, P. W. (2011). *Educational research: Competencies for analysis and applications* (10th ed.). Boston: Addison-Wesley.

George, A. L., & Bennett, A. (2004). *Case studies and theory development in the social sciences.* Cambridge, MA: MIT Press.

Gibson, W. J., & Brown, A. (2009). *Working with qualitative data.* London: Sage.

Gillies, R. M., & Ashman, A. F. (2010). *The teacher's role in implementing cooperative learning in the classroom.* New York: Springer.

Glaser, B. (1992). *Basics of qualitative research: Emergence vs. forcing.* Mill Valley, CA: Sociology Press.

Glesne, C. (2010). *Becoming qualitative researchers: An introduction* (4th ed.). New York: Longman.

Good, T. L., & Brophy, J. E. (2007). *Looking in classrooms* (10th ed.). New York: Longman.

Goodlad, J. I., Soder, R., & McDaniel, B. L. (2008). *Education and the making of a democratic people.* Boulder, CO: Paradigm.

Gort, M. (2006). Strategic codeswitching, interliteracy, and other phenomena of emergent bilingual writing: Lessons from first-grade dual language classrooms. *Journal of Early Childhood Literacy, 6*(3), 323–354.

Green, S. K., & Johnson, R. L. (2010). *Assessment is essential.* Columbus, OH: McGraw-Hill.

Greene, M. (1978). *Landscapes of learning.* New York: Teachers College Press.

Greene, M. (1995). *Releasing the imagination: Essays on education, the arts, and social change.* San Francisco: Jossey-Bass.

Gubrium, J. F., & Holstein, J. A. (2002). *Handbook of interview research: Context and method.* Thousand Oaks, CA: Sage.

Guillemin, M., & Gillam, L. (2004). Ethics, reflexivity and ethically important moments in research. *Qualitative Inquiry, 10*(2), 261–280.

Hancock, D. R. (2011). *Doing case study research: A practical guide for beginning researchers* (2nd ed.). New York: Teachers College Press.

Hansen, D. T. (2001). *Exploring the moral heart of teaching: Toward a teacher's creed.* New York: Teachers College Press.

Hatch, J. A. (2002). *Doing qualitative research in education settings.* Albany: State University of New York.

Hendricks, C. (2012). *Improving schools through action research: A reflective practice approach* (3rd ed.). Upper Saddle River, NJ: Pearson.

Herr, K. G., & Nihlen, A. S. (2007). *Studying your own school: An educator's guide to practitioner research* (2nd ed.). Thousand Oaks, CA: Corwin Press.

Hesse-Biber, S. N. (2010). *Mixed methods research: Merging theory with practice.* New York: Guilford Press.

Hinchey, P. H. (2008). *Action research primer.* New York: Lang.

Holley, K. A., & Colyar, J. (2009). Rethinking texts: Narratives and the construction of qualitative research. *Educational Researcher, 38*(9), 680–686.

Holly, M. L., Arhar, J. M., & Kasten, W. C. (2009). *Action research for teachers: Travelling the yellow brick road* (3rd ed.). Upper Saddle River, NJ: Pearson.

Holmes, R. (2012). The literary turn: Fiction and poetry. In S. Delamont (Ed.), *Handbook of qualitative research in education* (pp. 562–576). Cheltenham, UK: Elgar.

Hopkins, D. (2008). *A teacher's guide to classroom research* (4th ed.). Berkshire, UK: Open University Press.

Huck, S. W. (2012). *Reading statistics and research* (6th ed.). Boston: Pearson.

Jarvis, P. (1999). *The practitioner-researcher: Developing theory from practice.* San Francisco: Jossey-Bass.

Jenkins, J. R., Antil, L. R., & Vadasy, P. F. (2003). How cooperative learning works for special education and remedial students. *Exceptional Children, 69*(3), 279–292.

Johnson, A. P. (2011). *A short guide to action research* (4th ed.). Upper Saddle River, NJ: Pearson.

Johnson, R. S. (2009). *Developing portfolios in education: A guide to reflection, inquiry and assessment.* Thousand Oaks, CA: Sage.

Kahne, J., & Westheimer, J. (2003). Teaching democracy: What schools need to do. *Phi Delta Kappan, 85,* 34–66.

Kemper, A., Stringfield, S., & Teddlie, C. B. (2003). Mixed methods sampling strategies in social science research. In A. Tashakkori & C. Teddlie (Eds.), *Handbook of mixed methods in social and behavioral research* (pp. 351–384). Thousand Oaks, CA: Sage.

Klingner, J. K., Scanlon, D., & Pressley, M. (2005). How to publish in scholarly journals. *Educational Researcher, 34*(8), 14–20.

Krippendorff, K. H., & Bock, M. A. (2009). *The content analysis reader.* Thousand Oaks, CA: Sage.

Kuhn, T. (1970). *The structure of scientific revolutions.* Chicago: University of Chicago Press.

Kuntz, K. J., McLaughlin, T. F., & Howard, V. F. (2001). A comparison of cooperative learning and small group individualized instruction for math in a self contained classroom for elementary students with disabilities. *Educational Research Quarterly, 24*(3), 41–56.

Kvale, S., & Brinkmann, S. (2009). *InterView: Learning the craft of qualitative research interviewing* (2nd ed.). Thousand Oaks, CA: Sage.

Lamprianou, I., & Athanasou, J. A. (2009). *A teacher's guide to educational assessment.* Boston: Sense.

Lauer, P. A. (2006). *An education research primer: How to understand, evaluate, and use it.* San Francisco: Jossey-Bass.

LeCompte, M. D., & Schensul, J. J. (2010). *Designing and conducting ethnographic research: An introduction* (2nd ed.). Lanham, MD: AltaMira Press.

Lee, B. K., & Gregory, D. (2008). Not alone in the field: Distance collaboration via the Internet in a focused ethnography. *International Journal of Qualitative Methods, 7*(3) 31–46.

Lewin, K. (1946). Action research and minority problems. *Journal of Social Issues, 2*(4), 34–46.

Lewins, A., & Silver, C. (2007). *Using software in qualitative data analysis: A step-by-step guide.* London: Sage.

Lincoln, Y. S., & Guba, E. G. (1985). *Naturalistic inquiry.* Newbury Park, CA: Sage.

Lofland, J. Snow, D. A., Anderson, L., & Lofland, L. H. (2005). *Analyzing social settings: A guide for qualitative observation and analysis* (4th ed.). Belmont, CA: Wadsworth.

Machi, L. A., & McEvoy, B. T. (2009). *The literature review.* Thousand Oaks, CA: Corwin Press.

Madison, D. S. (2011). *Critical ethnography* (2nd ed). Thousand Oaks, CA: Sage.

Marshall, C., & Rossman, G. B. (2011). *Designing qualitative research* (5th ed.). Thousand Oaks, CA: Sage.

Marzano, R. J. (2003). *What works in school: Translating research into action.* Alexandria, VA: Association for Supervision and Curriculum Development.

Maxwell, J. A. (2013). *Qualitative research design: An interactive approach* (3rd ed.). Thousand Oaks, CA: Sage.

Mayer, E. E., & Moreno, R. (2002). Aids to computer-based multimedia learning. *Learning and Instruction, 12,* 107–119.

McMaster, K. N., & Fuchs, D. (2002). Effects of cooperative learning on the academic achievement of students with learning disabilities: An update of Tateyama-Sniezek's review. *Learning Disabilities Research and Practice, 17*(2), 107–117.

McMillan, J. H. (2011). *Educational researcher: Fundamentals for the consumer* (6th ed.). Boston: Addison-Wesley.

McMillan, J. H., & Schumacher, S. (2010). *Research in education: Evidence-based inquiry* (7th ed.). Boston: Pearson.

McNiff, J., & Whitehead, J. (2010). *You and your action research project* (3rd ed.). Oxford, UK: Routledge.

McNiff, J., & Whitehead, J. (2011). *All you need to know about your action research* (2nd ed.). London: Sage.

McQuillan, P. J. (2005). Possibilities and pitfalls: A comparative analysis of student empowerment. *American Educational Research Journal, 42,* 639–670.

Menter, I., Eliot, D., Hulme, M., & Lewin, J. (2011). *A guide to practitioner research in education.* London: Sage.

Merriam, S. B. (1998). *Qualitative research and case study applications in education.* San Francisco: Wiley.

Merriam, S. B. (2009). *Qualitative research: A guide to designing and implementation.* San Francisco: Jossey-Bass.

Mertler, C. A. (2012). *Action research: Improving schools and empowering educators* (3rd ed.). Thousand Oaks, CA: Sage.

Mertler, C. A., & Charles, C. M. (2011). *Introduction to educational research* (7th ed.). Boston: Sage.

Michelli, N., & Keiser, D. (2005). Education for democracy: What can it be? In N. Michelli & D. Keiser (Eds.), *Teacher education for democracy and social justice.* New York: Routledge.

Mikel, E. R. (2011). Deliberating democracy. In P. B. Joseph (Ed.), *Cultures of curriculum* (2nd ed., pp. 196–218). New York: Routledge.

Miles, M., & Huberman, A. (1994). *Qualitative data analysis: An expanded sourcebook.* Thousand Oaks, CA: Sage.

Miller, D. M., Linn, R. L., & Gronlund, N. E. (2009). *Measurement and assessment in teaching* (10th ed.). Upper Saddle River, NJ: Prentice Hall.

Mills, G. E. (2011). *Action research: A guide for the teacher researcher* (4th ed.). Upper Saddle River, NJ: Pearson.

Moore, D. S. (2009). *Essential statistics.* New York: Freeman.

Moore, D. S., McCabe, G. P., & Craig, B. A. (2010). *Introduction to the practice of statistics* (7th ed.). New York: Freeman.

Morgan, D. L. (1997). *Focus groups as qualitative research* (2nd ed.). Thousand Oaks, CA: Sage.

Myers, J. L., Well, A. D., & Lorch, R. F. (2010). *Research design and statistical analysis* (3rd ed.). New York: Routledge.

Nitko, A., & Brookhart, S. M. (2010). *Educational assessment of students* (6th ed.). Upper Saddle River, NJ: Prentice Hall.

Noddings, N. (1992). *The challenge to care in schools: An alternative approach to education.* New York: Teachers College Press.

Noddings, N. (2002). *Educating moral people.* New York: Teachers College Press.

Noddings, N. (2003). *Happiness and education.* Cambridge: Cambridge University Press.

Noffke, S. E. (1997). Themes and tension in US action research: Toward historical analysis. In S. Hollingsworth (Ed.), *International action research: A casebook for educational reform.* London: Falmer Press.

Onwuegbuzie, A. J., & Leech, N. L. (2007). Sampling design in qualitative research: Making the sampling process more public. *Qualitative Report, 12*(2), 238–254.

Opdenakker, R. (2006). Advantages and disadvantages of four interview techniques in qualitative research. *Forum Qualitative Sozialforschung/Forum: Qualitative Social Research, 6*(2), Art 11. Retrieved from *www.qualitative-research.net/index.php/fqs/article/view 175/392.*

O'Reilly, K. (2012). *Ethnographic methods* (2nd ed.). New York: Routledge.

Osterman, K. F., & Kottkamp, R. B. (2004). *Reflective practice for educators: Professional development to improve student learning* (2nd ed.). Thousand Oaks, CA: Corwin Press.

Palmer, P. (2007). *The courage to teach: Exploring the inner landscape of a teacher's life.* San Francisco: Jossey-Bass.

Parker, W. C. (2003). *Teaching democracy: Unity and diversity in public life.* New York: Teachers College Press.

Patton, M. Q. (2002). *Qualitative research and evaluation method* (3rd ed.). Thousand Oaks, CA: Sage.

Pearson, R. W. (2010). *Statistical persuasion.* Los Angeles: Sage.

Peshkin, A. (2001). Angles of vision: Enhancing perception in qualitative research. *Qualitative Inquiry, 7,* 238–253.

Phillips, D. K., & Carr, K. (2010). *Becoming a teacher through action research: Process, context, and self-study* (2nd ed.). New York: Routledge.

Pine, G. J. (2008). *Action research: Building knowledge democracies.* Thousand Oaks, CA: Sage.

Popham, W. J. (2010). *Classroom assessment: What teachers need to know* (7th ed.). Upper Saddle River, NJ: Pearson.

Prior, L. (2012). The role of documents in social research. In S. Delamont (Ed.), *Handbook of qualitative research in education* (pp. 426–443). Cheltenham, UK: Elgar.

Pritchard, I. A. (2002). Travelers and trolls: Practitioner research and institutional review boards. *Educational Researcher, 31*(3), 3–13.

Rallis, S. F., & Rossman, G. B. (2012). *The research journey: Introduction to inquiry.* New York: Guilford Press.

Ravid, R. (2011). *Practical statistics for educators* (4th ed.). Lanham, MD: Rowman & Littlefield.

Richards, L. (2009). *Handling qualitative data: A practical guide* (2nd ed.). Thousand Oaks, CA: Sage.

Richardson, V., & Fenstermacher, G. D. (2001). Manner in teaching: The study in four parts. *Journal of Curriculum Studies, 33*(6), 631–637.

Robinson, J. (2012). Focus groups. In S. Delamont (Ed.), *Handbook of qualitative research in education* (pp. 391–404). Cheltenham, UK: Elgar.

Rodriguez, N. M., & Rayave, L. H. (2002). *Systematic self-observation*. Thousand Oaks, CA: Sage.

Rossman, G. B., & Rallis, S. F. (2010). *Learning in the field* (3rd ed.). Thousand Oaks, CA: Sage.

Rubin, H., & Rubin, I. (2012). *Qualitative interviewing: The art of hearing data* (3rd ed.). Thousand Oaks, CA: Sage.

Russell, M. K., & Airasian, P. W. (2012). *Classroom assessment: Concepts and applications* (7th ed.). Columbus, OH: McGraw-Hill.

Ryan, J. B., Reid, R., & Epstein, M. H. (2004). Peer-mediated intervention studies on academic achievement for students with EBD. *Remedial and Special Education, 25*(6), 330–341.

Sagor, R. (2011). *The action research guidebook: A four-stage process for educators and school teams*. Thousand Oaks, CA: Corwin Press.

Salant, P., & Dillman, D. A. (1994). *How to conduct your own survey*. New York: Wiley.

Salend, S. J. (2011). Creating student-friendly tests. *Educational Leadership, 69*(3), 52–58.

Salmons, J. (2010). *Online interviews in real time*. Thousand Oaks, CA: Sage.

Samaras, A. P. (2011). *Self-study teacher research: Improving your practice through collaborative inquiry*. Thousand Oaks, CA: Sage.

Schär, S. G. (2002). Designing multimedia presentations for the learning content. In P. Barker & S. Rebelsky (Eds.), *Proceedings of World Conference on Educational Multimedia, Hypermedia and Telecommunications 2002* (pp. 673–674). Chesapeake, VA: Association for the Advancement of Computing in Education. Retrieved from *www.editlib.org/p/10095*.

Schreiber, J., & Anser-Self, K. (2011). *Educational research: The interrelationship of questions, sampling, design, and analysis*. Hoboken, NJ: Wiley.

Schutz, A. (2008). Social class and social action: The middle-class bias of democratic theory in education. *Teachers College Records, 110*(2), 405–442.

Seidman, I. (2012). *Interviewing as qualitative research: A guide for researchers in education and the social sciences* (4th ed.). New York: Teachers College Press.

Shank, G. D. (2006). *Qualitative research: A personal skill approach* (2nd ed.). Upper Saddle, NJ: Pearson.

Shermis, M. D., & Di Vesta, F. J. (2011). *Classroom assessment in action*. Lanham, MD: Rowman & Littlefield.

Sikes, P. (2012). Dance: Making movement meaningfully. In S. Delamont (Ed.), *Handbook of qualitative research in education* (pp. 577–590). Cheltenham, UK: Elgar.

Slavin, R. E. (2007). *Educational research in an age of accountability.* Boston: Pearson.

Somekh, B., & Zeichner, K. (2009). Action research for educational reform: Remodeling action research theories and practices in local contexts. *Educational Action Research, 17*(1), 5–21.

Spradley, J. P. (1979). *The ethnographic interview.* New York: Holt, Rinehart & Winston.

Spring, J. (2010). *American education.* New York: McGraw-Hill.

Stake, R. E. (1995). *The art of case study research.* Thousand Oaks, CA: Sage.

Steinberg, S. R., & Cannella, G. S. (2012). *Critical qualitative research reader.* New York: Lang.

Stenhouse, L. (1975). *An introduction to curriculum research and development.* London: Heinemann.

Stiggins, R., & Chappuis, J. (2011). *An introduction to student-involved assessment FOR learning* (6th ed.). Boston: Addison-Wesley.

Stringer, E. T. (2007). *Action research* (3rd ed.). Thousand Oaks, CA: Sage.

Stringer, E. T. (2008). *Action research in education* (2nd ed.). Upper Saddle River, NJ: Pearson.

Suskie, L. (2009). *Assessing student learning: A common sense guide* (2nd ed.). San Francisco: Jossey-Bass.

Tashakkori, A., & Teddlie, C. B. (Eds.). (2010). *Sage handbook of mixed methods in social and behavioral sciences.* Thousand Oaks, CA: Sage.

Taylor, C. S., & Nolen, S. B. (2008). *Classroom assessment: Supporting teaching and learning in real classrooms* (2nd ed.). Upper Saddle River, NJ: Pearson.

Teddlie, C. B., & Tashakkori, A. (2009). *Foundations of mixed methods research: Integrating quantitative and qualitative approaches in social and behavioral sciences.* Thousand Oaks, CA: Sage.

Tomlinson, C. A. (2001). *How to differentiate instruction in mixed ability classrooms* (2nd ed.). Alexandria, VA: Association for Supervision and Curriculum Development.

Tomlinson, C. A., & Eidson, C. C. (2003). *Differentiation in practice: A resource guide for differentiating curriculum, Grades 5–9.* Alexandria, VA: Association for Supervision and Curriculum Development.

Tomlinson, C. A., & McTighe, J. (2006). *Integrating differentiated instruction and understanding by design: Connecting content and kids.* Alexandria, VA: Association for Supervision and Curriculum Development.

Tozer, S. E., Senese, G., & Violas, P. C. (2009). *School and society historical and contemporary perspectives* (6th ed.). New York: McGraw-Hill.

Triola, M. F. (2006). *Elementary statistics* (10th ed.). Boston: Pearson.

Tyack, D. B. (1974). *The one best system: A history of American urban education.* Cambridge, MA: Harvard University Press.

Van Blerkom, M. L. (2009*). Measurement and statistics for teachers.* New York: Routledge.

Van Manen, M. (1994). Pedagogy, virtues, and narrative identity in teaching. *Curriculum Inquiry, 24*(2), 135–170.

Webster, L., & Mertova, P. (2007). *Using narrative inquiry as a research method: An introduction to using critical event narrative analysis in research on learning and teaching.* New York: Routledge.

White, M. L. (2012). Turning the camera on yourself: Digital video journals in educational research. In S. Delamont (Ed.), *Handbook of qualitative research in education* (pp. 325–341). Cheltenham, UK: Elgar.

Wolcott, H. F. (2005). *The art of fieldwork* (2nd ed.). Walnut Creek, CA: AltaMira Press.

Wolcott, H. F. (2008). *Writing up qualitative research* (3rd ed.). Thousand Oaks, CA: Sage.

Wolcott, T. G. (1997). Mortal sins in poster presentation or, how to give the poster no one remembers. *Newsletter of the Society for Integrative and Comparative Biology, Fall,* 10–11.

Wolford, P. L., Heward, W. L., & Alber, S. R. (2001). Teaching middle-school students with learning disabilities to recruit peer assistance during cooperative learning group activities. *Learning Disabilities Research and Practice, 16*(3), 161–173.

Wragg, E. C. (2012). *An introduction to classroom observation* (2nd ed.). London: Routledge.

Yin, K. (2009). *Case study research: Design and methods* (4th ed.). Thousand Oaks, CA: Sage.

Author Index

Subject Index

Page numbers followed by *f* or *t* refer to figures or tables.

About the Authors

Sara Efrat Efron, EdD, is Professor of Education at National Louis University, where she teaches courses in qualitative research, curriculum studies, and foundations of education to preservice, inservice, and doctoral students. Her areas of interest include teacher research, the role of the teacher's personal voice, and moral democratic education. Dr. Efron has presented extensively at multiple conferences, and her articles have been published in such journals as *Curriculum and Inquiry*, *Journal of Teacher Education*, and *Phi Delta Kappan*. She has also written several foreign-language instructional books for middle and high school students.

Ruth Ravid, PhD, is Professor Emerita of Education at National Louis University. Her areas of interest include educational research, action research, assessment, and school–university collaboration. Dr. Ravid's books include *Practical Statistics for Educators* (4th ed.), *Study Guide for Practical Statistics for Educators* (4th ed.; coauthored with Elizabeth Oyer), *Practical Statistics for Business: An Introduction to Business Statistics* (coauthored with Perry Haan), *Collaboration in Education* (coedited with Judith J. Slater), and *The Many Faces of School–University Collaboration* (coedited with Marianne G. Handler).